CW00642466

BSA TWINS & TRIPLES

NITON
PUBLISHING

BSA TWINS & TRIPLES

The postwar A7/A10, A50/65 and Rocket III

Roy Bacon

Published by Niton Publishing
P.O. Box 3, Ventnor, Isle of Wight, PO38 2AS

First published in 1980 in Great Britain by
Osprey Publishing Limited, 12–14 Long Acre,
London WC2E 9LP Member company of the
George Philip Group

A CIP catalogue record for this book is available
from the British Library

ISBN 1-85579-029-7

Original edition:–

Editor Tim Parker
Design Derek Copsey
Reprinted by Bookbuilders Ltd., Hong Kong

CONTENTS

Foreword by Bob Currie

Bob Currie on a BSA scooter in 1964 in the Isle of Man. He is competing in a scooter rally and the machine is powered by the 175 cc two stroke engine. In all other respects it is the same as the 250 cc model

Somewhere in the motorcycling lives of the majority of riders and ex-riders now middle-aged, there must have been a BSA. After all, not for nothing did advertisements for the Small Heath marque term it 'The Most Popular Motor Cycle in the World'.

Nevertheless, 'popular' is a relative term, and I know there were times when my brother was rather less than complimentary about his A7 twin. That was a 1947 model, one of the earliest all-iron jobs designed by Herbert Perkins, and it had an annoying habit of running-on lumpily for quite a time after the ignition had been switched off, due to a combination of poor cylinder-head design and almost indigestible 73-octane Pool petrol.

Like many servicemen returning from World War 2, he had blued his demobilisation gratuity on his first-ever brand-new motorcycle. He fell for the charms of the then-new A7. Just to be different, I plumped for another newly-announced twin, the 349 cc Triumph 3T de Luxe—a bit gutless but, I think, a rather sweeter machine taken all round.

Still, BSA soon learned, and with the coming of the A10 Golden Flash the picture began to change. Was there ever a more handsome vertical twin? Even now, a well-kept Flash in original trim is a magnet for reminiscent eyes.

As you'll discover when you get stuck into this book, Roy Bacon's homework is well worth a ten-out-of-ten mark, and certainly he has turned up information on experiments that have never before been made public. The 'hole under the floor of the development shop' mentioned in the opening chapter was the graveyard of many a failed experiment, but what Roy may not know is that in the 1960s, shortly after Ariel production had moved to Small Heath, Sammy Miller's workbench (on which he fettled the legendary trials 497 cc Ariel, GOV 132) stood on the planking covering that hole; if anyone wanted access to the hole—either to exhume one of the experiments or, more likely, bury yet another—then a grumbling Sammy had to move himself, his workbench, and his bike.

Among early BSA experiments with vertical twins, Roy Bacon refers to an in-line overhead-camshaft twin of the 1920s. Where that unit may be now is anybody's guess (most probably, smashed up for its scrap value), but I have been told on good authority that it was on a table in Erling Poppe's office, at the time that Erling was involved in designing the postwar S7 Sunbeam twin, so if not an ancestor, it was at least an influence on the Sunbeam.

And talking of Sunbeams, the Edward Turner-designed 250 cc vertical twin scooter was a rather better machine than many folk give it credit for, and if only the makers had given it quickly-detachable side panels (as on the Lambretta) it would have been better still. At one period I had a lot of fun by riding one of these—a 'works' job, tweaked by Brian Martin in the BSA competitions shop—in Midland scooter events, and I still have the cups to prove it. Get the hang of that single-pedal gear change, and one could leave a Vespa or Lambretta for dead in acceleration and stop-and-restart tests.

Today, in 1980, the BSA name lives on, but the machine the tank sides of which those familiar initials now adorn is a small-capacity two-stroke with a power unit of continental origin. And that is a long, long way from the A7 and its true descendants.

If any epitaph for the postwar BSA twin be needed, let it be 'This was a bike of its time'. It was born into a world far less sophisticated than that of today, a world when the motorcycle was still, very largely, a workaday transport and not a status symbol. Dad used his Golden Flash to get to and from the factory during the week and, possibly, hitched on a double-adult saloon chair at the weekend to take the family for a run into the countryside.

There was no such thing as a BSA Five Star Service Station, nor was there need for any. Design was uncomplicated, and maintenance could be (and was) carried out in the backyard—with the tools thoughtfully provided in the tool-roll. Superbikes, and the Japanese industry in general, have a lot to answer for . . . .

Bob Currie
Birmingham

Acknowledgements

How do you say thank you to people who have helped you write a book when without their assistance it could not have been done. The words always seem inadequate. However, thanks very much for help, advice, information, assistance and encouragement.

To Titch Allen who supplied most of the data on the prewar twins and impressions of the earliest A7s. Jack Harper of BSA who, together with Gordon Jeal and Bill Lincoln of the Vintage Club, dealt with my problems over that most awkward of subjects—engine and frame numbers. Jack also kindly sent me data on the A70 when I had nearly run out of sources.

To Brian Martin for his confirmation of various points from the past when he worked at BSA. Clive Stokes, now with Kawasaki, but who also once worked at BSA. Jeff Clew who advised on points regarding A7 and A10 construction and organized a photo of an early A7. Renold Chains Ltd for information. Blays of Twickenham for data on machine specifications. Bob Currie who wrote a kind foreword. Tim Parker who persuaded me to write the book and gave me help and advice when I needed it.

Obtaining photographs for a work such as this would be impossible, without the assistance of the motorcycle magazines who once again generously opened their files to me. The bulk of the pictures came from *Motor Cycle News* and *Motorcycle Sport* and from some 400 were selected the 160 plus finally used. Many of these taken (and returned I would add) from the files were marked as having been supplied by freelance photographers and in every case I have endeavoured to get in touch to clear the copyright. If by chance my letter failed to reach any photographer through a change of address I can only apologise for not reaching you.

In addition to the pictures a number of line drawings and brochures taken from BSA material have been reproduced and I would particularly like to thank the present BSA management for giving their permission so readily for this to be done. After the collapse of the Company in 1973 it was nice to see the name revived in 1979 and exhibiting once again at Earls Court.

The magazines and publishing houses that provided the pictures were: *Motor Cycle News, Motorcycle Sport, Motor Cycle Weekly* (and thus *The Motor Cycle* and *Motor Cycling*), *Haynes Publishing Group* and S. R. Keig.

The freelance photographers and other organizations whose pictures were used are: Arnold-Allan Photography, Braithwaite Photography, M. Carling, Reg Cave, Central Office of Information, Court Studio, Daytona International Speedway, Derek Evans, Dave Freidman, Kawasaki Motors (UK) Ltd., Nick Nicholls and Sports & General Press Agency.

Thank you everyone, I hope you think the finished result made it worthwhile.

Roy Bacon
Hampton, Middlesex
April 1980

1 Background

The story of the BSA vertical twins spans a period of nearly thirty years from the end of the Second World War, but has its roots in the immediate prewar period, with an additional echo from the twenties.

BSA existed for half a century with a reputation for producing reliable, un-exciting motorcycles with stolid performance and little to fire the imagination. They knew better than most that their first need was to stay in business and make a profit, and that however much motorcyclists of those times clamoured in the press for exotic specifications, they went out and bought the well known and reliable singles and vee-twins they trusted. The history of motorcycling is littered with names of companies who were foolish enough to provide what was requested, only to find that the conservative public always waited for someone else to buy first in case there were problems.

So BSA continued to build machines that people actually did buy, and did this well enough to be able to advertise that one in four was a BSA. Behind that careful business front, however, lay a wealth of diverse prototype models as exciting and technically advanced as those made anywhere else. From the experimental shop came a steady stream of machines and engines as the designer's fresh ideas were turned into hardware, many showing real brilliance both in thought and execution. Often, new ideas were tried out by adapting existing units sometimes in a drastic manner, cutting engines in half, fitting different top halves, turning engines round, and so on.

Few of these ideas ever reached the public even after development, as they were abandoned for one reason or another. In some cases the resulting performance would fail to come up to expectations and be too limited to compete with an existing range. If development failed to remedy this and there was no other good reason to pursue the particular line of inquiry, the offending unit was consigned to a big hole under the floor of the development shop. Often an idea would result in a real improvement but would have to be dropped due to its extra cost, or if it was judged to be too advanced for the buying public.

The Company's behind the scenes enterprise first turned to twin cylinders in formations other than the then common vee in the period from 1920 to 1925. During these years it built three different types, all using layouts that would not have been out of place fifty years later. Two of these layouts were to appear twenty years further on, just after the Second World War, and the third has become a standard layout used by most major firms.

The first was a four-stroke with an in-line form of construction as used by all the postwar Sunbeams. Like them, the BSA had an overhead camshaft and a unit construction gearbox bolted to the rear of the engine. This contained a bevel drive as the unit differed from the Sunbeam in having chain final drive, a layout identical in basic principle to that of the postwar 350 cc Douglas.

The second engine, like the Douglas, was a flat twin and a four-stroke but with more resemblance to the postwar LE Velocette or the first BMW, the R32. Like these, it was a side valve unit and had the gearbox built in-unit with the engine. Unlike the in-line it had shaft final drive.

The third engine was in its way more prophetic than the others for it was a vertical twin two-stroke of 150 cc. Since those days, few in-line twins have been built and the only well known transverse ones are those built by BMW in limited numbers. On the other hand, the twin two-stroke has been built since the War by companies ranging from Adler to Yamaha and is now looked on as a standard engine format.

None of these advanced designs were considered suitable for a public brought up on a stable diet of side valve singles so they were never marketed, and throughout the twenties and thirties BSA built and sold sound machines with single and vee-twin engines. After their one dreadful experience in the 1921 TT when all six of their fast but under-developed entries retired, they retreated even further from the sporting side that had brought their hard-won reputation so near to ruin in a single afternoon. They concentrated on bread and butter machines and it was not until the late thirties that this mood showed any signs of changing.

The first crack in the wall came with the unexpected entry of Wal Handley on a BSA at a minor midweek club meeting at Brooklands in 1937. This was more than unusual, for Handley was better known for his Isle of Man exploits than track-riding and had been retired for some years. BSA were well known for their dislike of racing, so the combination caused a considerable stir. He started well back in the handicap he rode in, as the timekeepers had seen him practising on an Empire Star running on alcohol and knew he would not have entered unless the machine was rather special. It proved to be so, winning the race and a gold star, by lapping at over the 100 mark. This led, of course, to the sporting Gold Star range introduced at the 1937 Show, and continued after the War up to 1963.

Another sign of the change was the move in 1939 by Joe Craig from Norton to BSA. Late that year, he wrote that BSA were interested in road racing and while the Italian opposition, not in the War at that time, were still developing their Gilera and Bianchi supercharged fours and the new blown Guzzi three, with a determined effort they could be caught as AJS had shown with their four in Ulster.

Nothing further came of this for Joe moved on to AMC and Italy were drawn into the conflict, but at that time BSA did have a machine with racing potential and Craig did do some work on it. It was the first of BSA's vertical twins, one of two built in response to the challenge that Edward Turner's Triumph had thrown down to the rest of the industry at the Earls Court Show in 1937. The Speed Twin looked so like a twin port single, was lighter and very little more expensive. Housed in the familiar Tiger 90 frame, it sold really well from the start. Every other firm knew at once that they had no option but to follow suit, although none were able to build other than prototypes before the War. After the conflict was over every major English firm was to produce their rival to the Turner twin.

BSA followed two separate lines with their prewar vertical twins with one designed to be sporting enough to win the enthusiasts away from Triumph and the other more sedate in appearance to appeal to the traditional BSA buyer who expected reliable, if uninteresting performance. A good few of those who wrote to the Press asking for advanced specifications could well have bought the second twin even if they would not have considered the first.

The 1938–39 prototype vertical twin of 500 cc and the only one with ohc. With 100 mph potential it could have given the Tiger 100 a run for its money

The sports engine was of 500 cc with a single overhead camshaft driven by shaft and two pairs of bevels on the right side of the engine. It was an imposing unit with ample finning to both head and barrel, these being held down by long through bolts. The cylinder head was cast in light alloy with the cambox integral and sealed by covers. One, of circular form retained by six screws, gave access to the top bevel pair while each pair of valves and rockers was covered by a rectangular plate lying at an angle in side view. The valves were closed by hairpin valve springs, these being the best available at that time, and the whole cambox lubricated with internal drillings.

The crankcase was split vertically, as was then standard practice, with the cambox drive contained in a tubular housing with gland nuts to case and cylinder head. Outboard of the timing case driving the camshaft and the oil pumps lay the drive up to magdyno unit, positioned behind the cylinders. The offside plug was tucked away behind the camdrive.

This advanced engine was mounted in a standard Silver Star frame with M type cycle parts and girder forks. The heavy duty gearbox with footchange was fitted along with the normal oil tank for the dry sump lubrication. Separate exhaust pipes and silencers were used, the latter standard tubular types mounted parallel to the ground.

From the offside the machine looked very much like the Excelsior of the period, while from the nearside it was only the rocker box size that made it easy to tell that it was not a standard overhead valve twin-port single.

Despite limited development, the twin went well, being capable of exceeding the 100 mph mark, a figure few machines of that size could reach in 1939 when carrying road equipment. The power band was very narrow so speed dropped away quickly on hills but work on the cam design could have dealt with that problem even if BSA had kept to the four speed gearbox. There can be little doubt that it would have given Triumph a very real headache in 1940 or 1941 as it could have been as fast or faster than the Tiger 100 with the added glamour of the overhead camshaft.

In addition to the conventional engine, two units were converted to use the Aspin rotary valve. This device was an inverted cone which formed the combustion chamber and rotated to open and close the ports to let the mixture in and out. It also exposed the plug at the correct time for the mixture to be ignited. Rotary valves for four-stroke engines were a popular exercise at that time, and on paper all worked well with substantial benefits to the engine's breathing and speed, or both. Sadly, all had the same Achilles heels of lubrication and heat. The rotating valve was subject to cool inlet and hot exhaust gases so was prone to distortion. The oil had to combat this, lubricate the ample running surfaces and not contaminate the mixture in the combustion chamber.

None would run happily over the wide range of conditions expected, and while the BSA's had plenty of oil supplied to the valve to keep it running happily, as soon as the throttle was closed the plugs would oil up. To stop the oil reaching the combustion chamber the valve spring loading was increased but the valve promptly seized.

Perhaps in the hopes that a steady running speed would overcome the problem, the then Ministry of Supply became interested in the use of the Aspin valved twins for light aircraft use and arranged for the two engines to go to Aspin. BSA were no doubt glad to let them go and they were never seen again. The ohc engines have all disappeared and are thought to have been lost when the BSA works were bombed during the War, a time when many such interesting prototypes vanished and the factory was mainly concerned with producing M20s for the services.

BSA was not a company to be carried away

by a potential sports image and in addition to the ohc twin they built another designed to sell to their existing customers. This was a very modern looking engine of 350 cc with pushrod operated vertical valves and a distinct resemblance to the postwar Ariel twins. This was most noticeable with the timing cover which was of the same broadly triangular form with well radiused corners, the rear of which extended back to take in the drive to the dynamo carried on the back of the engine at cylinder base level. This was the economy type which had the contact breaker housed in its end and usually ran at engine speed in order to generate enough output. This would have suited a 360 degree twin which could have run with a single pair of points firing both plugs together on the lost spark basis.

The engine was adequately cooled with five fins on the barrel and five more on the head. The exhaust ports were in the extreme front outer corners of the head, pointing straight forward, and led to separate pipes and silencers. The valve gear was totally enclosed by a square cover on the top of the head. Only one carburettor was fitted, without air cleaner, and lubrication was dry sump as normal then.

The remainder of the machine comprised stock items adapted to suit and were basically again the M type frame but with the lighter B forks. Again, a footchange gearbox was used along with the other standard parts so the prototype machine was fully equipped.

The engine came to light on a Redditch scrapheap in 1977, and is due to be restored for museum display.

Then came the War and the factory turned to producing M20s by the thousand while new machines were pushed to the back of everyone's mind for a year or two.

The 1938–39 prototype 350 cc vertical twin for the more traditional BSA market. Ohv and straightforward construction in the Company's tradition

2 First postwar twins

By 1939 BSA were well advanced on the true forerunner of the A7 twin, and visitors to the works that summer would occasionally see one of the development machines out on test. It was intended to unveil the new model at the autumn show at Earls Court that year and include it in the model range for 1940 but the outbreak of war prevented that. It was not until 1946 that it finally reached the public.

The basic layout of the engine unit has been generally attributed to Val Page for, although he left BSA to return to Ariel in 1939, the design bears a close similarity with that of the 650 cc Triumph Model 6/1 which first appeared in 1933. The design was also worked on by Edward Turner for a brief period during the early part of the War when he was at BSA and several detail points bore witness to his style. The separate rocker box caps fitted to the early engines are very typical of Turner.

In the postwar period Bert Hopwood was chief designer at BSA and it was his assistant, Herbert Perkins, who did much of the work on the early A7, together with David Munro.

The overall design concept laid down in the late thirties stood the test of time well, for in essence it remained unchanged from the first A7 to the last A65. All used the 360 degree twin cylinder format and all had a single camshaft located to the rear of the crankcase working pushrod overhead valves. All machines used a four speed gearbox.

According to the patent specification taken

out in 1945, the single camshaft was chosen to save both material and labour costs. In general the rest of the industry did not agree with BSA, for AMC, Enfield, Ariel and Triumph all used twin camshafts placed fore and aft of the cylinders. The method of driving them varied as did the cam position with gear driven Triumph cams sitting in the centre of the shafts, working the pairs of pushrods in tubes between the cylinder, while Enfield and Ariel cams were placed at the outer ends of the camshafts which were chain driven. Only Norton chose to use one camshaft, but unlike BSA they placed theirs at the front of the engine and drove it by chain.

In September 1946 the A7 was announced and went on sale to the public.

The first engines, which were to be used until 1950, were based on dimensions of 62 × 82 mm which gave a capacity of 495 cc. Although very similar in layout, the later engines do vary in their detail designs so not all parts are interchangeable. The early engines are most easily recognised by their screw-in rocker box caps.

The general construction of the early engines was quite straightforward, being based on a vertically split crankcase with separate cylinder block and head attached to it, and a semi-unit design of gearbox bolted to the rear of the crankcase. This was not a usual feature in 1946 when most manufacturers built the gearbox as a separate unit to be mounted behind the engine in plates which allowed it to be moved for primary chain adjustment.

At the top of the engine the cylinder head was a one-piece iron casting with two separate wells for the pairs of inlet and exhaust valves separated by a lateral air space. The base of each well contained a passage for the pushrods and these joined at the gasket face. The rear of the head was machined across to carry the inlet manifold, and this two into one casting carried a single type six Amal carburettor with the float chamber attached on the left and a drip shield fitted between the carburettor and manifold to prevent fuel dripping onto the magneto situated immediately below it. It was also possible to fit an induction bias washer at this point (BSA part 67-359), this being a distance piece shaped to fit the carburettor flange, and made with a tapered thickness to direct the mixture to the desired side. In practice this is not normally needed on the A7 but is occasionally found on the later A10.

Each inlet port was separate in the head casting but parallel to the other, while the exhaust ports were splayed out to allow the cooling air to easily reach the area between the cylinders. The exhaust pipes pushed into place, the finned rings being for appearance and not attached to the cylinder head at all.

The rocker boxes were separate alloy castings each retained by five fastenings. Each pair of rockers ran directly, without bushes, on a long spindle across the box which was supported by an internal rib in the centre and secured by a dome cap nut on the right side.

Early models relied on oil mist for lubrication but from 1948 the shafts were drilled and the left ends fed with oil from a feed taken off the oil return pipe. Each rocker was located sideways by spring washers and was forged into a cup at the inner end to fit the push rod. The outer ends carried square end adjusters and locknuts.

This arrangement of rocker box design was arrived at after a number of alternative layouts had been drawn up and several mock-ups constructed. One, which many a BSA owner would have been pleased to have, had a one piece cover which fitted over the whole of the valve gear. Accessibility would have been excellent but the problems of keeping such a cover oil tight in 1946 ruled that out. Thirty years later, knowledge of oil seals and gaskets had moved on enough for such covers to be commonly used on overhead camshaft engines despite their much more copious oil supply.

Access to the adjusters was via four separate hexagon headed caps similar to those used by Triumph then and Honda now which required a bent feeler to measure between adjuster mark and the hardened stem cap fitted to all four valves. These were closed by duplex coil springs seating on cups holding them clear of the head and retained by collars and split taper cotters. The valve guides were made from cast iron and pressed into the cylinder head.

A conventional copper and asbestos gasket was fitted between cylinders and head which was held in place by a total of nine bolts. Six of these were positioned at the cylinder corners with a further two either side of the pushrods, and the last in the centre of the engine between the bores. This was always the first removed and last fitted as it lay at an angle to the others, with its head in the exhaust valve well just in front of the pushrods.

The cylinder was also a one piece iron casting with the pushrod tunnel cast in, and despite its presence, air flow between the cylinders and round the tunnel was quite adequate and was to give no problems. The block was held down on the crankcase by eight nuts and had its bores hone finished while the pistons running in them were cast in a silicon alloy. Each carried two compression rings and one slotted oil ring. The compression ration was 7 to 1 and small valve cut-aways were machined in the pistons which were fully floating and had their taper-bored gudgeon pins retained by wire circlips.

The connecting rods were forged in an oil

The first A7 model of 1946 with the speedometer in the petrol tank and no cylinder head steady

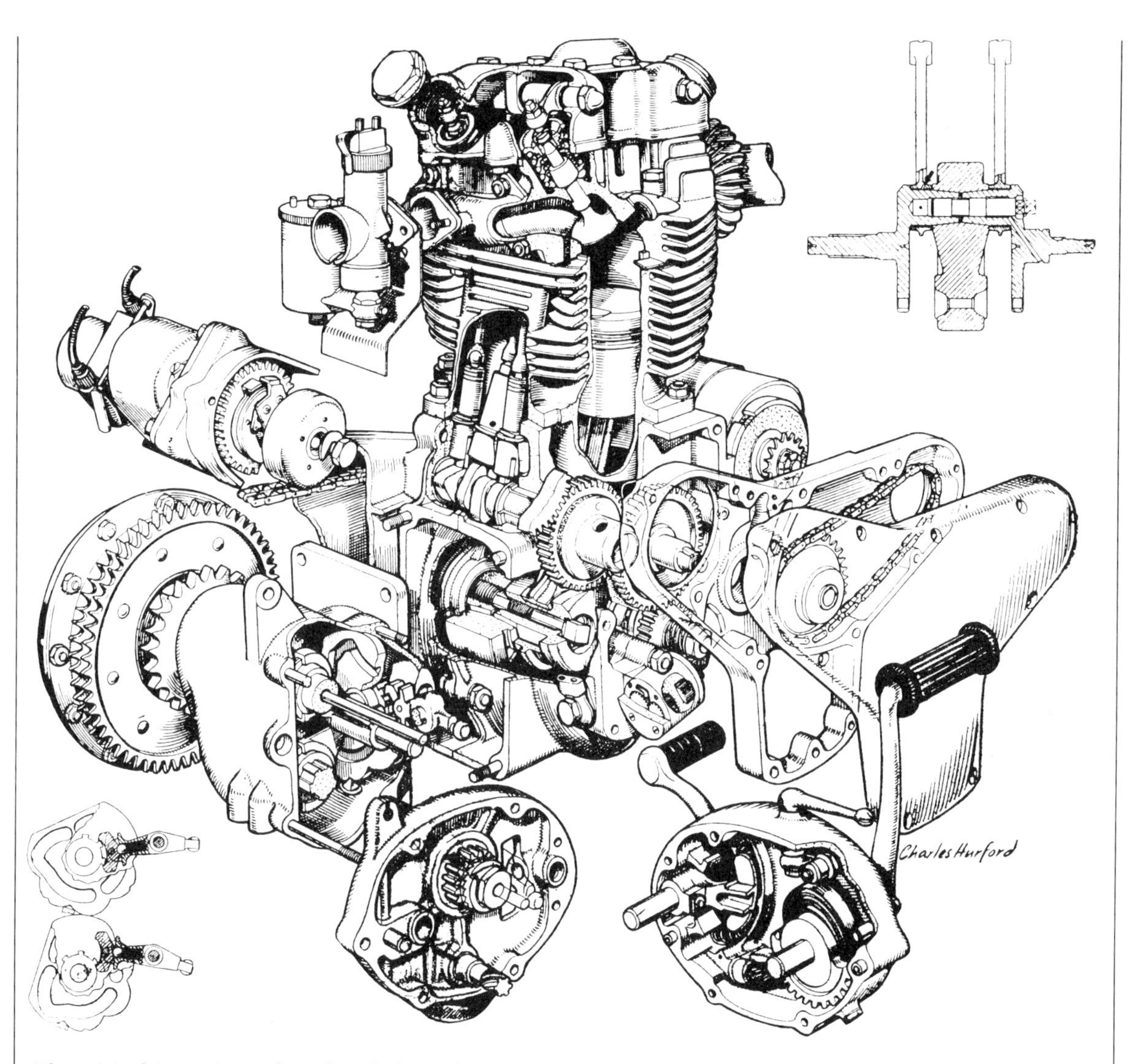

The original A7 engine and gearbox design with built-up crankshaft and plain big ends

hardening, high carbon, nickel steel with an H-section and conventional split big ends. These carried steel backed, lead bronze shells flashed with indium and the caps were retained by nickel chrome steel bolts fitted at first with slotted nuts and split pins and later self-locking nuts.

The crankshaft itself was forged in one piece in a toughened nickel steel with integral bobweights on each outer web. To the centre web was bolted a separate flywheel, also formed with additional bobweights, and this was designed to allow it to be threaded into place onto the crankshaft. The crankpins were drilled along their axis and blanked off with an inspection screw to provide an oil gallery which

Left **Nearside view of the 1946 machine showing primary chaincase, battery location and rear brake detail**

Below **The production A7 engine and gearbox with conventional split connecting rods and replaceable big end shells**

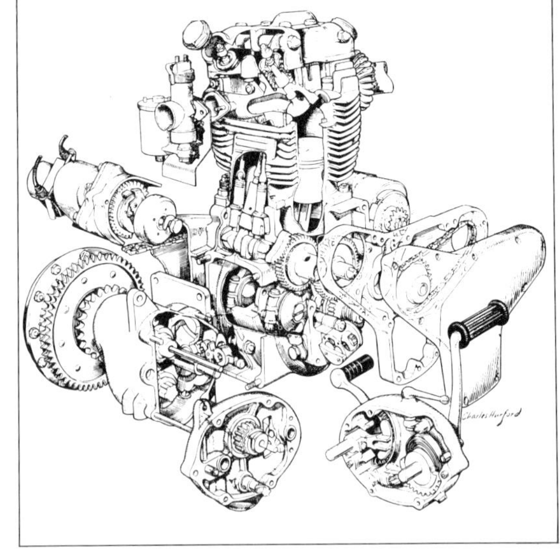

was fed via the timing side bearing and connected to the big ends by cross-drilling of the pins.

Thus all the production A7s had crankshafts which were straightforward and easy for the home mechanic to understand and service. Even when worn out it was simple to remove the central flywheel and have the pins ground so that undersize shells could be fitted to the rods just as in a conventional car engine.

However the prototype engines used an entirely different arrangement of built-up construction which allowed the use of one-piece rods with lead bronze bushes pressed into the big end eyes. The shaft was built up from three sections, the two outer parts each comprising a single forging of halfshaft, web and crankpin. Each crankpin was extended and the extension tapered to fit a corresponding hole in the central flywheel. The three parts were held together by a very special bolt fitted from the right and machined with a differential thread, that is, two threads of different pitch. The nett effect is to give a bolt of very fine pitch, and hence high clamping power, but to retain the normal thread section and strength. The construction concept can be found in Scott engines using a normal clamp bolt, while the differential screw is used in Hirth crankshafts which are built up from individual sections locked together with radial teeth. This complex and expensive design was quietly dropped in favour of convention by the time units reached the public.

The crankcase was an aluminium alloy casting produced in two halves split on the centre line of the engine. The left half extended back to form the inner section of the primary drive case and carried the deep groove ball journal bearing which located the crankshaft. The right half was smaller with a small rearward extension to carry the magneto and two semi-circular supports at the front for the dynamo. The timing side main bearing was steel with a white metal lining and very substantial. Combined, the bearings provided a bottom end good for over 30,000 miles of hard fast use, provided the oil was kept clean and changed frequently enough to prevent debris from wearing out the bush.

The crankcase halves also carried the camshaft in three bushes, one in the left and two in the right halves and the three tappet housings. The outer two housings were mounted vertically and each carried a single ball topped tappet which worked the inlet pushrods while the centre one carried the two exhaust tappets and was sloped forward to work the longer exhaust pushrods. All three housings were held in place by a single clamp bolted to the crankcase.

The timing shaft was ground to fit the bush in the case and then reduced in diameter to carry the timing pinion keyed to it. This was held in place by the oil pump drive worm threaded onto the end of the shaft while this in turn was locked by a nut. Both items had left hand threads.

The oil pump was bolted to the right side of the crankcase below the timing pinion, with the pressure relief valve screwed into the front of the crankcase just in front of the pump and the supply and return pipe union behind it on the rear face of the crankcase.

A dry sump lubrication system was used with the oil carried in a tank located on the right side below the seat. Oil passed through a filter mounted on the supply pipe in the tank to the engine and the gear pump which forced it into the timing bush and hence to the big ends. Pressure was controlled by the relief valve and a bleed-off from this fed oil to the timing gear. The remainder of the early engines relied solely on splash lubrication, so that up to engine number XA7-449 there are no external oilpipes apart from those to and from the oil tank, but from then on the feed to the rockers was taken from the return pipe. The scavenge pump feed pipe in the crankcase contained an anti-syphon ball valve located in its lower end, which had a filter fitted round it and was held in place by the detachable sump plate bolted to the underside of the crankcase.

From the start the engine had a rotary timed crankcase breather and this was turned by one of a train of three gears driven from the timing pinion all of which ran at half crankshaft speed, but varied in detail mounting and function. The first was positioned above the pinion and was keyed to its shaft, which ran in bushes pressed into the crankcase and the inner timing cover. Outboard of this cover the gear shaft carried a sprocket which drove forward to the dynamo

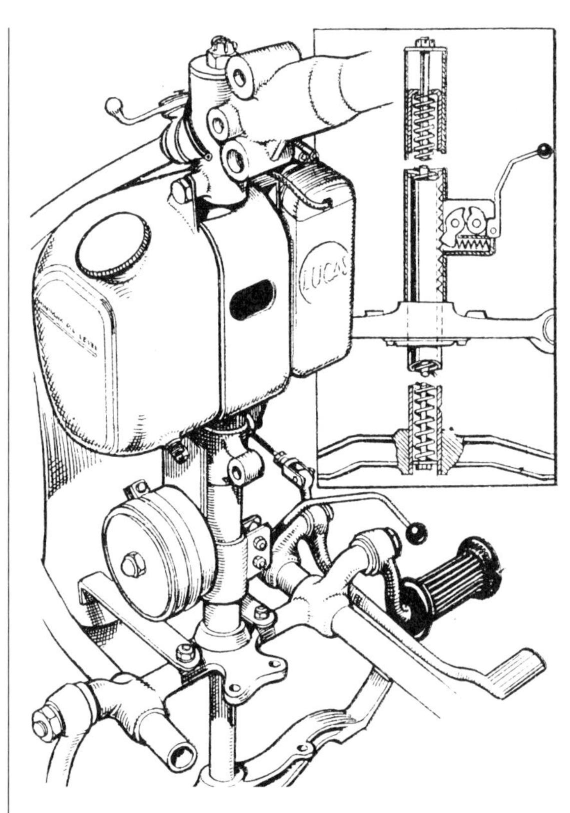

strapped to the front of the crankcase. Chain tension was adjusted by rotating the circular dynamo which had its driven sprocket offset from its own centre.

The inner timing cover was a casting that spaced the outer cover from the crankcase and followed the same general outline. Internally it was divided into three parts, the lowest of which had no inner wall as it surrounded the oil pump. The part containing the dynamo drive chain had an inner wall, as it extended forward out past the line of the crankcase, and this wall provided support for the drive shaft bush, and acted as a sealing face for the dynamo to abut against while separating the grease lubricated dynamo drive chain from the oil mist in the timing chamber. The hole through which the dynamo was driven could be sealed off with two large washers and a through bolt on later engines where the dynamo was dispensed with.

The third part of the cover extended to the rear and enclosed the first of the other two gears, which was keyed to the camshaft and drove the crankcase breather by a cheese head screw fitted to it. The breather was packed against the inner cover by a cork sealing washer between it and the gear and run direct in the cover. The last gear drove the magneto so was fitted directly to its shaft without any keyway, and carried the automatic advance and retard mechanism which protruded through a hole cut in the wall of the inner cover. The magneto itself was a twin cylinder Lucas instrument and fired 14 mm short reach plugs set splayed out about 45 degrees in the head. It was fitted on studs in the rearward extension of the crankcase and held by two standard nuts and one special long one underneath it.

Left **The seat stay with oil tank, air filter, battery, horn and air lever all attached. It contained the ingenious stand detailed in the insert**

Below **The QD rear wheel with straight spokes. A design concept that has seldom been bettered**

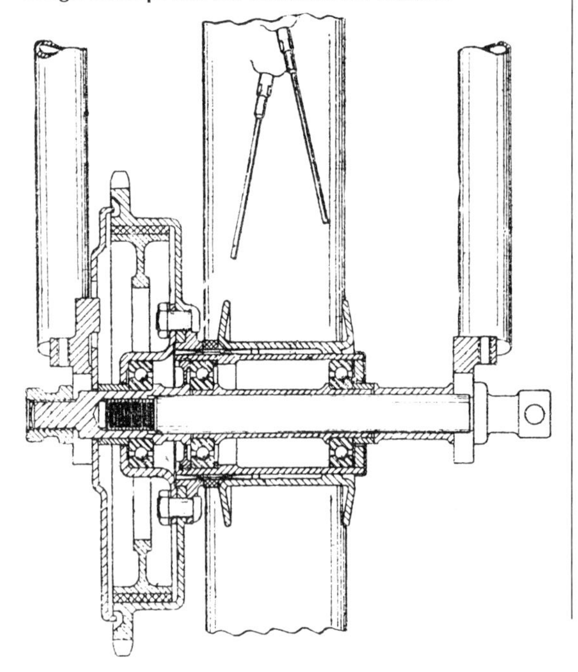

The three sections of the inner cover were sealed from each other and the outside world by the outer timing cover which set the whole engine off well with a shape that was totally characteristic of the range. In its centre it carried the piled arms trade mark and the Company name.

The drive side of the crankshaft carried a duplex sprocket incorporating a twin lobed cam-type shock absorber held in place by a sleeve nut locked with a split pin. When first announced, it was stated that a triplex chain would be fitted for overseas models but in fact

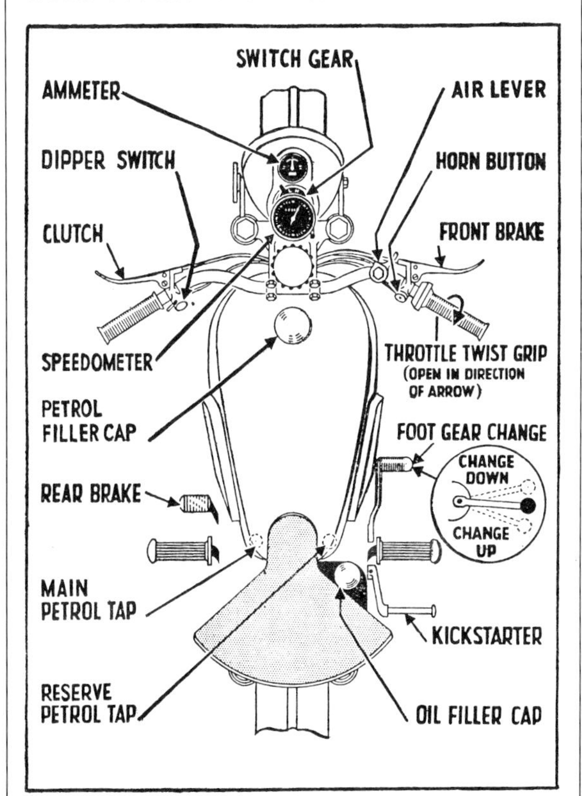

this was not done and only the duplex chain was used. The drive was to a dry clutch fitted to a four speed gearbox which followed conventional lines for the time with both clutch and output sprockets on the left, clutch fitted to mainshaft, sprocket on sleeve gear running concentric with and bushed to support mainshaft, and layshaft mounted below mainshaft.

This form of construction was virtually standard for most British machines at that time and the only unusual feature was the semi-unit construction achieved by casting a flange on the front of a standard gearbox shell and bolting this to a face machined on the rear of the crankcase. This meant fixed primary chain centres, so adjustment was by means of a curved slipper working against the underside of the lower run of the chain. This was adjusted by a jack bolt with locknut which screwed into the underside of the inner chaincase section of the left crankcase half. The primary drive and clutch was covered by an outer case, a polished alloy casting, which set off the nearside of the engine in fine style.

This outer case was fitted with a single screwed cap which gave access to the top

Left **The controls—taken from the rider's handbook**

Below **The oil tank and its connections**

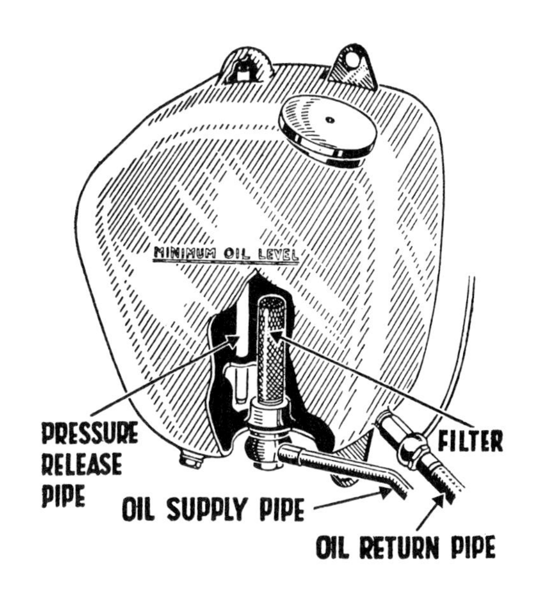

chain run for checking tension while two of the lower case screws acted as level and drain for the lubricating oil, being painted red for easy identification.

The oil level was critical as the clutch was designed to run dry, and the whole assembly was covered by an outer domed plate bolted to the body by twelve screws. Under this cover lay six clutch springs compressed with self locking shouldered nuts, and removal of these allowed the five friction and six plain plates to be removed.

In practice the oil level was too critical for anyone doing a high mileage. If allowed to drop too low the primary chain and the slipper tensioner suffered, while if too high the oil got onto the clutch linings and caused them to slip. The only answer to that was new plates or stronger clutch springs which only worked for riders with a grip of iron in their left hands. At that time BSA used dry clutches in most of their models so had no other answer. The knowledgeable enthusiasts copied Triumph and had their plates fitted with corks, filled the chaincase well above the normal level and had no problems.

The gearbox shell was closed on the right side by inner and outer covers, the first supporting the two gearbox shafts together with the selector fork rod and the selection pawl assembly. The mainshaft ran in a race in the cover and bushes in the sleeve gear, which was in turn run in a ball race fitted in the end wall of the gearbox shell with an oil seal. The layshaft ran in bushes at both ends with its right end extended to carry the speedometer drive skew gear. The centre pair of gears on each shaft was moved to select the ratios, not such an efficient method as used by other makers who only moved one gear on each shaft, so achieving a lighter feel to the change. The engagement dogs in the BSA were also rather numerous, a feature not found in the better gearboxes of that time which relied on three or

The oil system of the engine showing the pump and the pressure release valve

four dogs with plenty of backlash. This practice always felt bad in the workshop but changed gears like a hot knife through butter. The BSA design was not bad but fell some way short of the best in terms of feel and slickness.

The change mechanism, pivoted in the inner cover, worked a ratchet formed on the flat, circular cam plate which was attached to the inner front wall of the gearbox shell with the detent plunger locating it from below. The outer end of the change lever attached to the pedal shaft fitted into the outer cover. This incorporated the pedal return springs which were originally of the compression type worked in an arc. The outer cover also carried the quadrant kickstarter gear, and its clock type return spring, which engaged with a gear mounted on an extension of the mainshaft which protruded into the between covers space. This gear drove through a face ratchet to turn over the mainshaft and thus the engine. The clutch operating arm was mounted on a vertical shaft in the outer cover with a short lever at its lower end with adjuster and locknut which bore on the end of the clutch pushrod.

The speedometer drive gear was fitted in the bottom of the outer cover with its output shaft facing forward to drive the cable connecting it to the speedometer. Due to their situation these drive gears had to be changed if the final drive sprockets were altered for sidecar use or any other purpose.

The engine and gearbox unit was housed in a rigid frame built up from tubes brazed into forged lugs, as was normal at that time. It had single top and saddle tubes with duplex down tubes running from headstock to rear fork ends and saddle stays joining fork ends to seat lug. Sidecar lugs were incorporated, the oil tank fitted beneath the seat on the right with a toolbox behind and below it in the angle

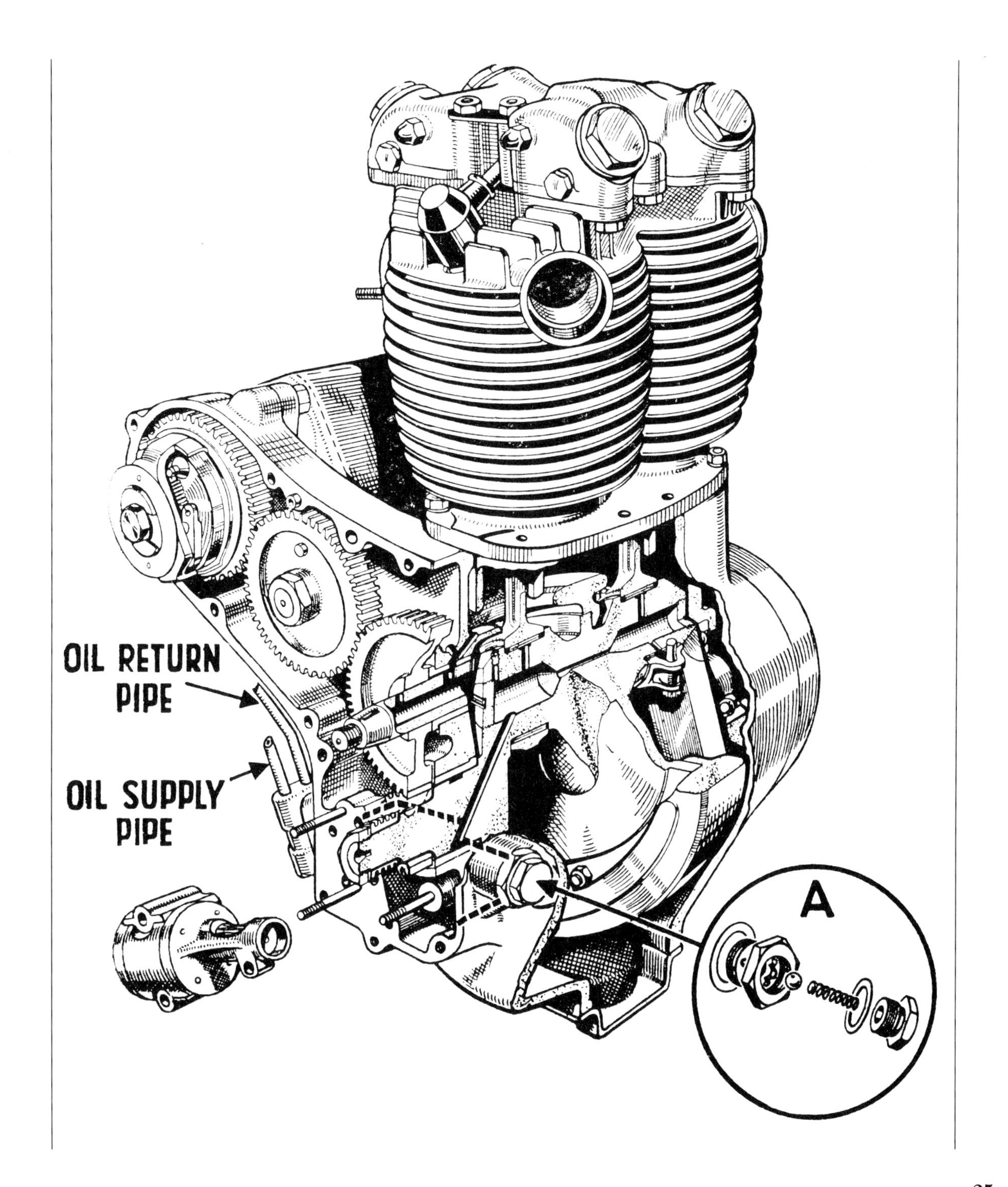
OIL RETURN
PIPE
OIL SUPPLY
PIPE
A

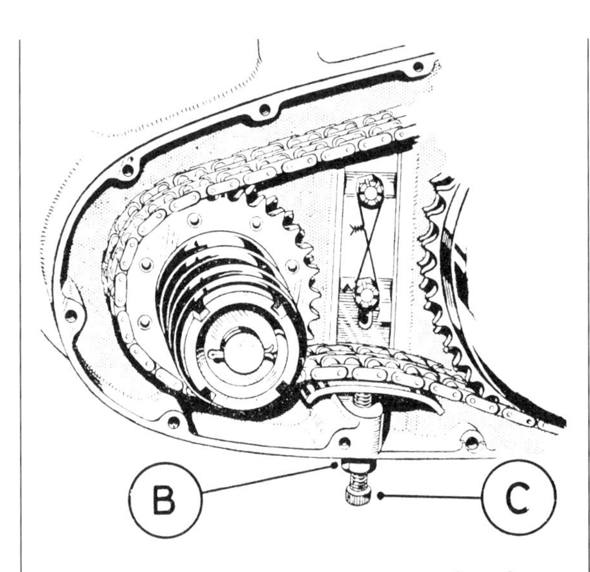

formed by the chain stays. The British industry was fond of giving its customers triangular toolboxes at that time, they were a straight carry-over from prewar days and usually very inconvenient to use.

The pillion footrests, an extra, were attached to the lower chain stays and the same fixing also held the tubular silencers clamped to the ends of the exhaust pipes. The pillion seat or an alternative tubular carrier were also extras to the standard rider only saddle. On the nearside was mounted the 6 volt, 12 ampere hour battery and sandwiched between the battery and oil tank was a Vokes-pattern air cleaner. The dynamo regulator was bolted to the rear mudguard, under the saddle, again very common practice at the time. Both runs of the final drive chain were protected by separate guards.

At the front were fitted BSA telescopic forks which were among the best available in 1946 and initially these carried a front wheel which was quickly detachable and interchangeable with the rear. By 1948 this had changed to a more conventional design with pull-out spindle which was still quick and easy to remove although no longer interchangeable with the rear wheel. The rear wheel design was used by many BSAs for a good number of years and the principle is still found on many modern machines. It consisted of a hub held in engagement with its drive built in the back of the sprocket and brake drum by a distance piece. Remove the spindle, knock out the spacer if it did not fall out and pull the wheel clear. The chain, sprocket and brake all remained attached to the machine.

Both brakes were 7 inch diameter with single leading shoes and both wheels 19 inch diameter with 3·25 section front and 3·50 section rear tyres of the studded variety. Little else was available in those years. Mudguards were reasonably well proportioned, the front held by two stays, the rear one of which could be hinged down to act as a front wheel stand, a commonly used hangover from prewar days. The rear mudguard ran from behind the gearbox to the rear of the machine where it carried the rear number plate and was supported by the chain stays and two other stays, one a loop with lift handle incorporated.

No rear stand was fitted but the early models

Left **Engine sprocket shock absorber, duplex primary chain and its slipper adjuster**

Below **The rigid rear hub. Note that chain guards were fitted to both chain runs**

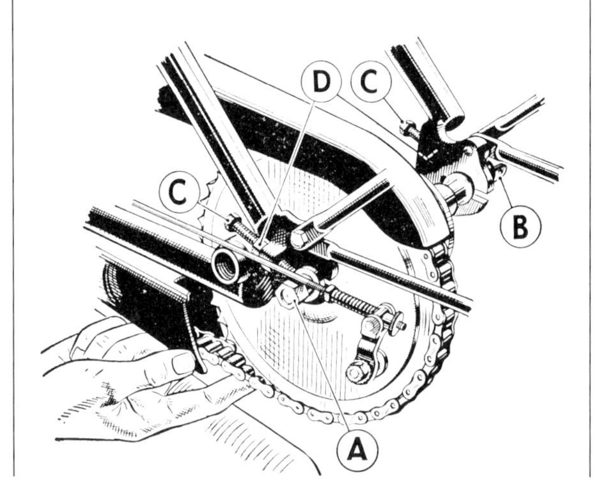

had an odd centre stand which telescoped up into the seat tube where it was retained by a tension spring. On paper it looked good as the rider merely pressed the peg on the end of the stand down to the ground and it then supported the machine until its ratchet was released by moving a small lever. In practice it was not very firm unless the machine was lifted a little so that some weight came onto the stand. For the rider to do this while holding the peg firmly on the ground fell into the art of lifting oneself by ones bootlaces. There was also the ever-present thought that as the seat tube was angled back, if the tension spring should fail while riding, the stand would become a first class sprag with results not to be contemplated. By 1948 it had been replaced by a conventional centre stand which pivoted back and if that lost its tension spring it did at least rattle over the ground to warn the rider before legging him off on the first corner.

The electrics for 1946 were all stock Lucas with negative earth and the 8 inch headlight on the early models had a flat glass and a separate reflector with means of moving the bulb for focussing. The same design with sealing bead between reflector and glass, and inset bulb continued for all the early A7s although from 1948 the headlamp glass became domed. The headlamp shell carried a separate panel with an ammeter and behind it a lighting switch with off, side and head positions.

The other electrical controls comprised dip switch on the left handlebar and horn button on the right, with the ignition cutout button mounted on the magneto contact breaker cover. The remaining controls followed normal practice for the time, with throttle and front brake controlled by the right hand, clutch by the left, gear lever and kickstarter pedals both on the right and the rear brake pedal on the left. Petrol taps were fitted to both sides of the tank at the rear. A steering damper was fitted below the steering head and controlled by a knob above the top fork crown (yoke). The air lever was fixed to the seat lug under the saddle.

The early models had the horn mounted on the right side below the oil tank and just in front of the tool box, while the speedometer was set into the top of the 3 gallon petrol tank. Both these items moved to other locations, the speedometer being attached to the fork crown from 1948 onwards and the horn moving to the left side by the front engine mountings via a position beside the battery where it resided for a short time.

The finish of the machine was in red or black, relieved with gold lines and chromium plate. The petrol tank was plated on the sides and these then painted with lined panels carrying the BSA badges, behind which were attached rubber kneegrips. The exhaust system and silencers were also plated as were the handlebars and some minor items. At that time chrome was in short supply, so that the finish of a machine would often reflect the current supply position rather than the salesman's optimistic brochure.

The power output was quoted as 26 bhp at 6000 rpm and the price was announced at £135 plus £36. 9*s*. 0*d*. purchase tax, with the speedometer a further £5. 1*s*. 7*d*. extra. Production was stated to be well in hand with prospect of delivery in November 1946. A rear sprung model was promised for later.

The late Graham Walker had ridden a prototype as early as June 1945 and his impressions were of a comfortable 80 mph machine with exceptional (for the times) roadholding and a high degree of mechanical silence. A production model ridden by another journalist confirmed these points, adding notes on easy starting, excellent tickover, quietness of engine, short movement of the gear pedal during changes and a non-snatch top gear speed as low as 7 mph.

All told the new BSA twin looked well and compared favourably with the only other twin then available, the Triumph. It looked similar enough to overcome the conservative nature of the motorcyclist, but its tank and timing cover were sufficiently different to distinguish it as a product from Armoury Road.

A road test of the A7 appeared in *Motor Cycling* in August 1947, written by the late Charlie Markham, in the enthusiastic vein that was common at that time. This spoke of steering to fine limits and of excellent roadholding that few unsprung frames could equal, also of a non-stop 190 mile run covered without fatigue.

Few modern riders realise how comfortable a machine with no rear suspension can be, when fitted with a good saddle and responsive front forks, both of which attributes the BSA had.

Despite the dreadful Pool petrol of the time, something akin to paraffin in octane value, the BSA could motor well enough for a 500 cc machine in 1947. In second gear it would run up to nearly 7000 rpm before valve float set in to act as an automatic engine speed limiter, and it only pinked if driven at the 70 mph mark for long periods in hilly country. Top speed was 84 mph at an engine speed of 5503(!) rpm, while it did 77 mph in third at 6133 rpm so was obviously overgeared to assist consumption. Driven hard, this averaged out at 60 mpg but if the cruising speed was held at 55 to 60 mph it improved to 68 mpg. In fact, a cruising speed of 60 mph was fast motoring by any standard in 1947 when few motorcycles and very few cars could keep up that sort of progress on the arterial lanes of England, and the roads themselves were seldom more than the width of two vehicles.

No vibration was reported. What there was must have been absorbed through the frame, saddle springs, footrest and handlebar rubbers, and the kneegrips. The tickover was slow and reliable as could be expected from a machine with one small carburettor, and this also helped the low speed pulling. These were both features

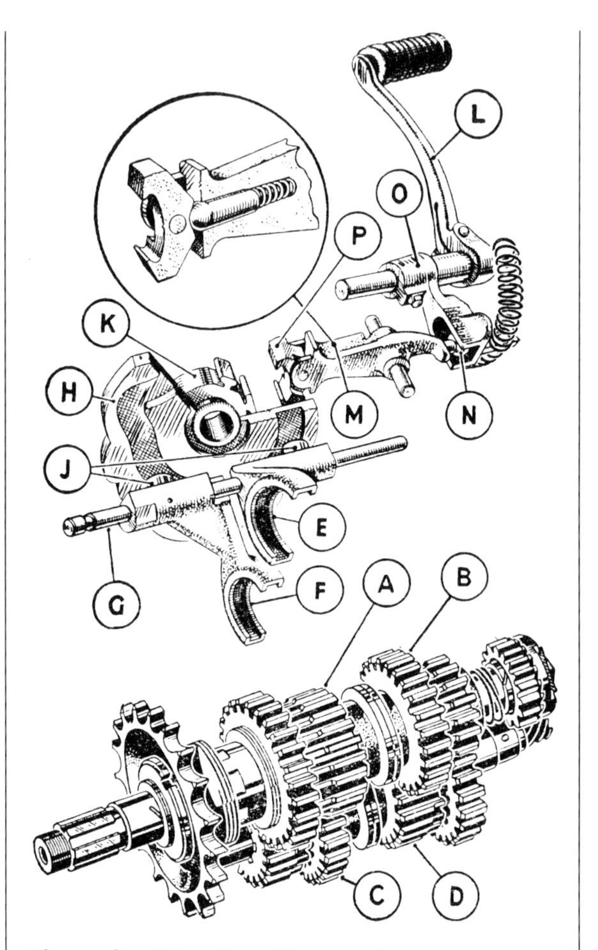

The gearbox internals and the gear change mechanism. Both selector forks work on two gears which move together although running at different speeds

on which great store was set in those times, all road tests giving the minimum non-snatch speed in top gear and reporting on the tickover.

The exhaust note, always an important feature in a machine's sales appeal, was a deep drone and the engine was very quiet. This was in contrast to the Triumph twin which had a less impressive exhaust note and a noisier engine, and the singles of the time, many of which rattled more than somewhat.

As sampled the machine weighed 373 lb and

the test persuaded a good few riders to part with some £175 in 1948 as soon as they became available on the home market. Very few of the original 1947 models with interchangeable wheels were sold in the UK; most went for export, although two ran in the Senior Clubmans TT that year.

The A7 built up a following and a reputation that endeared it to the traditional BSA owner. It was stolid and reliable. It would motor if you forced it to, but by its nature it preferred to settle for reliable cruising at whatever speed its rider had set the throttle for. With no vibration period, it ran at its set speed without pause as a good servant should but never gave any indication of life. The machine was popular, but riders who had also used the Triumph twin knew that the BSA lacked that vital spark that some engines have to make them alive and eager to run.

All the early BSA twins had this trait, but for most owners it was just what they wanted—a reliable and fast motorcycle even if the nil vibration turned out to be some vibration all the time, not much but enough to tire the rider on a long run because there was no escape from it.

One model not to be much publicised was an A7 modified for trials use early in 1948 and ridden by Bill Nicholson in a few events. He was never very happy with it and it only secured him a few class awards before it was put away and he reverted to a single, and outright wins.

At the end of 1947 most of the changes already mentioned were introduced with the speedometer moving so the tank capacity increased to 3½ gallons, the horn moving, conventional centre stand adopted, domed headlamp glass fitted and the oil feed to the rockers taken from the return line.

Also changed was the position of the air lever which moved onto the right handlebar, and the rocker box which gained four holes in its sides to provide direct access for a feeler gauge when checking the tappets. Light alloy bolts sealed the holes. A further modification not mentioned in the report of the time was the fitting of a cylinder head steady comprising two links bolted to the top of the cylinder head at the front and running forward to a single fixing on a lug fitted between the two down tubes.

The price had risen slightly to £177 16*s*. 0*d*. with the speedometer still an extra at £5 1*s*. 8*d*., which compared favourably with the Triumph Speed Twin at £180 and the Ariel Twin at £185.

During this period a further prototype twin based on the A7 was built for a specific but lucrative market. This was the then Ministry of Supply who were inviting tenders for a machine built to meet their specification for use by the Armed Forces. The specification called for twin cylinders and 500 cc with a performance of 70 mph, 80 mpg at 30 mph, 300 lb weight, braking of 35 ft from 30 mph, laden ground clearance of six inches, engine inaudible at half a mile, ability to ford fifteen inches of water, ability to climb a 1 in 2·24 gradient at 4 mph and to be able to stop and re-start on that gradient.

Both Triumph and Douglas had machines on test to meet these needs during 1946, but the BSA answer came along later and became known in 1948 when it and the other two were entered in the Scottish Six Days Trial by the Ministry.

The BSA engine was based on the A7 twin but with side valves at the front of the unit. A one piece detachable cylinder head was used and the barrels had tappet chambers covered by plates, each retained by a single knurled screw. An exhaust valve lifter was fitted and the camshaft ran across the front of the engine in the position normally occupied by the dynamo. This resulted in the timing cover being truncated at the front although the rear part still contained the drive to the magneto. It worked but ruined the appearance and balanced lines of the normal case.

With the camshaft fitted where the dynamo

normally went there was little option but to use an alternator and this was mounted in the outer half of the primary chain case which followed the normal A7 lines. The semi-unit construction gearbox was fitted, but only contained three speeds. It drove the rear wheel by a chain fully enclosed in a cast alloy case and this was adjusted by an eccentrically mounted jockey pulley as the rear wheel was fixed.

A dust and waterproof Solex carburettor with bi-starter device was fitted behind the cylinders and fed a gas passage which passed between them to the inlet valves. It was connected to an air cleaner mounted on the rear mudguard. The exhaust ports splayed out from the front corners of the cylinders and the left joined to the right to provide a siamesed system connected to a single, low mounted silencer.

The frame was a straightforward rigid, duplex one, the only unusual feature being the fixed rear wheel spindle. Telescopic front forks were fitted and drum brakes. The saddle could be adjusted fore and aft as well as up and down, and a pillion pad was mounted on top of the air cleaner.

The prototype was finished in service trim with pannier frames fitted either side of the rear wheel to take the standard canvas bags. A tool box was fitted in the top of the fuel tank but the oil tank was a standard A7 item.

Although the BSA and the other machines were good, the Ministry went another way and no more was heard of this venture.

Despite the austere times in the UK in the 1940s a sports version of the twin was announced and first shown to the public at the 1948 Earls Court Show. Originally it was called the Special but this was soon changed to the Star Twin, and it had the benefit of two carburettors and the slightly higher compression ratio of 7·5 to 1 which helped to increase the standard power output from 27 bhp at 5800 rpm to 31 bhp at 6000 rpm.

Lubrication chart for the A7 and the Star Twin. The plunger rear suspension must be kept well greased as must the saddle nose. Wear at either point can make handling feel odd

The Special was fitted as standard with plunger rear suspension and finished with matt silver and chromium tank and wheels with a star transfer badge on the tank, to distinguish it from the standard model. The price of the new model was £203. 4*s*. 0*d*. while the rigid A7 remained unchanged with the speedometer still an extra for both machines. The spring frame was priced at £12. 14*s*. 0*d*. when ordered as an extra on the A7 while pillion footrests cost 12/9d. and the pillion seat or alternative luggage carrier cost £1. 6*s*. 8*d*.

Early in 1949 a Star Twin was road tested by *The Motor Cycle* and received a very enthusiastic report, although the machine was no faster than the A7 had been in 1947, recording 84 mph in top and 75, 57 and 37 in the gears. Consumption at constant speeds ranged from 93 mpg at 30 mph to 65 mpg at 60 mph so an overall figure of 60 to 70 mpg would have been usual under normal to hard driving conditions.

Brakes and handling were reported on favourably and vibration only noticed at 50 mph in top and when above 70 mph. All the indirect gears, especially third, were audible and the gear change none too certain which indicated clutch drag, confirmed by the noise that occurred when bottom gear was engaged with the machine at rest.

The engine unit was reported as having no oil leaks but did pink on the Pool petrol under hard acceleration. Minor changes on the cycle parts were the deletion of the guard on the lower chain run and the addition of a lifting handle on the left side located between the saddle spring mounting and the top of the plunger unit.

The Star Twin was sold in this form for 1949 and 1950 but the BSA engine never really took to twin carburettors and usually went best with one, even when used for road racing. The twin

LUBRICATION CHART

For B.S.A. 500 c.c. O.H.V. Vertical Twin

(Model A7 and A7 Star Twin)

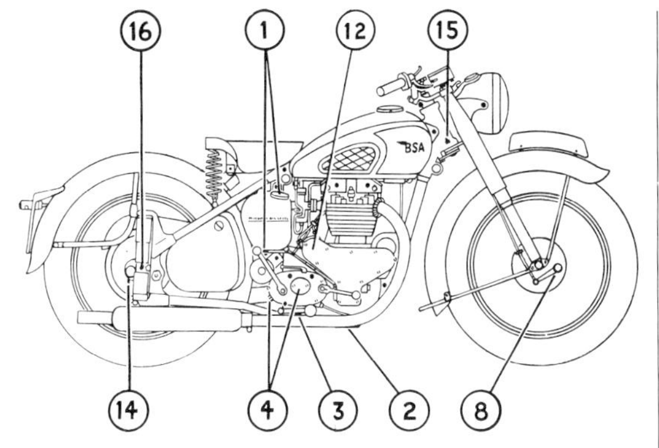

ENGINE OIL.		
No.	Part.	Pages.
1	Oil tank and filter	11 12
2	Crankcase and filter	12 17
3—4	Gearbox oil level	17
5—6	Primary chain oil level	15 17
7	Front forks (see table below)	18

THIN MACHINE OIL.		
No.	Part	Pages.
8	Brake cam spindles	15
9	Rear brake pedal	15
10	Saddle nose bolt	15
11	Control levers, etc.	15
12	Automatic advance mechanism	16
13	Magneto	17

GREASE.		
No.	Part.	Pages.
14	Wheel hubs	15
15	Steering head	15
16	Rear suspension (when fitted)	50
17	Central stand fulcrum	17

It is recommended that the following brands and grades of oil be used.

BRAND.	Summer.	Winter.	Front Forks only.	GREASE.
Mobiloil ...	D	BB	Arctic	Mobil-Grease No. 2
Castrol ...	Grand Prix	XXL	Castrolite	Castrolease Heavy
Essolube ...	50	40	20	Esso Grease
Price's Energol	SAE40	SAE30	SAE30	Belmoline D
Shell	Triple	Double	Single	Retinax CD

For extra heavy duty such as trials and competition work, slightly heavier grades of oil may be used if desired.

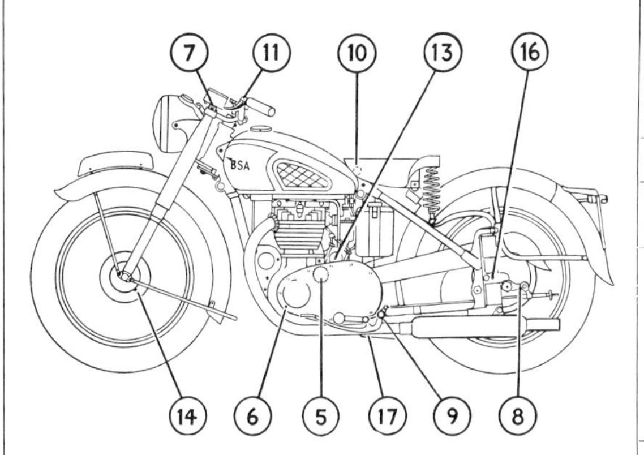

units ran without air cleaners and had an unfortunate tendency to catch fire unless gauze covers were fitted to the bellmouths.

From then on until 1950 the A7 and the Star Twin continued in these forms with little change, for it was a period when production was paramount and annual changes just a nuisance to the factory. In the main it was a seller's market with machines in short supply, so there was little incentive to introduce changes for the sake of them. However, behind the scenes BSA were, as usual, far from idle and the results of their work came to fruition in 1950.

3 Two twins—A7 and A10

In October 1949 BSA announced a new larger capacity twin to be called the A10. Although very similar in appearance to the early A7 it was in fact a new engine design using many of the original basic features. It was of 650 cc capacity and was soon followed by a 500 cc version, still known as the A7, produced by reducing the new engine's bore and stroke. Many parts of the two new machines were common but relatively few from the early A7 engine would fit the new

Right **A picture that typifies what the BSA vertical twin stood for in the 1950s. It took dad to work during the week and the family out into the country at weekends. The rigid frame was normal practice for sidecar use at the time**

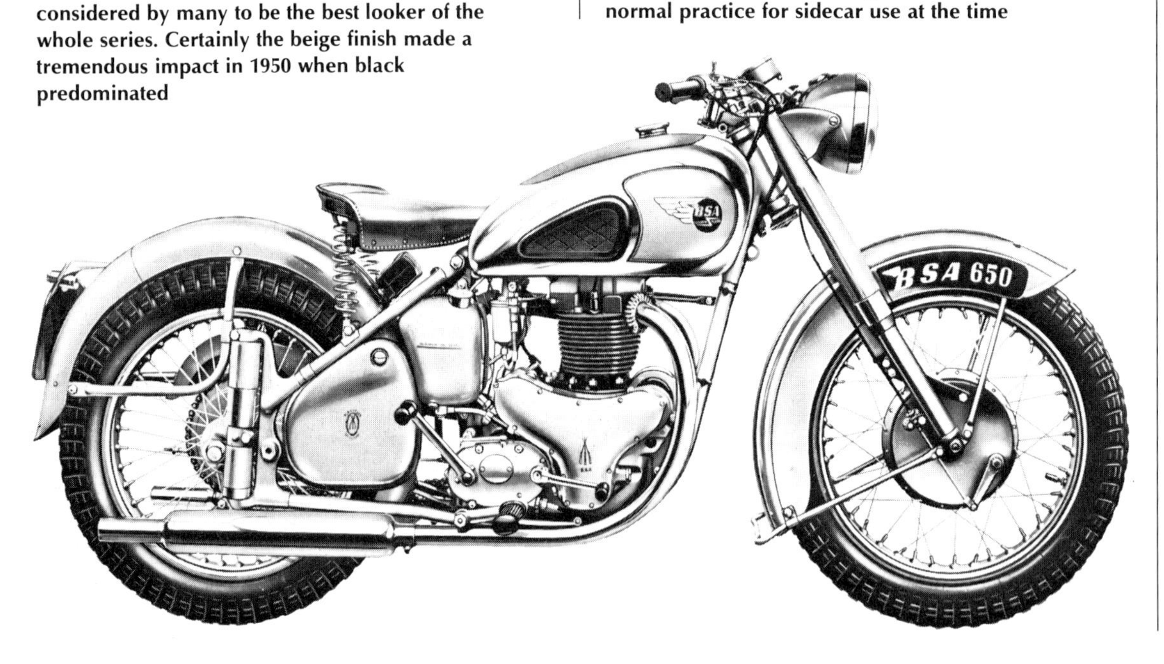

Below **The A10 Golden Flash in its early form, considered by many to be the best looker of the whole series. Certainly the beige finish made a tremendous impact in 1950 when black predominated**

one. Cycle parts remained common with detail changes only until 1954 when the swinging fork (arm) frame was introduced and at the same time the gearbox became a separate unit, as was common with most English machines of that period.

The new A10 engine and gearbox unit followed the same basic form as the 1946 design and used engine dimensions of 70 × 84 mm to give a capacity of 646 cc. The new A7 changed to 66 × 72·6 mm bore and stroke and 497 cc capacity for 1951.

The most immediate difference from the early engine lay in the cylinder head and rocker boxes. These were still cast in iron and light alloy respectively, but the head casting now included the induction manifold and the rocker box was a one piece affair with two covers each held by four nuts. Each exhaust valve now had its own well, although the inlets were still

combined and the cooling air that passed between the exhaust wells was guided round the inlet well by curved fins. The inlet manifold had a slight downdraught angle and provided for one carburettor only, a feature which stayed with the engine throughout its life. The detail design of the rockers and valve gear was unchanged from the earlier engine but with all four rockers in one casting, re-assembly of the rocker box to the cylinder while ensuring that all four pushrods had engaged correctly with their respective rockers became even more difficult. The answer was to use a BSA comb which would hold the pushrods in the correct positions while the box was lowered into place.

Apart from this snag, the assembly of the top end remained straightforward with the head still retained by nine bolts and the rocker box by bolts and nuts.

The barrel design followed the earlier pattern with the pushrod tunnel cast in the rear and the barrel held down by nuts on its flange. However their number had increased by one to nine. What was new was the tappets, their position and their method of fitting, as they now ran directly in holes machined in the barrel at the base of the pushrod tunnel. Each tappet was formed from a cylinder with each end chamfered and a flat machined on one side. They worked against each other in pairs, running directly on the cams and supporting the lower ends of the pushrods in recesses. The centre of each tappet was machined away, partly to reduce weight but also to allow for their retention, as without this they would drop out during assembly. The outer, inlet tappets were retained by grub screws inserted from each side but the centre, exhaust ones were held by a dowel with flats and groove, which pushed in place from the rear into a hole just below the base flange. The two flats on this dowel engaged with flats machined on the tappets to prevent them from dropping out and were themselves held by a locking ball bearing fitting into the groove from above and fixed in place by a further grub screw.

The pistons of the new engine were in a silicon alloy and of a flexible skirt design. The gudgeon bosses were very rigidly connected to the piston crown by internal webs but slots were cut in the skirt running parallel to the webs from the gudgeon pin centre line up to just below the oil control ring. Each pair of slots on front and back of the piston was joined by a thin horizontal slot cut parallel to the scraper ring. This held the heat in the piston crown, so allowing smaller skirt running clearances to be used with reduced noise and ring wear. The piston crown itself was concave on the original compression ratio of 6·5 to 1, and each piston carried two compression rings above the scraper.

The pistons ran on fully floating gudgeon pins, retained by circlips, and were attached to light alloy rods with bushed small ends. The big ends were split and lined with steel-backed shells in the conventional manner and the big end bolts located the caps to the rods.

The crankshaft itself was of the same design as before, being a one piece steel forging with the flywheel bolted to the centre web. It ran in the same timing side bush but on the drive side a roller bearing replaced the ballrace previously fitted, and the crankshaft was allowed a small degree of end float on assembly.

The lower half of the engine and the layout of timing gear, magneto drive, oil pump and dynamo closely resembled the 1946 design but some minor changes were incorporated in the crankcase castings. One of these allowed for the additional cylinder stud to be fitted, but the main change concerned the camshaft which had a trough cast under it to retain oil. This

A very well used police Flash which covered 120,000 miles on the original crankshaft. Note the car dynamo fitted in front of the engine to cope with the extra load

NOTTINGHAMSHIRE
CONSTABULARY
POL
BSA
OAL 984

provided constant and immediate lubrication for the cams, even if the engine was not started for long periods, and the surplus oil overflowed onto the big ends and was then flung up onto the cylinder bores. The amount and the direction in which it flowed were controlled by the shape of the trough which was arrived at after extensive tests.

The cams themselves had quietening ramps giving one thou lift in three degrees of crankshaft rotation which contributed to the quiet running of the engine. This was assisted by the careful detail design of the timing gears and their tooth form.

In the timing case the diameter of the timed breather became smaller and its path to the outside world more tortuous as it led, by drillways, across the timing cover and through both crankcase halves to a pipe which ran from a point above the camshaft left bearing housing down behind the crankcase casting, just in front of the final drive sprocket, finally exiting to the left of the sump cover.

The dynamo drive was unchanged but the new longer unit with a fifty per cent increase in output was fitted and at the same time the electrical system was changed over to positive earth.

The transmission design remained very similar but the gearbox was modified early in 1950 to improve gear changing. It was quite capable of handling the fairly modest engine power output of 35 bhp at 5500 rpm, with a maximum torque figure of 39 ft lb at 3900 rpm. With the fixed primary drive centres there was no option but to keep the same engine sprocket and clutch wheel, which are in fact common to all rigid and plunger frame A7s and A10s with semi-unit engine and gearbox construction. The gearbox sprocket for the A10 was given one more tooth than that used for the A7 but the rear wheel shed four teeth. Where sidecar gearing was specified both machines used the same rear hub with three

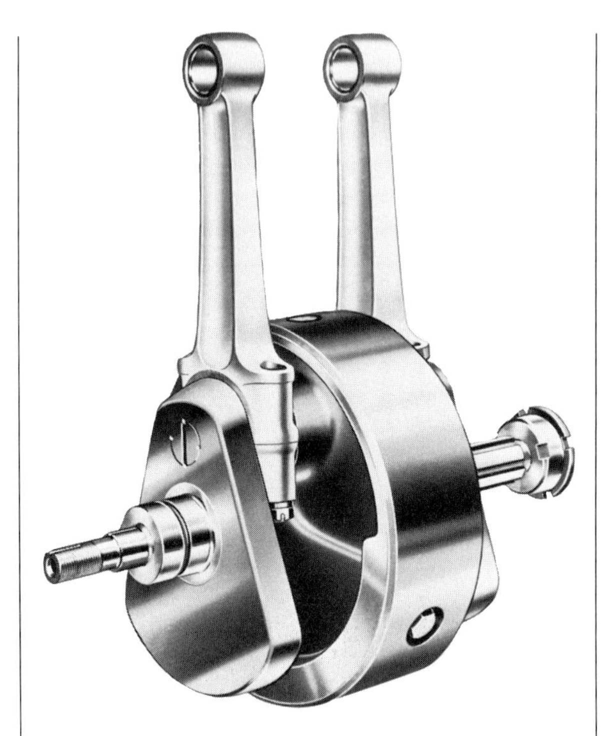

The crankshaft assembly used from 1958 onwards with the flywheel retained by three radial bolts

teeth more than the standard A7 but retained their normal sprockets on the other shafts.

The new engines were fitted into the existing rigid and plunger rear suspension frames and in most respects the cycle parts were unchanged. There was a little more chrome plating and the front mudguard was deeply valanced so that the registration numbers could be painted on its sides. The toolbox had a more rounded shape to fit in with the rear suspension and chain stays while the petrol tank was made more quickly detachable by slotting its front and rear fixing lugs so that the bolts only needed to be slackened for tank removal. The front brake size was increased to eight inches in diameter.

The most dramatic feature of the new model was its golden beige colour from which its type name, the Golden Flash, was derived. This model was fitted with the plunger frame as standard and with a larger capacity petrol tank. It was mainly destined for export in its early days. A version fitted with a rigid frame and the standard-sized tank was also available in a black finish but this was dropped from the range in 1951 when all the twins were fitted with the plunger frame as standard.

The Golden Flash proved tremendously popular, and like the A7 quickly earned a reputation for having a great capacity for hard work. It was particularly good with a sidecar attached when it would still exceed 70 mph and reach 65 mph in third while keeping to the right side of 50 mpg even when hauling a heavy chair about. Solo, it became a very fast and exciting machine with a top speed exceeding the one hundred mark and acceleration to match. It was road tested by *Motor Cycling* in 1950 and they recorded 104·56 mph over a flying quarter mile, with maximum of 89 mph in third and 66 mph in second. The BSA was the fastest road machine they tested that year and covered the standing start quarter mile in the shortest time, 15·82 seconds. The weight was quoted as 395 lb which must have helped to achieve this and the

The light alloy cylinder head used for the sports models running on higher compression ratios. All models from 1950 had the Siamesed inlet tract and only one carburettor

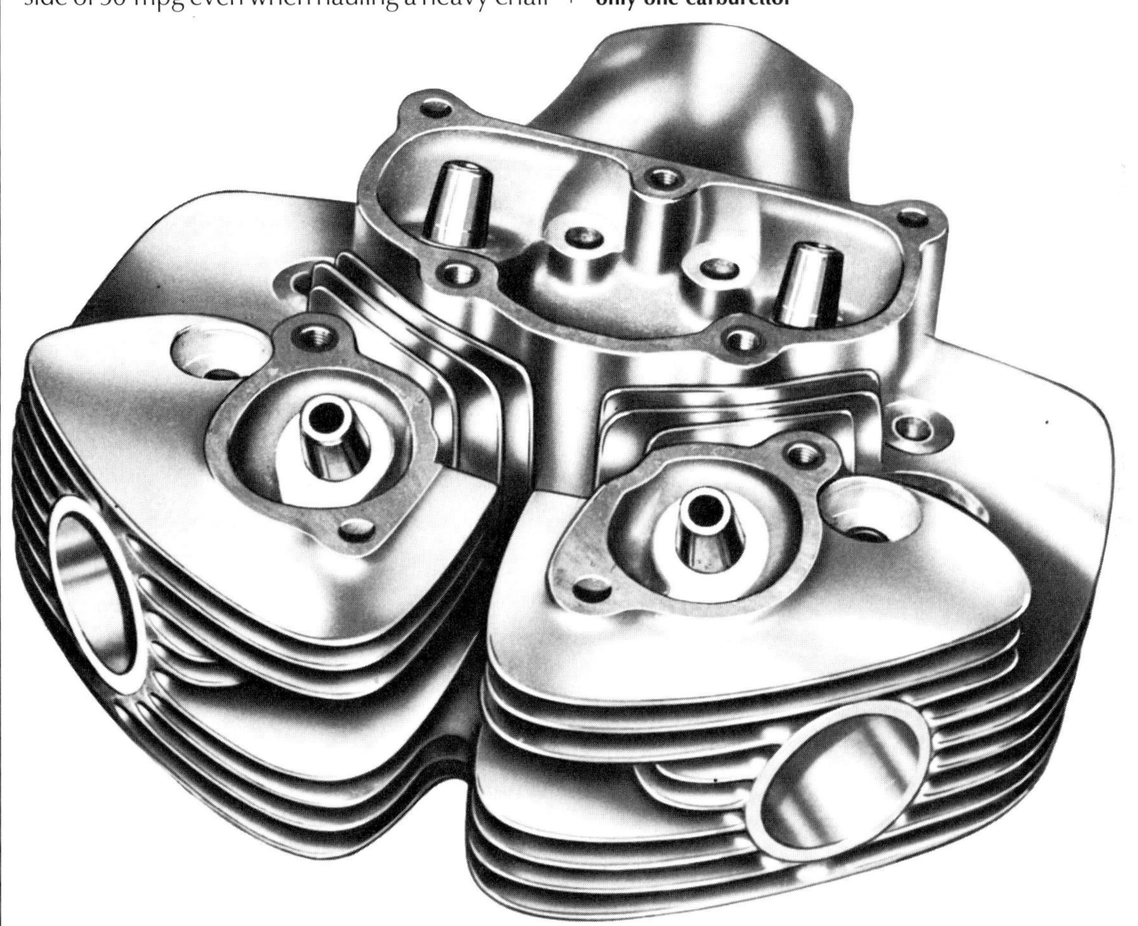

braking figure of 25·5 ft from 30 mph. Consumption at a steady 30 mph was 89 mpg but very few owners would have driven such a machine so slowly, so most settled for the 60 mpg they obtained while riding fast.

The machine tested was the home model with rigid frame and small tank and its listed dry weight was as low as 380 lb and its price including purchase tax £193. 0*s*. 10*d*. At the same time, the rigid A7 weighed in at 375 lb and £182. 17*s*. 8*d*., while the Star Twin with plunger frame ran out at 382 lb and £208. 5*s*. 8*d*. The spring frame for both A7 and A10 was listed as an optional extra at £12. 14*s*. 0*d*. As time passed, both figures were to creep up and by the end of 1952, the plunger framed A10 was up to 408 lb and £227. 8*s*. 11*d*. while the two A7 models, both with plunger frames, were at 400 lb and £220. 8*s*. 4*d*. for the standard model and 401 lb and £230. 0*s*. 0*d*. for the Star Twin.

The top end showing cylinder head with valves installed together with the assembled rocker box

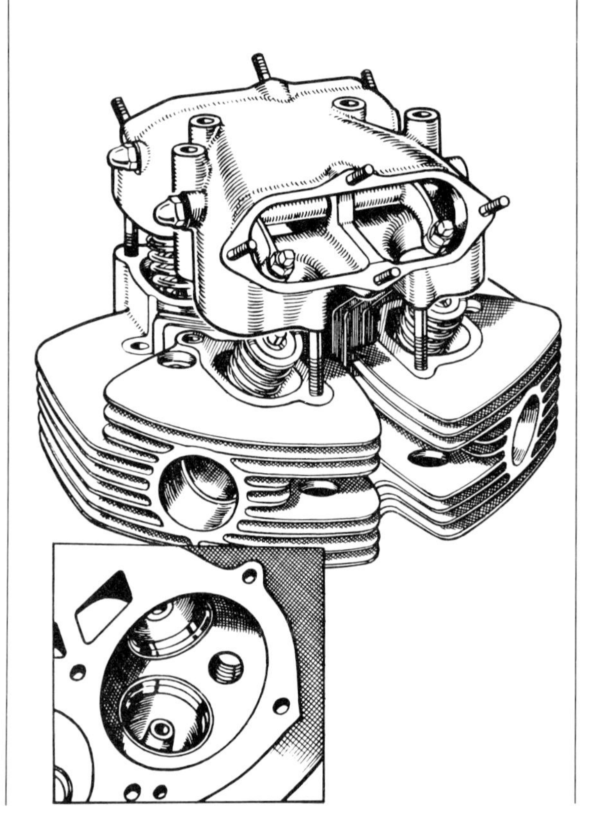

On the roads of the early 1950s, the new twins motored reliably with a bottom half that would withstand just about anything the average owner asked of it and would keep going for very extended periods. In fact, they required a considerable mileage to loosen them up to the point when they really felt free and keen to run fast. A few ran into a minor problem with carbon building up on the exhaust valve stem which slowed down the valve closing speed. In place of the squeak that such a problem would bring on a B31, on the A10 the power would begin to fade slightly while the exhaust note became much harsher and the tappets rattled furiously. The B31 cure was a finger over the oil return pipe in the oil tank to force the lubricant up to the valve gear, but on the twin the rider had rather more work to do as the answer was to counterbore the exhaust valve guides. Most owners would give the engines a decoke and new exhaust valves at the same time as the old valves suffered if the fault had persisted for any length of time.

The clutch and gearbox remained the same with the primary chain oil level still critical and the gearchange good if the rider matched engine and road speeds reasonably accurately. If he did not, the change would become quite audible.

The handling of the machines was typical of the times, adequate rather than good. The rigid frames steered well enough and would hold a set line through a corner even over the bumps provided the rider kept a tight rein on things. Where the road surface was smooth, the machine was very easy to hold to its line and the light weight allowed it to be banked from one side to the other quickly and smoothly.

The plunger frame was less successful and

Above **The full width front brake of 7 inch diameter and $1\frac{1}{2}$ inch width**

Right **The front wheel installed with full width hub**

could be a good deal more exciting for its only damping was that provided by the grease on the plungers, any rust that might have appeared on the spring covers and the fit of the wheel hub to the frame. Due to manufacturing tolerances, it was possible for the wheel to pull or push the sliding wheel carriers away from their true positions as dictated by the frame they were fitted to. Thus in one frame, the wheel could move quite easily while with a change of wheel or frame, the suspension could become fairly stiff. The uncontrolled movement at the back end began to make its presence felt on bumpy roads at between 60 and 70 mph, when it would send the whole machine into a weave. The result was that on fast bumpy stretches the rigid frame would often be faster and much less disturbing to the rider. Once on straight roads the added comfort of the plungers was worth having.

The Golden Flash suffered more from this problem due to the increased power and although faster than the 500 cc twin in a straight line, many riders preferred the smaller engine as it was the more pleasant of the two to ride solo.

In the main the cycle parts served very well, although the brakes were hard pressed when a heavy sidecar was attached to the A10 and driven fast for few, if any, chairs at that time were fitted as standard with a brake to their 'third' wheel and it was considered normal for sidecar braking to be much inferior to that of a solo. Sidecar users just had to anchor up well in advance but for solo use the BSA brakes were powerful, smooth and progressive. The wheels were not quite up to the hardest sidecar use but were faultless for the solo rider. With a chair attached the front wheel bearings could be

worn out quickly and the rear hub suffered. The old type of quickly detachable hub was built up from two pressings, formed with crinkle edges to take straight spokes of equal length on both sides, which were riveted to a central sleeve. Under hard sidecar work the rivets would work loose and eventually shear off.

The lighting was improved in 1950 with a higher wattage headlight bulb even though it was still fitted in the same style of holder that could be slid in or out for the best focus.

The two twins were built in this form for some years before a major change occurred when the swinging fork frame was introduced. Up to then, modifications were fairly minor although one of importance was introduced on the 1951 engines. This was the drilling of a small hole in the left hand connecting rod only, that ran from the centre of the big end shell off at an angle to emerge from the side of the rod at the lower end of the relieved section. A drilled big end shell to match the rod was fitted in the upper position, to the left rod, the other three shells remaining undrilled. If the rods are interchanged or the shells not fitted correctly, the left big end will be inadequately lubricated. Other minor changes for that year included a different carburettor slide for the A7 and a slightly bigger carburettor for the Star Twin.

1952 saw more small changes with the Star Twin made available with an Amal TT carburettor of increased size and some electrical changes. These included the horn which was changed to a Lucas type HF1234 which continued to be used up to the last of the A7 and A10 twins. The headlight was changed from the adjustable focus to the pre-focus type with bulb located into the rear of the reflector by its flange and held in place with an adaptor carrying the supply current wires. A less popular change was the adoption of the underslung pilot light, a short lived folly formed in the bottom of the headlamp shell which produced a small rectangular patch of light,

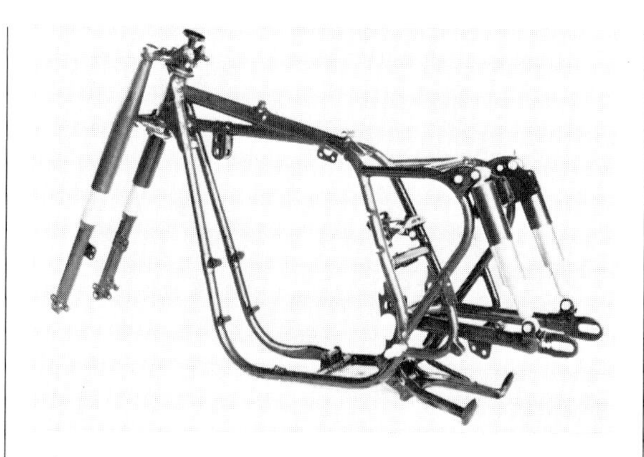

Above **The all-welded duplex frame with swinging fork rear suspension, shown bare with centre stand and forks**

Right **The QD rear wheel with full width hub as used in the swinging fork frame. The brake is cable operated from a lever attached to a shaft passing through the fork pivot**

partly obscured by the then obligatory front number plate. As anything other than a parking lamp, it was useless and the industry dropped them after a year or two. The Star Twin went over to manual ignition with high compression pistons and a special camshaft, while all twins had improvements made to the breathing system, petrol tank ties added and modified front fork damping.

1953 saw the introduction of the first headlamp cowling which carried the light unit and was flared back to be clamped in place by the top fork nuts and the lower crown clamp bolts. The pressing also carried the speedometer centrally, so doing away with its bracket, and the lighting switch on the left and an ammeter on the right. These two items were mounted at an angle, nearly on the sides of the cowling, which drew some caustic comments from both riders and press on the problems of reading the ammeter at all, let alone accurately, and reaching the light switch if a screen was fitted. The switch was less of a problem for the underslung pilot light was still fitted so most

riders only used the headlight and never needed to use the switch while riding. The ammeter was only of use when standing beside the machine as anything less than a substantial discharge was hard to detect.

The good news for 1953 was the introduction of a sports version of the A10 for the USA. This was the Super Flash and it featured high compression pistons, a special camshaft and an Amal TT carburettor. In addition to the modified engine which developed 42 bhp and pushed the road speed up to a genuine 110 mph, the machine had a different tank finish, paired speedometer and rev-counter, sports mud-guards and a new pair of handlebars.

This new model was shown in Europe at the Geneva and Vienna Shows early in 1954 and was the forerunner of the Road Rocket series which ran on to 1963, culminating in the highly regarded Rocket Gold Star model.

The Super Flash used the old plunger frame but BSA were well aware that this was hardly adequate for the twins so they introduced a new swinging fork frame for the Road Rocket, which was shown alongside the Super Flash at exhibitions abroad.

It was not until the 1954 Earls Court Show that the Road Rocket appeared in England as part of a line-up of twins with several major changes to engine, gearbox and cycle parts.

The engine and gearbox of the new machines reverted to separate units when fitted to the new swinging fork frame, the semi-unit construction being retained for the plunger frame machines which were gradually phased out. The engine design remained unchanged except for the actual crankcase castings which were modified to suit the needs of separate gearbox and engine plates. Both the sports models featured light alloy cylinder heads with compression ratios of 7·25 to 1 for the 500 cc engine and 8 to 1 for the 650.

1955 was the year that the Amal Monobloc carburettor was introduced in place of the old type six and the new unit was fitted to the new models. The A7 retained the same size it had always used and was to keep until the model was discontinued, while the sports model, which was re-named the Shooting Star, used the same carburettor size as the Star Twin had fitted. 1954 saw the end of the TT Amal on the 500 cc engine but it was continued on the Road Rocket up to 1957 and reappeared with a larger bore in 1960 and 1961. The Golden Flash followed the lead of the A7 and just changed over to the Monobloc while keeping to the existing bore size.

By changing to a separate gearbox, BSA were able to use their heavyweight unit which was fitted with its normal clutch. The old shell with mounting plate was replaced by the standard pivoted casting which provided for primary chain adjustment so the early slipper tensioner was dispensed with. In its place was provided a conventional draw bolt attached to the top fixing bolt on the right side engine to gearbox plate. As usual with such devices, actual adjustment was awkward, involving turning the adjustment nut one flat at a time, as it was impractical to use a ratchet or box spanner. Fortunately, it was not a frequent job and did not involve too much gearbox movement at any one time. Chain tension was still checked via a capped hole in the primary chaincase.

While the primary chain adjustment became more of a chore and filling and checking the gearbox oil level remained as awkward as ever, with oil having to be poured in a hole in

Left **The neat and effective chaincase used on the swinging fork models. This is a 1956 model**

Below **Top of the range A10 in Super Rocket form—a fast and stylish road-burner**

the end of the box until it drained from a level hole, the use of a standard box did eventually allow the choice of the full range of internal ratios. These covered wide (for trials), standard, scrambles, close and extra close. In time all became available in standard form or with needle roller layshaft bearings while the extra close box was also available with needle roller mainshaft bearings as well.

A further facility offered with the gearbox was a reverse camplate. This was a mirror pattern of the standard part and was intended to be fitted when rearsets were used and the gear pedal reversed, as it would retain the normal up-for-down change sequence in this circumstance.

The new frame was of straightforward construction with a single top tube and duplex down tubes which ran under the engine and gearbox and up to the rear of the top tube. The steering head was further braced by a tube running back from its lower end into the underside of the main top tube. The headstock was gussetted with plates while the subframe and most brackets were welded onto the main structure.

The swinging fork pivoted on two Silentbloc bushes, pressed into its cross tube, supported on a pivot bolt fitted to flanges welded to the main frame tubes. This bolt was fixed by its own locking bolt in addition to a substantial nut on the right side of the machine. The rear suspension units were supplied by Girling and fitted with a three position cam adjuster set by a 'C' spanner supplied in the tool kit.

The frame was listed with a saddle but from the start it was supplied with a dualseat so that the grease nipple thoughtfully provided to lubricate the saddle nose bolt was rather redundant. Also listed at a later date was a crankcase shield which was fitted to the Spitfire Scrambles model.

At the front end the frame carried standard BSA telescopic forks of the same appearance as

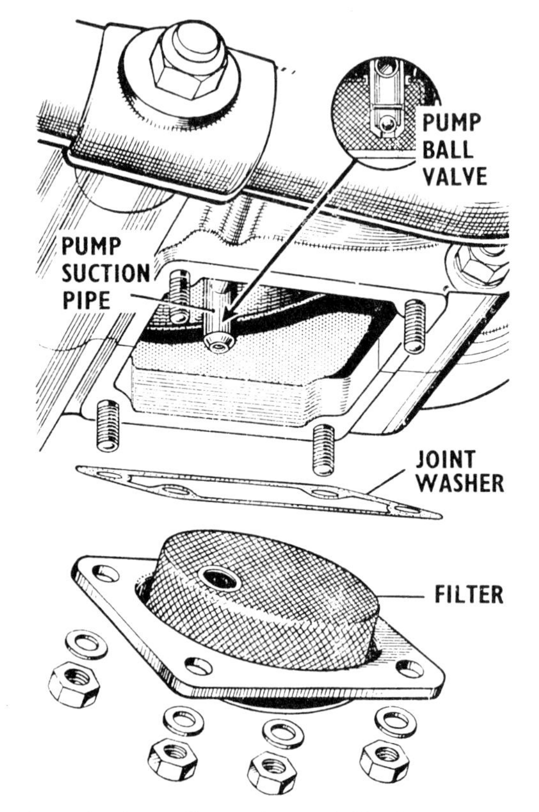

Above **Crankcase filter and pump ball valve. Used for years, this is the unit construction version. Many riders have prodded that ball free with a piece of wire over the years!**

Right **1957 BSA brochure showing many of the features used on the A and other ranges. All apply to the twins**

before but modified internally so that their fork oil content was nearly doubled. On the Road Rocket the forks were fitted with the earlier style of headlamp without cowl, but still with the underslung pilot lamp. The older ammeter and light switch were also used, and either side of them were located matching speedometer and rev-counter heads. The speedometer was still driven from the gearbox but the rev-counter drive was from the magneto gear, a right-angle drive box being attached to a suitably machined timing cover.

Total enclosure for rear chain for greater efficienc/ and longer life.
Extra on A and B models.
High - efficiency aluminium alloy cylinder head. *On A7 Shooting Star and Road Rocket.*
Only BSA gives you ALL these features
Full-width aluminium hubs with central cast - in iron alloy brake drums—extremely powerful.
On A and B models.
ome - panelled petrol k, 100% rubber nted, single-bolt fixing easy access to engine. *A and B models.*
f-proof headlock cks at acute e. *On C12, M, B A models. Extra D3 and C10L els.*
Swinging-arm rear suspension with hydraulic damping and silentbloc bearings is standard on *D3, C12 and B and A models.* The type illustrated incorporating duplex frame construction as used on *B and A models* possesses great lateral rigidity for high speed performance.
Detachable rear wheel.

Both petrol and oil tanks were new, the first a common four gallons for both engine sizes, and retained by a single bolt fitted into the centre of the tank top and covered by a rubber bung. The early models were fitted with a circular tank badge with the piled arms in the centre of the design except for the Shooting Star model which used the Gold Star design of badge. Kneegrips were still fitted and carried the Company name. Later models used a pear-shaped tank badge and different, anonymous kneegrips.

The oil tank was of completely new design with an increased capacity of $5\frac{1}{2}$ pints. It was shaped to fit to the right side of the machine in the triangle formed by the seat, subframe tube and saddle tube, and was matched on the left by a similar shaped toolbox. Between the two was fitted the battery under the dualseat which was removed for servicing. The oil tank cap occupied the top front corner of the container and to the rear of it was an oil breather tower with vent pipe pointing into the centre of the machine. The supply and return pipes fitted to the inner side of the tank while the combined drain plug and filter was fitted from the outside. As before, the feed to the valve gear was taken from the return pipe but the supply pipe was continued in the tank so that its end fitted into the filter.

The existing types of wheels were continued for the early swinging fork models and at the rear the quick detachable hub continued in use with the backplate moved round so that the cam pivot was directly above the wheel spindle and the cam lever hung down with the brake rod running alongside the swinging fork tube.

The change over from plunger to swinging fork frames took some time to complete so that for a while both were sold. The new frame and larger front brake were used first on the two sports versions and only later for the standard ones. Exports were still of prime consideration, so that the requests of the home market for the newer features were often relegated well behind other countries' demands. However, by 1955 the needs of production at the factory dictated that only one basic form of machine was built, so the new frame became standard and the models continued with only minor changes up to 1962.

In 1955 BSA introduced one major change and a number of minor ones, in addition to fitting the swinging fork frame as standard to all models. The main change was to the front wheel which was fitted with a full width hub, the brake diameter reverting to seven inches. The alloy backplate was anchored by a torque stay and carried a lug for the cable adjuster to screw into. In addition, a fulcrum adjuster was fitted to work on the shoe ends furthest away from the brake cam, so plenty of brake adjustment was provided.

Above **USA style Gold Flash with high rise handlebars and grab-rail behind the seat. Two US gallon petrol tank is smaller than that used in England and of a different finish**

Right **1957 Road Rocket fitted with rev-counter option. The silencer indicates that the slight oil leak of period road tests has afflicted it**

The other changes concerned the fitting of a steering lock in the top fork crown which held the front wheel on left lock when actuated, the fitting of a parking bulb in the headlamp shell that shone through a transparent spot in the reflector and thus did away with the underslung

arrangement, and the combining of dip switch and horn button into one control on the left handlebar.

For 1956 attention was turned to the rear wheel which was fitted with a full width hub in the same style as that used for the front with the brake moved to the right side. The rear hub remained quickly detachable in the same basic manner as before, with knockout spindle, but the hub and sprocket were held together by four special nuts which pulled up on studs secured in the hub. Their removal along with the brake details and main wheel spindle allowed the wheel to be removed as before.

The rear brake backplate was of the same form as the front with fulcrum adjuster, lug for cable adjuster and anchored by a torque stay. The operation was by cable which ran forward

Left **Rear chaincase used in the late 1950s—smart and practical**

BSA

Above **Headlamp cowl introduced for 1958 and used for most of the range**

Left **Shooting Star with revised headlight mounting and neat, cast iron front hub**

Top left **The revised silencer used on the later twins**

along the fork arm to a small lever attached to a spindle which ran right through the fork pivot bolt. To its left end was splined the brake pedal which curved forward and under the left footrest to bring its pad to the usual position under the rider's foot. Attached to an extension of the brake pedal above its pivot was a tension spring which operated the brake light switch bolted to the frame above the left pillion footrest.

A worthwhile option that year was a full enclosure chaincase, this continuing to be available for the twins up to 1962. It consisted of upper and lower sections which bolted to the swinging fork, a section that enclosed the gearbox sprocket, and a tail section the removal of which gave ready access to the chain and rear sprocket for inspection. Two holes were provided in the side, one for chain tension checking and the other to give access, one at a time, to the four nuts holding the sprocket to the rear hub. Both holes were fitted with rubber plugs carrying the BSA insignia and the case around the front hole was pressed to simulate the flying wing symbol BSA often used in their trade mark.

In July 1956 the first English road test of the Road Rocket appeared in *Motor Cycling*. The model tested was finished in black with a red tank with chrome panels, and other bright parts chrome plated including the mudguards. The price was £217. 10*s*. 0*d*. plus £52. 4*s*. 0*d*. purchase tax and with the fitted extras which included a very useful prop stand and a rev-counter the total cost came to £279. 15*s*. 8*d*. The power output was given as 40 bhp at 6000 rpm and on its 4·53 top gear it went up to 6200 rpm which recorded 109 mph. Third and second were good for 88 and 67 mph respectively while the standing quarter was covered in 15·50 seconds. Consumption came to 43 mpg when the performance was used but improved at constant speeds. Slow running was a trifle erratic due to the racing carburettor and high compression ratio but was improved by use of the manual ignition control. Handling was reported as excellent, as was the front brake, although the rear remained spongy throughout the test. The riding position suited both the test riders and the fittings and finish were favourably commented on.

Two months later the same magazine tested a Shooting Star finished in two-tone green and costing a total of £251. 2*s*. 0*d*. including purchase tax. This particular model was fitted with a rear chaincase in addition to a prop stand, so kept the area around the chain much cleaner than usual. The claimed power was 32 bhp at 6250 rpm and it was timed at 93, 84 and 59 mph in the three upper gears. The standing quarter time was 16·00 seconds and overall consumption 64 mpg. This was achieved using 100 octane petrol which had only just come onto the market at that time. The remainder of the test was rather similar to that of the Road Rocket with high speed cruising always available. The centre stand was commented on as rather strenuous to operate which could be taken that the 416 lb dry weight took very considerable effort to lift onto its stand.

The following year the same machine was tested by *Motor Cycle* by which time its price had risen to £264. 2*s*. 5*d*. The engine had apparently loosened up, or their rider was more tucked in, for speeds were up to 94, 90 and 62 mph in the upper gears. The quarter time was slower at 16·9 seconds and consumption

Right La Guarde Republicaine, **resplendent in full dress uniform, parade with their A7s with white wall tyres and crash bars**

Below **Petrol tank lifted off to show the single bolt fixing, rubber mountings and studs for front anti-vibration strap**

255 916

similar. Their comments on the machine confirmed their rivals, including the effort needed to use the centre stand, and when ridden hard they found that oil leaked from the tank filler onto the back of the rider's leg. One or two other minor leaks were also reported.

So the two twins in standard and sports forms ran on into 1957 with minimal change but for 1958 several modifications were announced late in 1957, a year when no Earls Court Show was held. The Road Rocket became the Super Rocket and its power output together with that of the Golden Flash and Shooting Star was increased by raising compression ratios. The Super Rocket engine also had redesigned inlet and exhaust tracts which helped to push the claimed power up to 43 bhp despite the use of a Monobloc Amal in place of the TT9, although this continued to be available for a short while if specified.

At the same time a Scrambles twin based on the 650 cc engine was introduced for the USA although it was not generally known of at home. Further changes in the larger engine included a considerably stiffened crankshaft assembly with improved sludge trap and centre flywheel retained by three radial bolts.

The brakes were also new and worked in full width cast iron hubs supported by straight-pull spokes. The front brake size was back up at eight inch diameter on all the twins except the A7 tourer and the backplates located on the fork legs so that the torque stays were no longer required.

Also changed were the silencers which were of improved performance, and the headlamp mounting. This became of cylindrical form with the front end of the tube carrying the pre-focus light unit, and the rear end bolting to a flat cover fitting round both fork tubes between the upper and lower yokes. The headlamp support continued to carry the centrally mounted speedometer but the ammeter and light switch were transposed and sited to left and right respectively. The ammeter was still awkward to read with any accuracy.

Finally, the centre stand was modified to make it easier for the rider to lift the machine onto while the rear chaincase remained available for £3. 4*s*. 0*d*., as were legshields and an air cleaner for the Shooting Star.

Both prices and weights had crept up with the A7 tourer at 425 lb and £257. 12*s*. 2*d*. The

Below **On the factory assembly line. Politicians finding out how they go together in early 1958**

Bottom **Unusual rider at the White City Tattoo where Johnny McTurk is pursued by his owner Mollie Badham, dressed as a policewoman. The BSA was remotely controlled by the Army Mechanical Transport School. A rehearsal picture, hence background**

Above right **Casual English style publicity picture**

Right **More posed US picture of the twin and twins. The Road Rocket is in its US style and the girls are the Toni Twins, Marianne and Charlotte**

sports version was lighter at 416 lb and cost £265. 14*s*. 5*d*. while the A10 was the heaviest at 430 lb but only cost £261. 19*s*. 6*d*. The new Super Rocket scaled 418 lb and was listed at £283. 3*s*. 8*d*. including purchase tax.

It was in this guise that in 1958 *Motor Cycling* tested an A10 with Watsonian sidecar. With its sidecar sprockets fitted, it was still well over-geared reaching 72 mph in top at 4700 rpm, 67 mph in third at 5200 rpm, and 58 mph in second at 6700 rpm, nearly 1000 rpm above its maximum output engine speed. It returned around 55 mpg during the test and got off the mark well enough to cover the standing quarter in 19·56 seconds, slow by solo motorcycle standards, but fast by 1958 car ones. With a brake fitted to the sidecar wheel, the stopping figures were fair and the added brake could be

independantly used to help the outfit round left hand corners. Both machine and sidecar body were finished in a matching BSA beige colour.

Late that year *Motorcycle News* tested a Super Rocket which proved just as fast as its predecessor and returned 52 mpg over some 3000 miles. It was constantly cruised at between 70 and 90 mph and would accelerate smoothly from as low as 40 mph in top gear. The front brake was first class but the rear spongy, thought to be due to the cable control. Handling and comfort for both rider and passenger were praised but the exhausts were deemed rather noisy at high speed.

1958 was the last year that the old type 6

Above left **Golden Flash with Avon fairing, windtone horns and general equipment for M1 motorway use by the Bedford Police**

Far left **Airfield testing a Road Rocket at speed. Note Siamesed exhaust, rev-counter and optional fuel tank**

Above **BSA Owner's Club members attending a rally at the Small Heath factory**

Left **Spitfire Scrambler for the USA. Neat exhaust pipes but it must have taken muscle to handle over the rough**

Amal was used on the Golden Flash and the year the Rocket was fitted with a Monobloc of larger size than before. During this period the method of adjusting the clutch was changed and some models were equipped with a primary chaincase with an extra hole which allowed the clutch springs to be adjusted without removing the outer case.

For 1959 a stiffer camshaft was fitted to all the 650 cc twins and the high lift cams fitted to the sports models were made standard for all.

Introduced at the Earls Court Show late in 1958 was the Spitfire twin, specifically designed for the USA to follow on the earlier Scrambles twin. The new model was fitted with open exhausts, high-rise handlebars and competition tyres, and equipped with an engine using a larger bore Monobloc, bigger valves opened by high lift cams and an 8·75 to 1 cr.

In 1960 further changes were introduced, both large and small. The more obvious ones concerned the carburettors fitted to various models, most of which were of increased size at which they were to stay to the end of the model's production run. Also re-introduced was the racing TT Amal for both Rocket and Spitfire models as an option.

Less obvious was a change of clutch design to one using only four springs adjusted by self-locking nuts. The clutch drum itself no longer had inserts fitted to it and ran on twenty rollers while the method of holding the clutch centre was also altered.

The primary chaincase oil level and drain were incorporated in one combined plug screwed up into the underside of the case. The larger of the two concentric hexagons was the drain, and extended up as a standpipe, whose top came to the required oil level. The smaller hexagon was a bolt whose removal allowed any excess oil to run down the standpipe until the required level was obtained.

Minor changes for the year included the fitting of another type of Lucas battery and the moving of the front brake adjuster from the backplate to the handlebar lever. Also moved was the air lever which returned near to its original starting point, it being positioned under the nose of the dualseat.

Towards the close of 1961 details of further changes to the Super Rocket were announced but the remaining twins were given as remaining unchanged. In fact, they were soon to be joined and then replaced by the new A50 and A65 series, although the 650 cc engine was to run on in a new guise for a while.

For 1962 the changes to the Super Rocket mainly concerned the silencers which had been redesigned to reduce the exhaust noise without affecting the top end power. In fact, the new units, known as BSA-Burgess silencers, gave an increase in power at the bottom and top of the engine speed scale. The machine was also made available with a Siamesed exhaust and single silencer, the left pipe passing between engine and front down tubes, in a very tight bend, to join the right pipe at crankshaft level.

Also changed were the brake shoes to a fully floating design, which worked well enough to require the leading edges of the brake shoes to be taken back $1\frac{1}{4}$ inches to prevent them biting too fiercely. The gear ratios were modified in the gearbox to give a lower bottom ratio with virtually no change to the other three.

It was in January 1962 that the new range of twins was announced so that the old became obsolete. However, although the A7 in both forms was dropped from the lists during that summer along with the Golden Flash, the Super Rocket continued on for another year until the middle of 1963 while in February 1962 its final form was introduced.

This was the Rocket Gold Star brought about by marrying the 650 cc engine in its most highly tuned form with a Gold Star type frame and forks. With it were offered a long list of options based on experience with both the twin and the Gold Star single.

The engine was the Super Rocket type with light alloy cylinder head and sports camshaft but with the compression ratio lifted to 9·0 to 1. Ignition was by magneto with manual control and the old dynamo was still used. The carburettor was a Monobloc of the size already in use on the Spitfire and the Siamese exhaust system was fitted as standard. In this form the engine developed 46 bhp at 6250 rpm with another 4 bhp available when a special track silencer was used. This was virtually a me-

Left **Police A10 in winter time fitted with saddle and luggage grid**

Below **The Rocket Gold Star, the final version of the A10 in sports guise. Many options were available for this model which was built for two years only**

1962 Super Rocket with same engine as RGS but fitted to normal A frame and cycle parts

gaphone exhaust incorporating a tail pipe.

The gearbox was the BSA heavy type fitted with the needle bearings and extra close gears as standard. All the other gears were available as options along with the reversed gearchange camplate described earlier.

The frame was the duplex loop Gold Star type with one change in the lower right tube. This ran straight under the engine and did not have the kink in it demanded by the oil pump on the Goldie single cylinder engine. The front forks were also from the Gold Star with gaiters and chromium plated shrouds carrying the quickly detachable headlamp. The wiring contained plug and socket connection to the lamp and the shrouds could also be removed to allow the fitting of clip-on handlebars. The normal Girling suspension units were fitted at the rear and alternative springs were available as options.

Fuel was carried in a standard four gallon tank finished in silver with chromium side panels carrying the round Gold Star badges and fitted with a quick action filler cap and racing pattern breather pipe. Also available was a two

The full brochure cover as used on the dust jacket of this book—a handsome illustration of the Golden Flash

gallon tank in steel or light alloy, and a five gallon racing tank in light alloy.

Further choice existed with the wheels, which as standard used the eight inch front and seven inch rear brakes, the rear rod-operated, and in the old type quick detachable hub with the crinkle edges for the spokes. Options included light alloy rims, racing tyres and the 190 mm front brake with alloy hub and cast iron sleeve.

Also available as options were a rev-counter driven from the timing case and mounted to match the speedometer, rear mounted footrests and brake pedal, air cleaner, and separate exhaust pipes only to be used when the footrests were mounted in the forward position. In its standard form its price was £299. 19*s*. 5*d*. but most were sold with one or more of the options fitted.

By the middle of 1962 the Super Rocket also had the 9·0 to 1 compression ratio and by September it was priced at over £300, a figure the Rocket Gold Star had reached in March, a bare seven weeks after its introduction a few pence under that level.

Although primarily built as a super-sports solo cum production road racer, the RGS could also be used to very good effect when fitted up as a sidecar outfit. In this guise, the gearing was lowered, upturned handlebars fitted and a studded front tyre used in place of the normal ribbed. Harnessed to a sports sidecar, it was capable of over 80 mph, returning a fuel consumption figure just below 50 mpg.

So the A10 engine ran its course and during 1963 production of it in its final forms, the Super Rocket and the Rocket Gold Star, came to an end. Its unit construction successor was already eighteen months old and was soon to branch out into the gap left by the old sports models.

HOME EDITION
BSA 650
From Bantam to Golden Flash
BSA
THE MOST POPULAR MOTOR CYCLE IN THE WORLD

4 Final big twins—A50 and A65

Front view of a fast motorcycle with ball-ended levers and ventilated front brake

January 1962 was only a few days old when the new BSA twins were announced by the motorcycling Press. The new machines were considerably lighter than the old models and featured true unit construction, very clean lines and an updated specification.

In essence the engine design followed the same lines as before with a 360 degree crankshaft, camshaft mounted behind the cylinders, overhead valves and dry sump lubrication. However, it also featured coil ignition, an alternator, triplex primary drive and an integral rocker box.

The new engines were both based on a stroke of 74 mm with a bore of 65·5 mm to give a capacity of 499 cc for the A50, and a bore of 75 mm to give a capacity of 654 cc for the A65. In most respects the two models were identical, each having a compression ratio of 7·5 to 1, and power outputs of 28·5 bhp at 6000 rpm for the smaller engine and 38 bhp at 5800 rpm for the larger.

In a four-stroke engine, the design of the cylinder head is of paramount importance as it can have a great effect on the breathing capability of the engine. By careful design, BSA were able to achieve the power output they sought using a very modest compression ratio so knew they had good breathing. The result was an engine less demanding of high octane fuel and capable of considerable tuning as and when required.

The cylinder head was a one piece light alloy

Unit construction engine showing oil circulation and separate oil tank

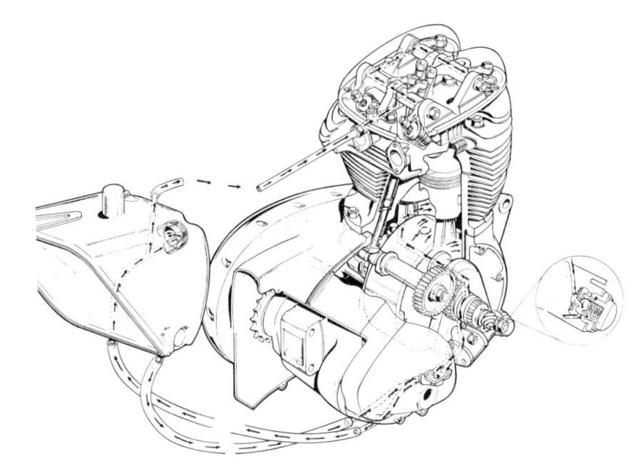

die casting with separate inlet and exhaust ports. As on the 1946 cylinder head, the inlets were parallel to each other and supplied by one carburettor bolted to an alloy manifold attached to the head while the exhaust ports splayed out. Compared with the earlier cast iron head, the new one was much more extensively finned with ample passage for the cooling air between the exhaust ports and fins round and between the inlet ports.

The rocker box was formed integrally with the cylinder head with a floor above the head fins carrying six trunnion supports, three for each rocker shaft which was thus supported at its centre as well as each end. The rocker box floor at the rear of the head contained two wells which joined at head gasket level to form the passages for the pushrods.

The rockers were of conventional type, located by thrust washers and springs, unbushed and worked directly on their respective spindles which were locked in position by end nuts. They were hollow and supplied with lubricant from the oil return pipe as before, the supply connecting to the rear of the cylinder head on its centre line. The supply entered the inlet rocker spindle via the centre trunnion, passed along it to the left trunnion which was joined to its companion supporting the exhaust spindle and so to the exhaust rockers. A bleed-off controlled by a loose split pin allowed some oil to escape straight down the pushrod tunnel onto the tappets and camshaft as a back-up to the main lubrication system. The whole of the rocker box assembly was sealed by an unstressed cover held down by six nuts.

The actual combustion chambers were hemispherical and had the valve inserts cast in. The inlet valves were slightly larger than the exhausts and both set at 37 degrees from the vertical. The inlet valve stem had a hardened tip while the exhaust used a brazed-on Stellite tip. Both valves worked in pressed in valve guides and were controlled by duplex coil springs with separate seats and retained by conventional collars and split cottars fitting into single grooves machined in the valve stems.

The cylinder head was retained by four nuts and five bolts to a one piece cast iron cylinder barrel very similar to the earlier ones. The pushrod tunnel was still cast in and the tappets still ran direct in its base. These were, however, changed to simple round pins with block feet which worked against each other to prevent them rotating. Each ran in a plain drilled hole in the barrel and was retained by a circlip to hold it in place during assembly. Solid light alloy pushrods with hardened steel end caps transmitted movement to the rockers. The cylinder was retained by eight nuts at its base.

In the cylinder bores ran conventional solid skirt pistons with two compression rings, the second with a taper face, and one oil scraper all above the gudgeon pin. The pin was fully floating and retained by wire circlips. Connecting rods were light alloy with a bush in the small end and bearing shells at the big end. The cap was retained as before by fitted bolts which provided the location between cap and rod.

The crankshaft was made in exactly the same way as before, being forged in a manganese-molybdenum steel with the timing side bearing area hardened. A central flywheel was still used and retained by three radial bolts, one of which also located the sludge trap fitted into the crankpin and sealed in place by an end plug. On the left side two changes occurred, the first that dictated by the adoption of an alternator and the second the fitting of a ball race on the drive side in place of the earlier roller race. The timing side bearing was increased in size from that used in the A10 as was the crankpin diameter but the fittings on the end of the crankshaft remained unaltered with a keyed timing gear retained by the oil pump drive worm and lock nut, both of which screwed onto the shaft with left hand threads.

The crankshaft gear drove the camshaft via an intermediate gear, which was supported in bushes in both crankcase and inner timing cover, and this drove the contact breaker cam. The camshaft ran as before in two bushes in the right crankcase half and one in the left, but was also hollow with a timed breather at the left end which opened at the point of maximum crankcase pressure. The feature of casting a trough beneath the camshaft to retain a reservoir of oil for its lubrication was continued.

The crankcase was cast in two halves, split on the centre line. The left half was very similar to that used for the semi-unit construction engines, with the inner wall of the primary chaincase formed with the case and carried over the final drive sprocket to the centre of the engine. One noticeable change was the addition of a circular, bolted-on flange, whose removal gave access to the gearbox sprocket without the need to dismantle the unit further.

The right crankcase half was a little unusual in that while the front half followed normal practice, the rear half embodied the gearbox casting and the rear engine mounting. The gearbox internals were carried on a basically circular plate which bolted onto the crankcase from the right, and thus worked in a shell formed in that casting half that lay behind the main crankshaft casting. The plate carrying both gear shafts also had the change mech-

anism mounted on it so an internal wall separated all the gearbox parts from the timing gears and hence the engine lubrication system.

Onto the right side of the crankcase was bolted an inner timing cover which continued to separate the gearbox from the rest of the engine. It supported the intermediate timing gear to which was keyed an ignition cam assembly, complete with automatic advance and retard mechanism. A contact breaker plate was bolted to the inner cover and carried two sets of contact points and capacitors. The rear part of the cover supported the outer ends of the gear change and kickstart shafts and carried the simple clutch operating lever. The engine was finished off by a smooth outer cover which encased the mechanism, and had a small circular plate provided to give access to the contact points.

Due to the change of casting, the oil supply and return pipes were moved to a position under the engine and convenient to the gear oil pump which was situated in the same position as before. The sump with gauze filter and pick-up pipe with ball valve in it remained as on the A7 engine.

On the left side of the engine, the crankshaft carried a sprocket driving a triplex chain, adopted to cover all eventualities including American drag racing. The sprocket was clamped in place by the alternator rotor, itself held in place by a nut with lock washer. The stator was mounted on studs fitted into the crankcase and its wires fed through a pipe also screwed into the case. The chain drove a five plate clutch compressed by four springs, and incorporating a triple vane shock absorber with rubber elements, which worked by being distorted. The drive chain was tensioned by a curved slipper blade pivoted at its front edge and adjusted with a hollow bolt, which allowed a thin rod to pass through it to check the tension. This was screwed into the inner case wall from below and fitted with both a locknut and a sealing cap. The slipper was faced with rubber which initially worked on the chain link

Left **A50 nearside in 1962. The rather large sidecover, pear shaped tank badge and nondescript knee grips make less impact**

Below **A65R Rocket, offside. Introduced in 1963 to replace the sports A10 models it has Siamesed exhaust pipes and front fork gaiters**

plates until grooves formed and contact was taken up by the rollers. This occurred without the rubber wearing away and becoming debris in the case, as it gradually moved into the desired shape.

The primary chaincase was completed with a polished cast aluminium outer cover attached by a dozen screws. It contained a plug to provide access to the clutch adjustor screws in the centre of the pressure plate, and separate level and drain screws. A second plug gave access to the clutch spring nuts, and the two plugs were covered by a small pear shaped plate which blended into the outer chaincase.

The gearbox followed normal BSA lines with the speedometer still driven from the end of the

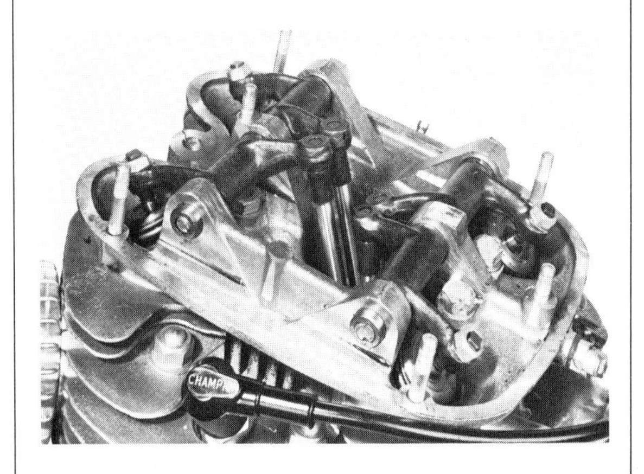

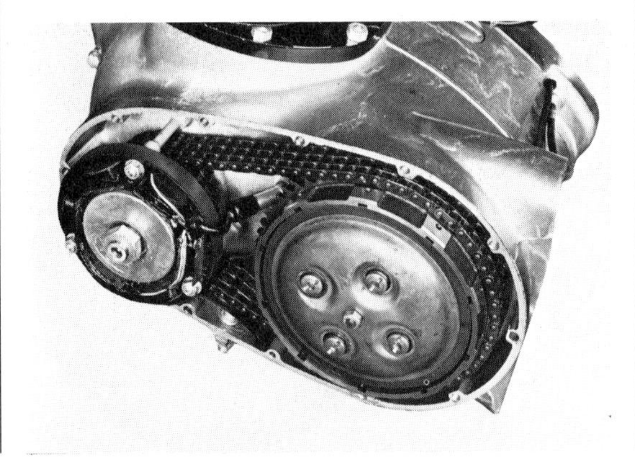

Above **Rocket rear with single silencer**

Above left **The valve mechanism of the twin with well supported rocker spindles fed with oil from cylinder head rear**

Left **Primary drive with triplex chain, slipper tensioner and four spring clutch**

layshaft. The gears were moved by a transversely mounted quadrant plate carrying the cam tracks to one side, and the change slots to the other of its pivot in the end mounting plate. The quadrant detent plunger and spring were located in the gearbox shell while the kickstart mechanism remained much as before, with a sector gear turning a gear on the mainshaft which drove through a face ratchet. The whole was lubricated separately from the engine with a filler plug in the top of the right crankcase half behind the cylinder, and the level and drain combined as a standpipe as used before in the primary chaincase.

The one aspect of the gearbox that was totally different for most riders of that time was a change to the pedal movement to give up-for-up changes, the reverse to that used on the earlier twins.

The new engines were fitted into new frames based on the A10 swinging fork type but with the wheelbase reduced by two inches. The frame retained the single, braced top tube with duplex members running from the headstock, under the engine and up to the top tube at the seat nose. The subframe was welded on with the rear mudguard cantilevered out and mainly

Road test A65 Rocket with long serving *MCN* staff member Peter Howdle at the controls. The relatively low seat height enables him to have his left foot flat on the ground

supported by its own valances. The three position Girling rear units controlling the swinging fork were laid forward at a small angle.

The front forks were as used on the later type A7 and A10 models, with cylindrical nacelle carrying speedometer, ammeter and, for the new models, separate lighting and ignition switches. A steering damper and steering head lock were fitted.

The wheel size was reduced to 18 inches while tyre sizes remained at 3·25 inch front and 3·50 inch rear. Fully floating brake shoes were used in full width hubs with straight spokes, and brake sizes were seven inches except for the A65 front which was eight.

Both tanks were rubber mounted, the petrol tank being held by the single bolt fixing already in use and having chromium plated sides carrying a pear shaped BSA star badge. The capacity remained at four gallons. The oil tank was fitted in the triangle formed by the right side saddle and seat tubes with the seat itself, and was concealed by a pressed steel panel which left the oil filler cap exposed but extended forward to encase the Amal Monobloc carburettor, air filter and twin ignition coils bolted to the frame. It was matched by a similar pressing fitted to the left side of the machine and this covered the battery and rectifier. A small space for tools was provided behind the oil tank.

Rocket publicity picture taken in 1964. The obvious association has to be airplane and motorcycle speed

Finish for the frame, forks and headlamp shell was black, while the hubs were silver. The colour schemes for the mudguards, side covers and petrol tank were polychromatic green for the A50 and sapphire blue for the A65. Either model could be supplied in black as well as the standard colours, and a flamboyant red finish was an optional extra for the A65 at an extra £2. 15*s*. 0*d*. Weight of the A50 was given as 385 lb and its original price £264. 7*s*. 10*d*., while the A65 scaled 390 lb and cost £268. 13*s*. 9*d*. Options included a prop stand at £1. 4*s*. 7*d*., a rear chaincase at £3. 4*s*. 9*d*., Siamesed exhaust system, legshields and whitewall tyres.

First road impressions of the new twins were published at the same time and were generally favourable, commenting in particular on the excellence of the handling. The new alternator was viewed with some suspicion but as it balanced the lighting load and kept the battery healthy enough for first kick starting on a cold day, it could not be faulted. Seat height was felt to be a little high, but was in part due to the need to keep everything off the ground when heavily laden and cornering briskly. No speed checks were taken of the machines, as the engines were not fully run-in, but acceleration was very brisk and three figure top speed for the A65 seemed a reasonable assumption with the A50 good for about 90 mph.

1964 Rocket with racing seat rear set footrests and clip-ons parked outside the London showrooms. The small petrol tank makes it for the US market

Further informal testing followed quickly with *The Motor Cycle* taking an A65 with Watsonian Monosport sidecar to various parts of North Wales. In the course of 305 miles over which the outfit was driven one way only—very hard—the speedometer went to 75 mph in top and 60 mph in third while consumption came out at 50 mpg.

A month later *Motor Cycling* conducted the first formal road test on an A65 and summed it up as an outstandingly good machine especially in view of its competitive price. At MIRA it just failed to achieve three figures, recording a best speed of 99 mph with the rider prone but under gusty wind conditions in drizzle. It did however return 62 mpg over 500 miles of hard driving. Handling and braking were both commented on favourably, as was the gearchange, despite a clutch that gave signs of not freeing as cleanly as it might have. The side covers were not liked as their fasteners were too narrow to accept any but the smallest coin, which was unable to provide the required purchase to turn them. One cover was easy to replace but the other not, and the toolbox considered far too small, so that removal of the tools was hard and their replacement even harder. These minor points failed to detract from the overall picture of a very sound motorcycle.

Next up was an impression written for *Motor Cycle News* by Eddie Dow, better known for his competition successes with Gold Star models, but as a specialist BSA dealer more than a little interested in all the sports BSAs. He covered over 300 miles and was very impressed by the power, torque, handling and comfort. Criti-

Dunstall-BSA in 1966. A very nicely customized example of the period

1965 Lightning with twin carburettors, rev-counter and humped back seat

cisms were minor, although he felt that the stand could be grounded too easily. The rear brake was not considered as good as it could have been, although the front was very effective, while the rear suspension units were awkward to adjust and the toolbox very difficult to use.

The *MCN* staffman agreed with most of Eddie Dow's impressions but had more problems starting it, and found both brakes very effective.

It was then the turn of the A50 and *The Motor Cycle* gave the same machine two write-ups. The first was a high speed run from the south of England to Scotland for the last day of the Scottish Six Days Trial and served to emphasise the comfort, good handling and fast touring abilities of the machine. Over 1100 miles the A50 returned 66 mpg, used half a pint of oil and the only attention then required was to adjust the rear chain.

The formal tests report followed soon afterwards and confirmed the points already made in respect of fast riding with few criticisms. These amounted to the grounding of the stand on left corners, the heavy pressure needed to make the front brake work possibly due to its smaller size compared with the A65, a tendency for the rear wheel to lock when braking, and an unreadable ammeter. On test it reached 95 mph in good conditions with nearly 90 mph obtainable in third and over 60 mph in second.

In the middle of the year *Motor Cycling* confirmed most aspects with a tourer test of an A50 fitted with windscreen and legshields. Their addition took the wind pressure off the rider, so that the standard handlebars were positioned too far forward for this application. Again the point was made that the A50 with its high performance and similar weight to the A65 really warranted the same front brake. The toolbox was condemned! Otherwise the test confirmed the others that the A50 was a fine motorcycle.

The two new twins continued unchanged into 1963 and both were tested by *Motor Cycle Illustrated* in the course of that year. *The Motor Cycle* again tested an A65 with similar results as before, and photographed an example fitted with a new option, 12 volt electrics achieved by fitting two 6 volt batteries and controlling the

generator output with a zener diode. The test machine managed to reach 102 mph and was equipped with the full chaincase option.

Towards the end of the year, in October, BSA announced a new version of the 650 cc twin, the Rocket A65R. This featured a higher performance engine achieved by fitting a high lift camshaft, special valve springs and increasing the compression ratio to 9 to 1. To cope with the added power, the machine was fitted with a heavy duty clutch tested in International Six Days Trials. The engine was fitted with a folding kickstarter, and the appearance of the machine enhanced by the use of chromed upper fork shrouds. These carried a detachable headlamp while the fork sliders were protected

The 1965 500 cc Wasp—no lights but fitted with low level exhaust pipes and silencers. Large tyres and small petrol tank for the US market

by rubber bellows. A Siamesed exhaust system was standard with twin pipes available as an option, and the finish was flame red set off by chromed blade mudguards.

A rev-counter was available as an option but had to be ordered with the machine, as it was driven from the end of the oil pump spindle and so necessitated the fitting of a modified timing cover. When fitted, the rev-counter matched the speedometer and both were mounted on a suitable bracket; a different headlamp shell was used without the normal speedometer mounting hole in it. This extra cost £8. 18*s*. 6*d*. while the complete machine was listed at £308. 11*s*. 0*d*. with the twin exhaust pipes a further £2. 12*s*. 3*d*.

The appearance of all the twin cylinder models was modified slightly by a change of the side panels which were made more bulbous. This was to accommodate the additional battery fitted when the optional 12 volt system was specified for the larger machines at an added £4. For this the customer also received a 50/40 watt headlamp bulb in place of the usual 30/24 watt one.

Early in 1964 *Motor Cycle* road tested an A65R achieving a highest speed of 108 mph and reporting favourably on the machine's performance, comfort and handling. Complaints were limited to the weak horn note, the need for the steering damper at very high speed and lack of bite in the front brake at low speed. The handlebar layout was approved although vintage in appearance with separate levers, twistgrip, dip switch and air lever as was normal at the time. The centre stand was a great improvement over earlier models, being easy to use, and a prop stand was available for

Right **The 1965 Spitfire Mk II, top machine of the twin cylinder range with a super sports specification**

Below **The 650 cc Hornet in 1965. As with the Wasp no lights are fitted but it does have high level exhaust pipes without silencers**

£1. 6*s*. 5*d*. extra although not fitted to the test machine.

The same machine was tested by *Motor Cycle News* in the middle of the year and they confirmed the speed and overall performance, reporting more favourably on the front brake which had, no doubt, bedded down more by then. They returned consumption figures of 45 mpg driven hard and 55 mpg when cruising at 70 mph. As this model was fitted with the rev-counter option, its ammeter was clearly visible in the centre of the headlamp shell. A central steering lock was fitted in the top fork yoke.

During 1964 variations of the standard twins had been supplied to the USA for competition purposes, and in October, four new machines were unveiled for the home market. Each capacity twin was available in sports or production racing trim, the 500s being coded A50C, Cyclone and A50CC, Cyclone Clubman, while the larger twins were typed as A65L, Lightning and A65LC, Lightning Clubman.

All four engines featured new light alloy cylinder heads with twin, splayed inlet ports fitted with carburettors with individual air filters, while compression ratios on both engine sizes were 9 to 1. A sports camshaft was also fitted together with the Siamesed exhaust system from the Rocket while all the engines were individually bench tested, a practice previously reserved only for the single cylinder Gold Stars.

A close ratio gearbox was specified with the reversed camplate fitted in the Clubman's version to retain the normal gear pedal movement, as those models were equipped with rear mounted footrests and a reversed pedal. Internally the new machines benefitted from a change to stub form gear teeth, this modification being incorporated throughout the range for highly stressed gearbox pinions. It increased the strength by up to twenty per cent.

The cycle parts followed the established

lines used for the Star twins but with 19 inch front wheels fitted in place of the normal 18 inch ones. Brakes were as fitted to the Rocket twin while the petrol tanks were of four gallons capacity. The Lightning Clubman was finished in metallic gold with chromium plated side panels lined in red and carrying the pear shaped BSA star badge. The side covers were smaller than before as they left the two carburettors and air cleaners exposed and were made in glass-fibre laminate, gold finished to match the tank. The frame was black but the headlamp shell chromed as were the blade mudguards and top fork shrouds. The forks themselves had protective gaiters fitted, and carried matching speedometer on the left and rev-counter on the right, the latter fitted as standard.

The sports twins were fitted with straight handlebars and a dualseat but the Clubman models had dropped bars, not clip-ons, and a racing seat. The most potent was the Lightning Clubman whose engine produced 51 bhp at 6750 rpm which in a machine of 400 lb made it a very fast motorcycle indeed. Its price was

£345. 16*s*. 0*d*. while the sports Lightning was £4 less but was also down 3 bhp on power. The 500 cc sports engine produced 38·5 bhp and cost £331. 16*s*. 0*d*. while the Clubman model cost a futher £4. As might have been expected, the larger capacity machines were the more popular and, in fact, very few Cyclone models were to be built before the range was renamed.

With four new models to launch, it is hardly surprising that the only changes to the existing twins were to adopt folding kickstarters and to modify the centre stand to provide better ground clearance.

In addition to the European style, the 650 was also produced in two special versions for the American market, one very similar to the Lightning and the other a street scrambler called the Spitfire Hornet and fitted with upswept exhausts, and equipped for cross-country work. It was finished in red, and shown to the UK public at Earls Court in 1964. The following year it was made available in the UK as part of a revamped model line-up announced in September for the Brighton Show held that month.

Left **A Lightning in the BSA workshop with road racers Mick Boddice, on the left, and Bob Heath**

Below left **1968 Thunderbolt with high bars. This had the single carburettor engine which many riders preferred**

Below **1967 Lightning fitted with alloy rims, folding kick start and rev-counter**

The new range was very influenced by the requirements of the American market and comprised six models, two 500s and four 650s. The touring models which replaced the Star twins were both fitted with a single Amal Monobloc and were the A50 Royal Star at £299 and the A65 Thunderbolt at £320. 13*s*. 10*d*. The A65 Lightning model continued although fitted with two separate exhaust pipes and silencers as the Siamesed systems were dropped from all models. The top of the road model was the Spitfire Mark Two Special in the style of the previous year's Lightning Clubman, but with the compression ratio raised to 10·5 to 1 and fitted with racing cams, twin Amal Grand Prix carburettors, alloy wheel rims and the 190 mm front brake. It was listed at £389. 10*s*. 0*d*. and weighed 382 lb, nine pounds less than the

Thunderbolt, Lightning and Royal Star.

The two street scramblers were typical of the requirements of the USA at that time, the larger A65 Hornet using the Spitfire engine fitted with Monobloc carburettors. A straight-through exhaust pipe was fitted to each side of the machine and this was swept up to run back at kickstart pedal height to the rear wheel spindle. Each pipe carried a heat shield to protect the rider's leg. No lights were fitted and ignition was by the energy transfer system while only a rev-counter was fitted to a central bracket carried on the top fork yoke. To meet the American taste, large section tyres were fitted, the front a 3·50 × 19 Dunlop K70 and the rear a 4·00 × 18. The racing seat was of the same type as used on the other models but to suit the use for which it was intended, the Hornet was equipped with a crankcase shield and a small glass-fibre petrol tank holding only two US gallons. The finish of the machine was mandarin red with chrome plated upper fork shrouds and mudguards while the frame was black. It weighed 386 lb and was listed at £339. 10*s*. 0*d*.

The 500 cc version, the A50 Wasp, weighed the same but cost less at £325. 0*s*. 0*d*. It was built to a slightly different specification as, although it had the same 10·5 to 1 compression ratio and twin Monoblocs, the exhaust system was downswept and with silencers. The remaining Hornet features of energy transfer ignition, no lights, larger tyres and small tank were the

An RAF Police BSA used in the *Daily Mail* Air Race. Motorcycles were of particular help in reaching the aircraft quickly

Below **1969 Lightning pictured at Silverstone. It has the American style grab-rail and side reflectors, front and rear**

Bottom **Close up of the Lightning engine. The balance pipe between the exhausts can be clearly seen together with the twin horns and the finned zener heat sink**

same but the basic colour scheme was sapphire blue.

All the road twins now had 12 volt electrics with the generator output controlled by a zener diode and the headlamp nacelle replaced by a chromium plated separate unit. New features were a balance pipe between the units on the twin carburettor models, twin throttle cables which did away with the need for a junction box, a dipstick attached to the oil tank lid, a new six plate clutch with three springs and gauze instead of felt air cleaners.

Detail improvements were also made to the stands, the control levers which became ball ended and the ignition lock which was changed to a Yale type in place of the old one which any screwdriver would turn.

The front forks on all models were from the Victor and incorporated two way damping, while only the Royal Star featured a non-racing dualseat without a rear hump. Finally, after nearly twenty years, the speedometer drive was taken from the rear wheel and not the gearbox.

Early in 1966, a five gallon racing style petrol tank was made available as an option for the Spitfire, which was roadtested to 120 mph, and a standing start quarter-mile in 13·6 seconds during the year. That year both the Wasp and Hornet models were dropped in the UK so that for the November show at Earls Court, the twin cylinder range was reduced to four models, one 500 and three 650s, plus the export-only Hornet.

This was to be a turning point in the Company's history for behind the facade of a successful motorcycle business, the holding Company was in the process of massive diversification and a whole series of Company acquisitions and sales. Many of these deals were ultimately very costly to BSA, and together with many changes of key personnel, led to the firm's final closure.

However, in late 1966 this was all in the future and the motorcycle division was making money, although very reliant on its American sales. To this end, both the styling of the machines and their promotion began to become more and more orientated to USA whims, although relatively little was to be done on the technical front to meet the Japanese challenge rising up over the horizon. Two years later the 500 cc Kawasaki three and the 750 cc Honda four reached the market and created the 'superbike', a machine with both speed and reliability but also a machine with style and all the features so many customers had clamoured for.

In retrospect, the new features for the 1967 BSA twins were a little limited. All models were fitted with finned rocker box covers which were a straight replacement for the earlier plain ones. Ignition timing continued to be set in the same manner as had been used since 1965 with a timing plug which fitted into the front of the crankcase and locked the crankshaft in the correct position. In addition, a line was now provided on the alternator rotor to indicate the correct full advance position when aligned with a fixed pin fitted into the primary chaincase cover. A small circular plate gave access to this and allowed the timing to be set with a strobe.

Other changes included the provision of a

Top **1968 instruments for the 650. The 10,000 rpm is perhaps as optimistic as the 150 mph speedometer. Note steering damper, light flick switch and inaccessible steering lock**

Above **1969 Firebird 650 cc street scrambler. Street legal, with lights, but for use off road. With the American market in mind**

Left **1969 Royal Star, also at Silverstone, fitted with humped back seat. It has the same twin cam brake as the other models**

finned heat sink for the zener diode, improved fork damping, 4·00 inch section rear tyres on all models, a 150 mph speedometer, a single 12 volt battery in place of the two 6 volt ones, a change to blade type rear mudguards, and improved tool kit. Both instruments were mounted in rubber cups to provide better insulation from vibration, while the rider, was similarly treated with the provision of cushioned handlebar grips. The oil tank dipstick gained high and low level marks which should have been there in the first place.

The touring Royal Star was finished in flamboyant blue and listed at £303. 17*s*. 4*d*. while the Thunderbolt was in black at £325. 18*s*. 3*d*. The 53 bhp Lightning still had twin Monobloc carburettors and was supplied in flamboyant red at £360. 15*s*. 7*d*. but the Spitfire was now coded the Mark Three and fitted with the new Amal Concentric carburettors. These were of 32 mm bore and with a 10 to 1 compression ratio helped the engine to produce its 55 bhp. It was fitted with light alloy rims and control levers, the 190 mm front brake, finished in royal red and listed at £395. 16*s*. 10*d*.

During 1967, both *Motorcycle Mechanics* and *Motor Cyclist Illustrated* roadtested the same model Thunderbolt and both acclaimed its smooth power, tractable nature and ease of riding. It proved good for over 100 mph and rather queried the need for the Lightning model with its two carburettors. The old fashioned eight inch front brake came in for particular praise and was preferred to the 190 mm unit used on the Spitfire. Handling was generally good except for a slight weave, which occurred on long sweeping bends tackled two up in the high 80s. It was never disconcerting. Petrol consumption varied between 40 and 65 mpg, depending on whether the model was thrashed or not. The new clutch worked very well indeed, the lights were particularly good and both magazines liked the machine.

In the course of 1967, the Spitfire was given a small power boost to 56·5 bhp at 7200 rpm while retaining its low down pulling power. The model tested by *Motor Cycle News* was fitted with American high rise bars which possibly accounted for their comments that the machine felt light at the front and sometimes shook its head in fast corners.

The Earls Court Show was held in September

in 1967, so the changes to the four twins for 1968 were not shown. They were announced in November and the most noticeable was the adoption of the Triumph twin leading shoe front brake on the Lightning and the Spitfire, now up to Mark Four. The brake was an eight inch diameter unit in a full width hub with cooling fins and the two cam levers were joined by an adjustable rod, the front lever being pulled by the brake cable.

A number of engine modifications were carried out at that time, the obvious one being a change to Concentric carburettors on all models not so fitted. The contact breakers were changed to the later Lucas type with both sets of contacts independantly adjustable for more accurate ignition timing. The condensers were no longer mounted with the points so moved closer to the coils in a pack fixed below the seat. The crankcase was modified to support the alternator stator directly and more accurately than the earlier stud mountings. The cylinder head gasket became solid copper and the oil supply to the rockers was improved by taking it from a point near the crankcase instead of the oil tank, and by minor changes to the oilways. The gearbox oil level was no longer checked with a level tube but by a dipstick attached to the filler cap.

There were minor changes to the cycle parts with the Spitfire's quick action fuel filler cap being fitted to the steel tanks of the other three twins. All the machines were built to the export specification to avoid production line problems, so came with high rise bars, side reflectors on the tail lamp housing and beneath the fuel tank nose, and without the front number plates, then obligatory in the UK. The tank badges were changed from acrylic mouldings to a three dimensional light alloy casting with an anodised finish, and the light switch changed from a rotary to a toggle action but still mounted centrally in the headlamp shell. In the main the finish remained unchanged except

Top **Thunderbolt engine for the 1968 season when it was fitted with a Concentric but not the exhaust balance pipe**

Above **Front wheel with revised brake linkage for 1969. Earlier models had the cable swept down to connect directly to the extended front lever**

Left **1967 Spitfire Mk III fitted with the then new Amal Concentric carburettors**

for the Royal Star which became flamboyant red while all prices stayed as they were.

For the USA the Hornet continued to be offered as a street scrambler but with a new name, Firebird, and the new front brake. The specification had changed for it now had lights and silencers fitted, the latter both on the left side, one above the other, the upper serving the right cylinder and the lower the left. A mesh shield was fixed to them and ran from the cylinders back to the rear dampers to make a styling feature on that side of the machine. A sump guard was fitted and the usual small fuel tank but otherwise it was a 650 cc BSA twin and must have been a heavy handfull over the desert scrub.

Late in 1967 *Motor Cycle* tested a Royal Star and despite the high rise bars achieved a best speed of 93 mph under rather adverse weather conditions. The bars did not help the handling which required more mental effort than usual when cornering while the increased ground clearance had also lifted the seat to 32 inches which made it a stretch to the ground for even average height riders. Consumption ran between 50 and 75 mpg and the brakes were first class. The clutch required freeing first thing in the morning, or it would refuse to free until the rider had stalled the engine at least once by forcing it into gear. It was not very quiet, with both valve gear and exhaust more intrusive than desirable in the touring machine it sought to be, but comfort was very good indeed.

In the autumn of 1968, the new three cylinder BSA was announced as described later so for 1969 the Spitfire was dropped from the range leaving only three twins for the UK, the Royal Star and the 650 cc Thunderbolt and Lightning. Also continued was the Firebird scrambler but for export only.

The changes to the twins were minimal although the 650 cc roadsters all gained a balance pipe between the exhausts close to the engine, and new silencers with redesigned internals which resulted in quieter machines. The scrambler could not accommodate a forward balance pipe but had the two exhausts joined just in front of the silencers. A blue oil pressure light was added to the headlamp, and turned off at 12 psi by a rubber-covered switch screwed into the front of the timing cover just below the rev-counter drive outlet.

In the engine, various joint faces were made broader to reduce further any chance of oil leaks and a seal was added to stop oil leaking into the inner timing cover via the idler pinion spindle bearing. The frames incorporated mounting points for a fairing, while petrol taps with reserve positions were fitted. At the front end, the brake cam operating lever was changed by adding a second arm at an angle to the short arm, linked to the second cam lever. This allowed the operating cable to run up behind and parallel to the right fork leg. The forks themselves were shortened and employed the shuttle valve and restrictor design from the new triple. The front hub nave plate was also restyled. On the Lightning model only, but provisioned for in the wiring harness of all machines, was fitted matched windtone horns and relay. The Lightning was also fitted with a stop light switch operated by the front brake cable, and its styling reverted to English, with flat bars in place of the high rise ones fitted to the other twins and the triple.

Early in 1969 *Motor Cycle* roadtested a

Rare 750 cc A70 twin engine housed in cycle parts put together by Devimead

Lightning which achieved 104 mph in both third and top. They were impressed by the power and good acceleration in all gears but less pleased with the signs of vibration which were tiring on long runs and fractured one of the horn brackets. The new method of operation of the front brake also gave rise to problems as the operation was spongy, and it was hard to adjust so that it did not bind slightly. It was, however, powerful, fade free, and totally unaffected by wet weather.

The same machine was tested by *Motorcycle Sport* in June 1969 and severely criticised for its vibration. Up to 75 mph in top and 5500 rpm in any gear all was fine, but going on to 6200 rpm cost a headlamp bulb each time. An attempt was made to reach the rated peak rpm of 7500 in third gear but failed as the rider's numbed hands prevented it. Top speed was not reached, only known to be over 100 mph. However, for touring up to 75 mph it proved a most pleasant machine, returning a reasonable fuel consumption of around 45 mpg.

Comfort was rated high, both the good suspension and the comfortable dualseat contributing to this while the seat grab rail proved useful and not just an ornament. The same comments were made on the front brake regarding sponge and binding, so it seemed that the new lever was not really adequate for its job.

Despite the vibration, it was rated a very satisfactory motorcycle.

Also tested about the same time was a Thunderbolt by *Motor Cycle* and a Royal Star by *Motor Cyclist Illustrated*. Both these single carburettor touring machines performed their tasks well and both were equipped with the English style flat bars. The Star had acquired the same dualseat with hump and grab rail as fitted to the other models.

The 650 proved as fast as the Lightning tested earlier, achieving a mean speed of 104 mph and a best of 107 mph at which the slow reading speedometer only showed 102. Fuel consumption was round the 50 mpg mark so it became hard to justify the extra cost of the Lightning on the grounds of performance. Vibration was still present and the highest grade of petrol was required to prevent pinking. The engine was very tractable and an easy starter at all times. Steering and road holding were praised although the effect of the machine's high centre of gravity when changing direction in a series of bends was commented on. The brakes were very powerful, although as supplied for test the front one juddered and continued to do so until the drum was skimmed out.

The 500 had a less happy test as it also vibrated, pinked on anything other than the best petrol, was none too fast and consumed rather more fuel than expected. The tester also fell off when a pedestrian ran into him. Despite these setbacks, it was enjoyed and labelled as a comfortable long distance tourer that was tough and reliable in the best BSA tradition.

At the end of the year, the changes for 1970 were announced and were concentrated on the internals of the engines. The model range remained the same but in an effort to reduce the effects of vibration the flywheel and crankshaft were fully machined so making accurate balancing easier. The connecting rods were also changed to the larger dimensions of a high performance racing specification rod. The cylinder barrel was modified to improve oil tightness and joint strength at the head, while the area of the base flange and crankcase joint was increased. Larger fixing studs were introduced in revised positions and the barrel was held down by nuts of a new design to improve the joint clamp pressure.

The carburation was improved by the fitting of a new needle jet assembly while clutch operation was changed to a three ball cam ramp design. An improved oil pump was fitted with internal changes which further eliminated any chance of air leaks and the oil pressure release valve was changed from a ball to a plunger type.

Apart from the engine changes, the front forks received attention in the form of hard chroming the legs, and holding their size to closer tolerances, to improve fork action and oil seal life. The brake and clutch lever housings were modified to allow mirrors to be fitted and the Lightning received a new style of glass-fibre fuel tank.

The result of all these changes was a better ride with less vibration for the rider but more for the machine. One tester of a Lightning had the two horn brackets fracture followed by the death of both speedometer and rev-counter. Otherwise the machine behaved much as any other A65, or in fact an A10, with its air of solid dependability, a possible maximum of around 100 mph, but a consumption that could easily be held above the sixty mark. It handled well, was comfortable and the brakes worked. The old style, very quickly detachable rear wheel was still fitted, but the ignition was up to the minute, as the optional capacitor discharge system was supplied in place of the normal arrangement.

By this time the whole Company was in serious financial trouble due to a number of

Right **The 1972 fold out sales brochure. A sad end to the line for a company that could once say that 'one in four is a BSA'**

Below **Frame drawings for A50, A65, A65R and A65T models taken from BSA workshop manual**

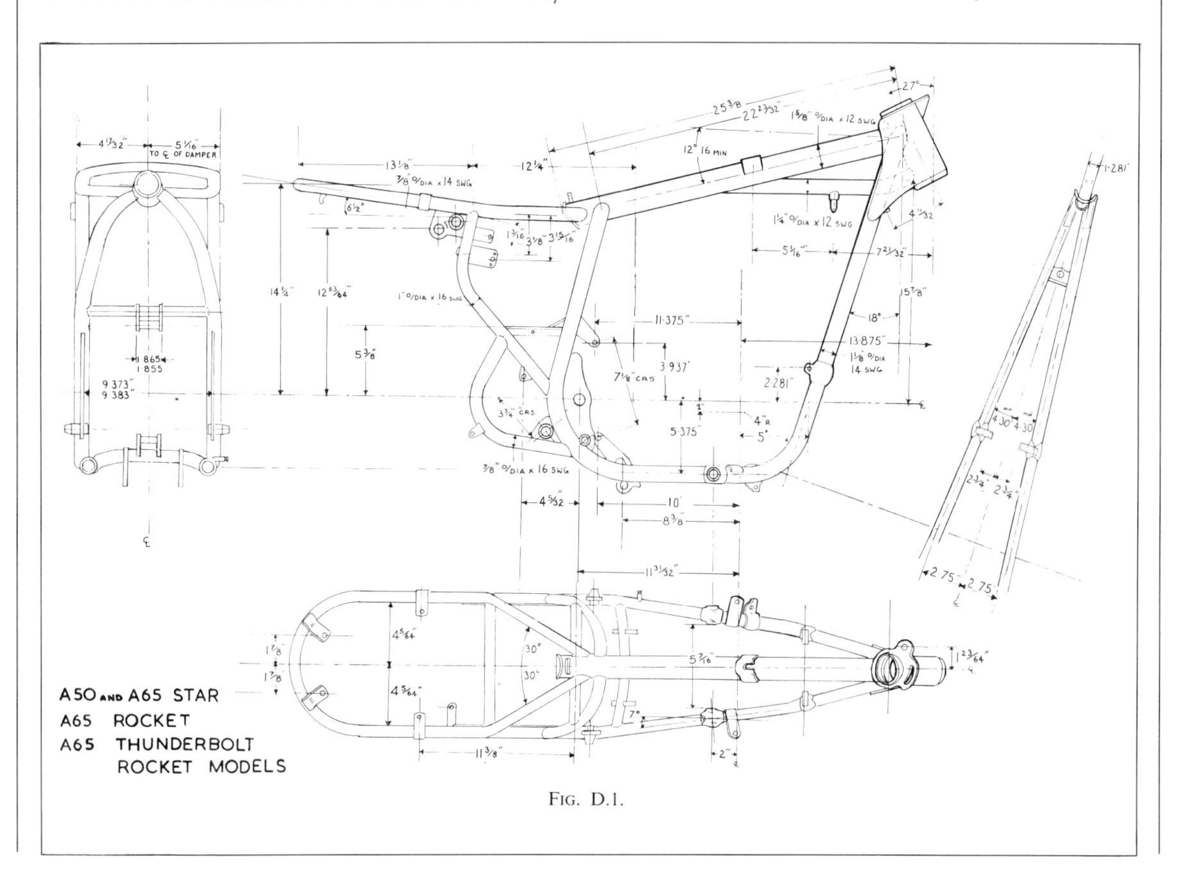

Fig. D.1.

LIGHTNING 650

- 650 cc OHV Twin Cylinder Engine
- Welded Frame with Oil Containing Top Tube
- Superb Forks with Two-way Hydraulic Damping

BSA's wide racing experience is the key to the success of the dynamic Lightning 650.

Sporting good looks with twin-cylinder twin-carburetter performance to match. Twin leading shoe 8" front brake for stopping power to match performance. Immensely tough all welded frame with large diameter main tube which also carries the engine oil. New in dramatic Firebird Red with chromium plated guards and polished forks. Dependable, rugged and fast – that's the Lightning 650.

POWER IN PLENTY, LIGHTNING POWER

The famous Lightning engine: two cylinders, two carburetters and tremendous performance. Alloy head, twin contact breakers and large capacity gear type oil pump. An engine that will go and keep going!

THUNDERBOLT 650

- 650 cc OHV Twin Cylinder Engine
- Single Carburetter ● 12 Volt Electrics
- Twin Megaphone Type Silencers

One of the world's most popular long-range machines. The vertical twin-cylinder engine gives the best of both worlds – the thrust from a large capacity engine plus the flexibility of a single carburetter configuration.

With its immensely strong frame and two-way hydraulically damped forks the '72 Thunderbolt comes in Etruscan Bronze with chromium plated guards and polished forks.

Mechanical simplicity, unobtrusive power with dynamic acceleration and a top speed of over 100 m.p.h. – that's the BSA Thunderbolt 650.

CONTROL LAYOUT OF THE THUNDERBOLT

Bars designed for maximum comfort and controllability. Powerful headlamp carrying warning lights for Main Beam, Direction Indicators and Oil Pressure. Switches grouped for easy use. Alloy brake and clutch levers.

BSA Motor Cycles Ltd.
Armoury Road, Birmingham B11 2PX
Telephone: 021-772 2381
Telegrams & Cables: Selmoto, Birmingham
Telex: 33315.

Printed in England by The Upton Printing Group

750 ROCKET 3

- 750 cc 3 Cylinder Engine
- 3 Carburetters ● Diaphragm Clutch
- 12 Volt Electrics ● Duplex Cradle Frame

A Rocket 3 won Daytona '71 at a new record average speed of 104.7 m.p.h. John Cooper beat Agostini to win the '71 'Race of the Year' and 'Race of the South' and won the Ontario 250 Mile Classic on a Rocket 3. The BSA expertise that produces this type of performance on the race track is built into the machine you buy. Rocket 3's three cylinder, three carburetter engine gives smooth, effortless acceleration (0 – 100 m.p.h. in 13.75 seconds) and Rocket 3 has a stunning maximum speed and many other exciting features. Two-way damped forks give a smooth controlled ride. Now in new colours for 1972.

Rocket 3 . . . The big bike with performance that speaks for itself.

CONTROL LAYOUT OF THE ROCKET 3

Comfortably shaped bars for maximum control. Light alloy clutch and brake levers. Horn, flasher and dip switches in neat groupings. Speedometer and Tachometer easily visible. Warning lights for Main Beam, Direction Indicators and Oil Pressure.

GOLD STAR 500

- 500 cc Single Cylinder OHV Engine
- Alloy Head and Barrel
- Welded Frame with Oil Containing Top Tube
- Upswept Black Finish Exhaust

A Gold Star 500 won the 500 cc class in the Thruxton 500 miles*, and the Barcelona 24 hours Race* and won the Zolder 24 hour Race* outright. A tough no-nonsense street scrambler which is as much at home off the road as on it. Gold Star 500 has an extremely rugged race-proven frame, a willing 4-stroke power unit giving tremendous torque at low r.p.m. – the right power at the right time. New colours for '72 with polished front forks and hubs, make the 500 Gold Star a machine that looks good . . . and works hard.

*Entered by Mead & Tompkinson of Hereford, England and ridden by Nigel Rollason and Clive Brown.

AN ENGINE WITH MOTOCROSS BREEDING

Unique, the four-stroke Gold Star 500 engine is the direct result of many years of successful competition on the international motocross scene. Four-stroke power means tremendous torque . . . and terrific engine braking – the right power at the right time.

Right **1971 Thunderbolt with tank removed and seat lifted to show the oil in frame filler, new style air filter boxes and battery compartment**

Below **1971 Firebird Scrambler with the new frame, forks and wheels. Built for export only it was essentially a Lightning with scrambles modifications as required in the USA**

major technical and managerial blunders, but in November 1970 there was a last ditch stand with a massive trade and press launch in London. Some thirteen new or revised models were shown and among them were the 350 cc twin covered in a later chapter, the Ariel 3 and the continuing twin cylinder range of Royal Star, Thunderbolt, Lightning and Firebird, the last reserved for export only.

The range of twins was extensively modified with a new frame carrying the oil within it, new forks, new hubs and a host of detail changes. The new frame was based on a very large diameter tube which ran back from the headstock and at the saddle nose turned to drop vertically behind the engine unit. It carried the engine oil and was closed at its lowest point by a plate which located a gauze filter onto the outlet pipe and carried a drain plug in its centre. The oil return pipe was located in the bend of the frame tube with the filler cap with its dipstick above it.

The remainder of the frame comprised duplex tubes which ran from the headstock under the engine unit to be braced to the large oil tank tube at its base, before continuing on to the top of the rear suspension units. A tubular loop ran back from the main tube to tie the duplex tubes and continue back to form a mudguard loop.

The new forks had fully exposed stanchions without gaiters or shrouds and the internals were of a new design. Alloy sliders were used with wheel spindle caps, held by four nuts on each leg, in place of the earlier arrangement with a detachable pullout front wheel spindle.

New conical hubs graced the new frame and forks, the front containing a new design of eight inch diameter twin leading shoe brake operated by a single cable, whose outer pushed the rear cam lever forward while the inner pulled the front one back. Adjustment was by a serrated cam turned via a hole in the conical part of the hub, which was sealed with a plug.

The rear hub contained a conventional single leading shoe brake in its new conical housing but in the process the quick detachable feature went, so the change was hardly for the good.

Most of the remaining changes were of a cosmetic nature and included rectangular, cast aluminium alloy, air filter boxes connected by hose to the carburettors, revised side covers, megaphone style silencers, light alloy clutch and brake levers, switches built into the control lever housing and restyled tanks. The export only Firebird followed the same lines and was, in fact, a Lightning with minor changes to handlebars which were high rise, the addition of a sump guard and the raised exhaust system which was finished in black.

Sadly, all this activity was only the last desperate effort of the dying giant. The introduction of so many new and revised models played havoc with production schedules and the twins had an additional burden to carry. The riding position was a good inch too high and despite adverse comment from works testers and the press who had ridden the pre-production models, it was launched without change and helped to tip the balance against BSA even further.

By August 1971, the 500 cc Royal Star had been dropped, so the long and proud line of hard working half litre twins came to an end. The larger road machines continued with a drastic price rise, the Thunderbolt from £475 to £558 and the Lightning a round £100 up to £614 while the Firebird was dropped from the range.

Late in the year the final BSA catalogue, a single, twice folded sheet, showed only four models, two of them twins, the Thunderbolt in Etruscan bronze and the Lightning in firebird red. They continued to be advertised during 1972 although by then production in quantity had ceased.

What was not shown in that catalogue or, in fact, mentioned in the English press of the day, was the final derivitive of the A7 concept, the A70L. This was a longstroke machine of 750 cc built at the request of BSA (Inc.) of America to provide a suitable basis for a US dirt track racing machine. These events were for motorcycles based on road machines so BSA had to build 200 of them in order to claim that they were a production model, and all were shipped to America.

The capacity was achieved by lengthening the stroke to 85 mm which with the standard bore, gave 751 cc. The compression ratio was also increased to 9·5 to 1 which in turn led to jet changes in the carburettors and a different big end shell anti-friction coating. The gearing was raised by the use of a gearbox sprocket with one extra tooth.

A few of these engines were left in England and some of them eventually found their way into the hands of dealers who fitted them into existing rolling chassis. At least one of the pre-production machines also came onto the UK market. These models are sometimes referred to as the Lightning 75 but are seldom seen.

This activity had little bearing on the main events that had taken place in the early 1970s and so the line of vertical twins came to an end.

Right **The new conical rear hub used on both BSA and Triumph models in 1971**

Below **Twin leading shoe front brake with conical hub, also new in 1971, and fitted by both marques**

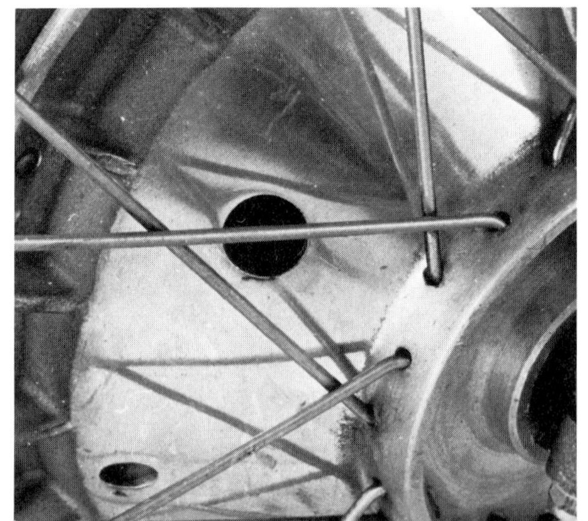

5 The triple

1969 Rocket 3. The machine has the group forks and twin leading shoe front brake. Note the finned heat sink for zener diode under headlamp

During the late 1960s there were a number of rumours that a larger capacity machine was under development at BSA and Triumph, to be produced by both companies. In time these hardened up and it became known that the machine was to have three cylinders and be of larger capacity than either the existing 650 cc twins. It was, however, not until 1968 that details of the two machines were finally released to the Press and public and initially all output went for export so that it was 1969 before they were sold on the home market.

The two machines followed the same general specification with many common detail parts but were different in the appearance of both engine and gearbox unit as well as the cycle parts and finishing touches.

The triple was designed at the Triumph works at Meriden and the chief architects were Bert Hopwood, Doug Hele and Jack Wicks. The engine followed Triumph practice more than BSA, and was designed by adding a third cylinder to the existing twin. Valve gear followed the pattern of Edward Turner's prewar Speed Twin with two camshafts fore and aft of the cylinder block, driven by gears and operating pushrods enclosed in vertical tubes laying between the cylinders.

The three was based on a forged crankshaft which after the initial operation was reheated and twisted to give the 120 degree crank throws. Balance was by the integral webs, no flywheel being fitted. The big end bearings were plain as were the two inner mains, but the ends of the shaft ran in drive side ball and timing side roller bearings. The stroke of the crank was 70 mm which with a 67 mm bore gave a capacity of 740 cc.

The crankshaft was carried in a three-piece aluminium crankcase, split vertically into a centre section to which two outer parts bolted, with these seeming much like two halves of a pre-unit Triumph twin crankcase. Like the early pre-unit cases, they carried the two camshafts in plain bearings with an intermediate gear, driven by the crankshaft gear, meshing with gears attached to the ends of the two camshafts.

The centre crankcase section was open at the top so that the crankshaft dropped into place with the two main bearing caps clamping it down into position. This section extended to the rear to include the gearbox shell which was closed on the left side to carry the main and layshaft bearings. The finned underside of the case carried a finned sump plate which retained a gauze filter as on the twins.

The BSA and Triumph engines were not identical as the BSA had cylinders sloping forward while the early Triumph had them mounted vertically, later models changing to the BSA layout. Thus the cases were also different as were the timing side and gearbox covers, these two items being designed to appear as a single flowing shape on the BSA and as two distinct covers on the Triumph.

The cylinder block was an aluminium alloy casting with pressed in steel liners forming deep spigots for the pistons to run in. These were of conventional design, giving a 9 to 1 compression ratio, and carried two compression and one scraper rings. The gudgeon pins ran direct in the forged, light alloy connecting rods which had steel backed, white metal lined, big end shells. The big end caps were retained by fitted bolts which located the caps and were clamped up with lock nuts. The cylinder casting also carried the pressed in, aluminium alloy, tappet guide blocks, one being housed between each cylinder at front and back of the block. The two on the right each contained a pair of tappets while that on the left had one only. Each tappet moved an aluminium pushrod fitted with hardened steel ends.

The cylinder head was a one-piece aluminium casting to which the two separate rocker boxes were bolted, one containing the three inlet rockers and the other the three exhausts. The head had the three separate inlet stubs bolted to it but the exhaust stubs were screwed in and were generally never disturbed. The casting was very well finned with six wells formed in its top surface for the valves, which were each controlled by two coil springs held by a conventional collar and collet arrangement.

The rocker boxes were also well finned with lids finished to match and fitted to the angled outer faces of the boxes. The vertical inner faces of these each carried a pair of inspection caps positioned to allow the fit of the pushrod cup onto the rocker end to be checked. The rockers had adjusters with locknuts at their outer ends and pivoted on fixed shafts lubricated by an external oil pipe connected to the scavenge pump fed to the oil cooler.

This cooler was mounted just below the steering head and was part of the original equipment. The lubrication was otherwise by a conventional dry sump system with separate oil tank with filter, which fed the gear pump located in the left crankcase and gear driven by spurs from the crankshaft. The oil was passed through a second filter located in the centre crankcase casting behind the engine and below the gearbox. From there it supplied the two centre main bearings which connected to the other crankshaft bearings in turn. Originally the main bearing caps carried feed pipes to the

Left **1970 Rocket 3 with high rise bars and original type silencers with triple pipe outlets**

Above **The two triples when first launched. The two engines are distinctively different although they are based on the same concept. Front forks and hubs are the same but frames are different**

tappets and cams, but this feature was discarded, as those parts were lubricated by splash as were the pistons and timing gears. Removal of the oil pipes when they were found to be unnecessary enhanced crankshaft life. Oil drained into the crankcase from where it was scavenged by the second oil pump which passed it through the oil cooler before it returned to the oil tank. This was vented to the primary chaincase while the return in the tank incorporated a drip feed adjuster and supply pipe for lubricating the rear chain. The engine lubrication system also maintained the primary chaincase oil at its correct level.

A rev-counter drive housing was bolted to the top centre of the crankcase and the drive spindle was skew gear driven from the exhaust camshaft. This also drove the contact breaker cam and advance and retard mechanism from its right hand end, the plate carrying the three

BSA
ROCKET
ROX

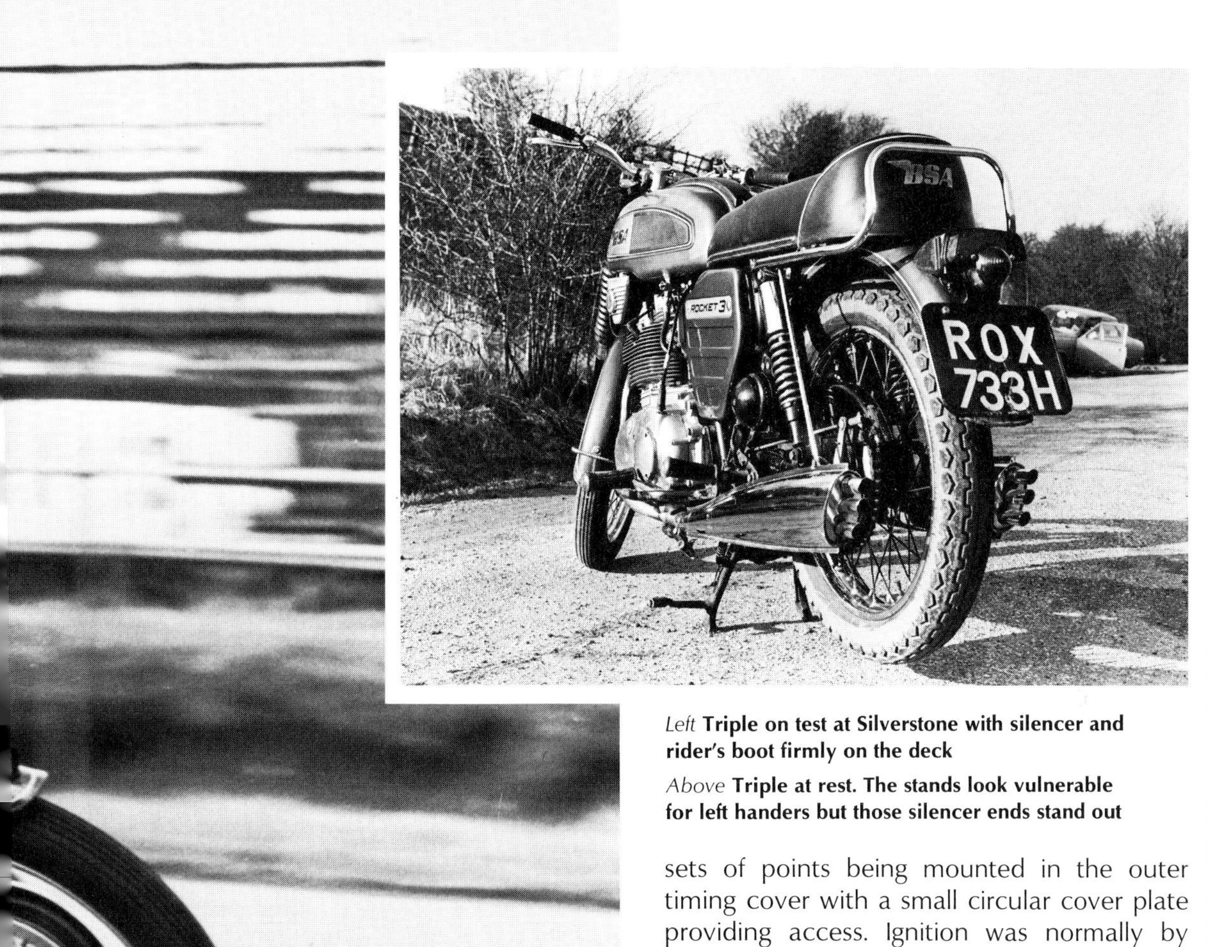

Left **Triple on test at Silverstone with silencer and rider's boot firmly on the deck**

Above **Triple at rest. The stands look vulnerable for left handers but those silencer ends stand out**

sets of points being mounted in the outer timing cover with a small circular cover plate providing access. Ignition was normally by battery and three separate coils mounted in a pack beneath the seat, but some machines use the Lucas capacitor system which relies on the generator to provide the ignition power, so allowing the 12 volt battery to be dispensed with if desired, but retaining the points to act as a trigger. Many triples have been converted to full electronic ignition, usually using the Boyer system, which dispenses with the mechanical advance and the points, these being replaced by an electro-magnetic trigger which connects to an electronic box incorporating ignition advance circuits.

Three separate Amal Concentric carburettors were used, fitted to a manifold which connected to the inlet ports with short rubber hoses. The carburettors were without throttle springs, each slide being positively connected to a throttle linkage mounted on the manifold and this in turn being coupled to the twistgrip and returned by a single spring. The air slides were originally controlled by a single handlebar lever which was later moved to a position next to the carburettors. Two petrol taps supplied the three units but neither had a reserve position, while all three carburettors were supplied by a common air cleaner.

The exhaust system was a three into four into two device as the pipe from the centre cylinder split and was connected into both the outer cylinder pipes, which then swept back into individual silencers on each side of the machine. In their early form, these were instantly recognisable, for they terminated in a laid back flat plate with three small outlet pipes with their ends cut off at an angle.

Right **The view most riders got in 1969 as the triple went past and dwindled into the distance**

Below **Rocket 3 engine in all its glory. The block is held down by special nuts but the chrome trim has come adrift from the air cleaner box**

The engine produced 58 bhp at 7250 rpm in this form and the power was transmitted by a triplex chain from a sprocket mounted outboard of the oil pump drive. To save space on that side of the engine and to avoid too much shaft overhang, the alternator was fitted to the opposite end of the crankshaft in the timing case. The primary chain was tensioned by a blade fitted in the bottom of the chaincase and adjusted from the front. It drove a shock absorber unit which in turn was coupled to a Borg and Beck diaphragm clutch with single plate, which lay within a casting fitted between the inner primary chaincase and the gearbox housing. The clutch was lifted by a ball and ramp device carried in the outer chaincase and drove a conventional four speed, direct top, gearbox.

The gearbox contained the usual main and layshafts with the latter running on needle races, and had the gear selector forks moved by a circular camplate geared to a quadrant worked by the positive stop mechanism. As on the twins, the quadrant pivot lay in the fore and aft direction in the inner cover. Alternative outer covers were fitted to suit the two makes of machine but both supported the outer ends of the gear pedal and kickstart lever shafts. The kickstart quadrant operated the normal BSA arrangement of mainshaft mounted gear driving through a face ratchet. The final drive sprocket was mounted inboard of the clutch in the normal English fashion and drove the rear wheel by chain on the machine's left.

The new engine and gearbox unit was mounted in a frame with single top tube braced by a second tube from the bottom of the headstock, and duplex down tubes which curved under the engine unit and up to the rear suspension top mountings. Saddle tubes connected the end of the top tube to the duplex tubes in the region of the swinging fork pivot, and a rear mudguard loop linked the suspension unit mountings to the top tube. The Triumph used a single down tube with bolted on sub-frame.

The front forks of the new three were similar to those used on the twin at the time, with gaiters protecting the sliders and brackets attached to the shrouds to support the headlamp. A friction steering damper was fitted as standard. The fork ends were split to clamp on the front wheel spindle, the wheel containing the Triumph eight inch diameter, twin leading shoe brake with air scoop and linked cam arms. Like the BSA twin unit, the cable was connected to the extended front cam lever and lay horizontal at the wheel. The front rim was a WM2 of 19 inch diameter shod with a 3·25 inch section Dunlop K70 tyre. At the rear a 4·10 inch Dunlop K81 was fitted to a 19 inch WM3 rim, both rims being steel. The rear brake was a seven inch diameter single leading shoe type. Movement of the rear wheel was controlled by a pair of Girling spring units with pre-load adjustment and exposed, chrome plated springs with chromed top covers only.

The oil tank was located behind the right side panel and contained six pints of oil while the petrol tank had a capacity of 4·25 gallons. On the BSA the side panels incorporated both the motif and the kneegrip within the same outline. A plain dualseat was fitted with a suggestion of a hump at the rear and a grab rail fitted behind that. The first machines had high rise bars to suit the US market, small chrome plate headlamps and matched speedometer and rev-counter heads. The front mudguard was a shaped affair with an arrow head front, supported by the forks and a single stay at the bottom while the rear mudguard was of normal type.

Side reflectors were fitted, those at the front being fixed to small side panels on the ends of the oil cooler while those at the rear were fitted to the sides of the rear light housing. Controls followed the fashion of the time with steel, ball ended clutch and brake levers, combined horn button and dipswitch on the left and air lever on the right handlebar. The ignition switch was located on the right side headlamp support.

The finish was black with chrome plated bright parts, only the petrol tank, mudguards and side covers being painted. The normal

colours were red with white lined mudguards, but some models were produced with a lime green finish and these had red lining applied not only to the mudguards but also to the tank round the combined badge and kneegrip panel, and round the decorative depressions in the side panels. These also carried 'Rocket 3' motifs in black on aluminium which matched the finish of the tank sides.

When first announced, the Rocket 3 or A75 as it was typed, was not available in England, but by early 1969 they were beginning to reach the home market and the price was given as £614. 3*s*. 5*d*. A road test of one appeared in *Motorcyclist Illustrated* at that time and reported very favourably on the machine's performance. Speed, acceleration, handling and brakes were all praised and complaints were limited to minor points concerning the light switch, the accessibility of the prop stand and the effort needed to use the centre stand. Some low speed vibration was noted and the point made that the twin horns directed their notes to the rear of the machine so were less effective than they might have been.

One minor alteration had already been incorporated, the front brake forward cam lever having changed to the two armed version used on the twins to allow the brake cable to lay parallel with the forks. The backplate was also changed to suit.

The test machine had first been run with the throttle linkage fouling one of the oil pipes and it was re-tested with the fault cleared which produced even more impressive performance and speeds around 50, 80, 110 and 125 mph in the four gears. This type of performance was confirmed later in 1969 when *Motorcycle Sport* published a test.

Unfortunately, the BSA triple appeared about the same time as the four-stroke Honda CB750 and the 500 cc Kawasaki two-stroke triple of immense performance and less impressive handling. Both the Japanese machines

Left **Triples in Italy. The Milan Show in 1969 and two triples to delight the natives**

Below **Drive side of the triple engine and gearbox unit. The clutch cable sweeps in neatly and rev-counter drive is from exhaust camshaft**

Bottom **Rocket 3 in presentation form on a plinth stand. Polished and pristine for Press and trade to view**

had five speed gearboxes, while the four cylinder Honda had an overhead camshaft, a disc front brake and electric starting, all of which were almost unheard of in 1969 in what was basically a mass-produced motorcycle with volume sales. At that time, only the rare exotica had such features and none had the established Honda name and reliability.

Despite this setback, the BSA and Triumph triples sold very well, boosted by some racing successes, and quickly earned themselves a good reputation with their owners.

For 1970 the triple received attention to a number of detail points but otherwise remained unchanged. The gearing between kickstarter and crankshaft was slightly lowered so the task of turning the engine over became fractionally easier. The engine joint faces were broadened to improve oil sealing, and the cylinder base nut design was changed to allow a greater clamping force to be developed. The cylinder base studs

were also moved to new positions. Finally, the overall gearing was lowered a small amount by changing the rear wheel sprocket for one with a tooth more, so that the power came in lower down the road speed range. In this form it ran on for another year with a top speed capability of 110 to 115 mph and a consumption that would rise to 30 mpg if it was cruised at 105 mph.

One further modification was introduced around that time to cure any tendency for the clutch to slip. This was dealt with by ensuring that its housing was ventilated and the later models had holes drilled in the casing to make sure it could breathe.

Late in 1970, BSA launched what was to be the final version of the Rocket, along with many other new and revised models. The Rocket engine remained basically unchanged, al-

though it had had minor improvements added from time to time. One such was a change in the shape of the clutch chainwheel shock absorber rubbers, and another concerned the type of bolt used to hold the plate which retained the rubbers. These originally had countersunk heads but were changed to hexagonal ones which allowed the addition of tab washers to ensure positive locking.

More noticeable changes were to the gearbox sprocket which went down one tooth to further lower the gearing, and the air lever was moved onto the left end of the carburettor manifold in which position it fouled one of the petrol pipes. The silencers were also changed to a conventional slow taper megaphone shape, so lost their distinctive ends with the three small outlet pipes. The frame remained as before but the front forks and wheels were changed to the same types used on the large capacity twins. Thus the front forks lost the gaiters and assumed the popular slimline look, while the front wheel gained the twin leading shoe, conical hub brake with the very short cam levers. The front tyre became the same section as that used by the rear wheel. At the rear, the suspension units lost their top covers so the springs became fully exposed.

Left **Triple with tank removed to show fixing and oil cooler line with the take off to feed the rockers**

Below left **The 1970 range line-up with singles, twins, triple and one two-stroke**

Below **Bulmer's MD, Peter Prior, arriving at work on his triple**

Further changes were mainly cosmetic but did include the adoption of indicators. Both mudguards were changed in shape and mount-

ing and their finish became chromium plating. The side cover styling was also changed to a simpler and more elegant form.

With this specification, it was better geared than before so that it would run happily in the 30 mph limit area in third gear which also took it into three figures. Top speed was over 120 mph and acceleration was even better, especially in top gear between 40 and 70 mph, just where it was needed.

Sadly, the BSA triple was nearing the end of the line along with the rest of the range, as already described. At the end of 1971, the Rocket 3 was one of the four machines listed in the BSA Company's final broadsheet, and was changed only in the finish of the front brake backplate, which was black, while the tank and upper part of the side panels were listed as Burgundy.

While this was to be the end for the BSA triple, the Triumph continued for some years, and late in 1972 a specially styled machine, the X75 Hurricane, was revealed at Earls Court. This used the BSA version of the three cylinder engine with a five speed gearbox mounted in a Rocket frame. The machine was styled by Craig Vetter from Illinois and caused something of a sensation at the time both for its lines and the UK price of £895 at a time when a CB750 cost £761. The styling theme was vaguely chop-peresque and the forks were extended, which increased the wheelbase to sixty inches.

Right **1972 Triumph Hurricane fitted with BSA Rocket 3 engine and special styling. A publicity exercise, hence both model and photographer**

Below **1971 three with the new forks and silencers**

Most photographs taken were of the right side as all three exhaust pipes were taken that way to run together under the gearbox and terminate in three reverse megaphone style silencers stacked one on top of another. The small steel fuel tank was enclosed in a glass-fibre cover which flowed down and back from the rear of the tank into the side panels and the

seat base. Front and rear wheels together with their mudguards were standard Triple, while high rise bars were fitted along with a dualseat that complemented the style but was rather short for two. Colour was red, with a pair of yellow strips running through the tank and sidecovers, and the usual parts chromed but the wheel rims alloy. It was of course designed for boulevard cruising and to 'show', but handled moderately well with a riding position that was comfortable at 70 mph. It had good brakes but a very large turning circle and was intended to be a limited edition machine.

Like the other machines, it was in the end overtaken by events within the Group as a whole.

6 The scooter twin

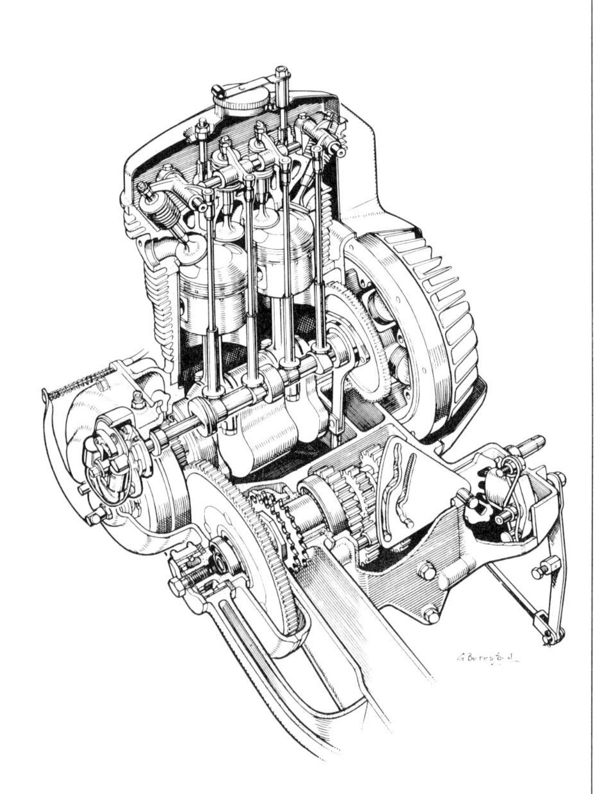

Line drawing of the 250 cc twin cylinder scooter engine and gearbox unit with attached rear suspension arm containing duplex chain drive

BSA were often castigated for missing the scooter boom, but their problem was that they were first too early, then too busy and finally too complicated and late. They built a prototype scooter in the early 1940s with small wheels and fat tyres, running it with a variety of small engines and alternative transmission types including, it was rumoured, a fluid flywheel. This would no doubt have been derived from the experimental motorcycle unit shown at a prewar show. The scooter had plunger rear suspension but was rigid at the front and known as the Dinghy. It sank in the postwar boom when BSA were stretched to their production limit building conventional motorcycles and nobody, in England anyway, believed that such things as scooters would ever sell.

They did, and in 1955 BSA revealed two scooters at the motorcycle show. One, called the Beeza, had a 197 cc single cylinder side valve engine laid flat across the frame driving a four speed gearbox and hence to the rear wheel by shaft. Twelve inch disc wheels were fitted along with electric starting. With it was shown the Dandy 70, a scooterette with 70 cc two-stroke engine with two speed gearbox operated by a form of pre-selector mechanism combined with the clutch.

Neither of these machines were very successful; in fact, the Dandy failed to reach the market until late in 1956, although it continued in production until 1962, while the Beeza never made it at all, being withdrawn before it went into production. Despite these setbacks, BSA persevered and a year later were able to announce that another prototype scooter, designed by Edward Turner, had been undergoing tests. The press statement of the time was made by the chairman, Jack Sangster, who stated that the scooter would go into production in the Triumph and Sunbeam ranges by the middle of 1958 and would offer not only excellent weather protection but a striking performance as well.

It was, however, not until October 1958 that a formal press presentation was made of the new models, although their existence had been an open secret for many months. Two versions were shown, both available either as the BSA-Sunbeam or the Triumph Tigress, one equipped with a 175 cc two-stroke engine based on Bantam engine dimensions, and the other fitted with a twin cylinder, four stroke engine of 250 cc.

Aside from the two engine types which were fitted to either make, the only differences between the two were the nameplates and the colours, the BSA being metallic green and the Triumph shell blue.

The twin cylinder engine incorporated a number of unusual features and was built in unit with a four speed gearbox. An electric starter could be supplied as an optional extra but the kickstarter was still retained on all models. The rear wheel was carried by a single swinging arm on the left of the machine formed

The Dandy 70 scooterette announced in 1955 and sold from late 1956 to 1962

by the castings enclosing the final drive chain and pivoted on the gearbox mainshaft axis.

The engine was of oversquare dimensions at 56 × 50·62 mm to give a capacity of 249 cc. It was based on a single light alloy casting which formed the cylinder block, crankcase and gearbox shell. To this was fitted the cylinder head, end covers to the crankcase and a pressed steel sump. The crankshaft was a one

Above **250 cc BSA scooter outside the company front door. Seated is Hap Alzina from Oakland while standing from the left are A N Brealey, R J Fearon, W L Rawson and Bert Perrigo**

Left **The Beeza scooter announced in 1955 but never to go into production. Pictured at Earls Court in November with model Josephine Griffin**

piece forging in manganese-molybdenum steel incorporating a massive central bobweight between the cylinders and a sludge trap within the crankpin. It ran in a deep groove ball race on the left side and a plain bush on the right and was assembled into the crankcase from the drive side. The connecting rods had conventional split big ends with shell bearings and supported full skirted pistons carrying two compression rings and one scraper. The gudgeon pins ran in bushes in the small ends and were retained by circlips. Compression ratio was 6·5 to 1.

The cylinder head was cast in light alloy with the cast iron valve inserts placed in the mould so that they were cast and locked into the cylinder head. The valve configuration was unusual, for the four valves lay in a line along the crankshaft axis across the engine. The two inner inlet valves were arranged vertically and operated by rockers, which pivoted on a spindle laying parallel to the crankshaft. Thus the rocker arms were brought straight back to the pushrods situated at the rear of the engine. The two exhaust valves were, however, laid out at an angle to give short exhaust ports to the ends of the cylinder head as distinct from the inlets which joined to a single port at its rear. The exhaust rockers were individually supported on spindles which ran across the head in the fore and aft direction. Thus the rocker ends also terminated at the pushrods at the rear of the engine. All three rocker spindles were supported by lugs standing up from the cylinder head, and all four rockers carried screw adjustors and locknuts at the valve end. An oil gallery ran along the rear of the rocker box and was fed at both ends by two pipes connecting it to the crankcase. The valves were closed by dual springs held in collars and split cotters, ran in pressed in guides, and the whole assembly was enclosed by a rocker box cover carrying the oil filler cap in car style. The two spark plugs were fitted into the front of the cylinder head between each pair of valves.

The camshaft was positioned at the rear of the engine and operated the valves via flat base tappets and pushrods. It ran in three bearings, one at its centre, to ensure stiffness at high speed, and was driven by a pair of gears from the right-hand end of the crankshaft. The right-hand end of the camshaft drove a simple plunger oil pump by means of an eccentric on the shaft inboard of the driving gear, and a connecting piece. At its other end, the camshaft drove the contact breaker cam and its automatic advance and retard mechanism by a tongue and slot arrangement which connected the two shafts. The cam opened two separate sets of points mounted on a single backplate that could be rotated to set the timing, and the whole assembly was sealed by a small circular cover.

The alternator was mounted on the right-hand of the crankshaft and its rotor incorporated both a cooling fan and the starter gear ring. The starter itself was a Lucas pre-engaged type, bolted to the crankcase right side end cover and positioned in front of the engine. It was operated by a knob on the machine's front shield, connected to the starter motor by flexible cable. The electric switch was mounted on the starter and made contact once the starter gear had been moved into mesh.

The cooling fan was enclosed with a cowl which connected to a shroud fitted over the front of the engine. It was claimed that the use of forced draft cooling allowed the fins of the cylinder block to be at a closer pitch than normal which helped to reduce engine resonance and so gave a quieter machine.

The clutch was mounted on the left hand end of the crankshaft and contained three bonded and three plain plates. Pressure was applied by three springs and the plates released by a simple lever arm operating a pushrod. The back of the clutch drum carried a gear which

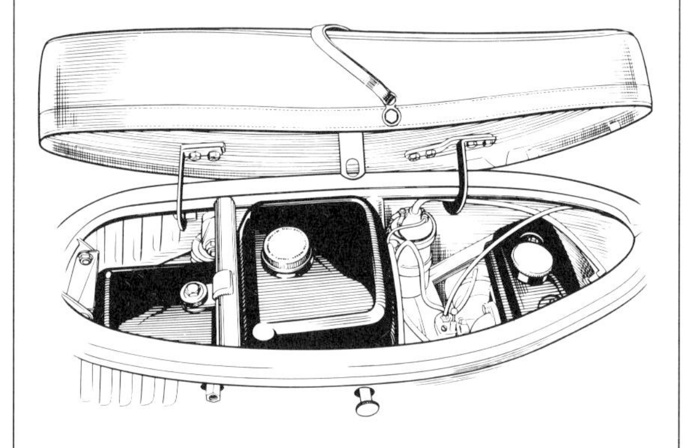

meshed with another on the gearbox mainshaft so the engine ran backwards, and the primary drive was enclosed by two light alloy castings, the inner acting as the left crankcase door while the outer also carried the contact breaker assembly as well as the clutch release lever.

The gearbox followed conventional lines with the output sleeve gear concentric with the mainshaft and the layshaft positioned below it. The gears were selected by two forks moved by a sector shaped camplate. This was shifted by a

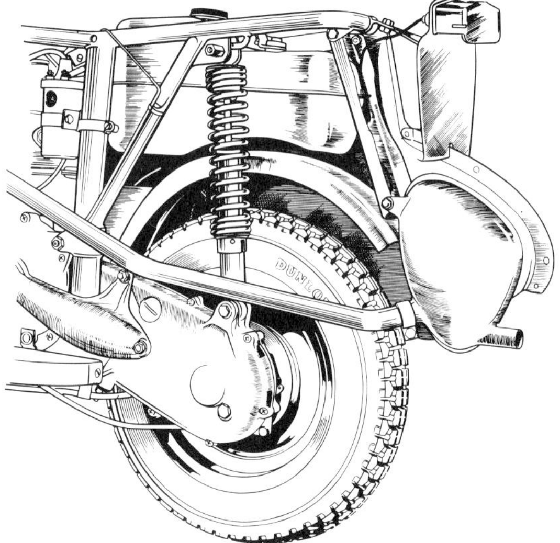

Top **Engine bay with offside panel removed. This clearly shows the chain linking kickstart pedal to gearbox**

Above **Line drawing of nearside rear of the scooter showing combined chaincase and suspension arm together with damper unit**

Left **Under the scooter seat which lifted to give access to the fuel tank and engine**

conventional positive stop mechanism connected by a rod to a pedal protruding from the right floor panel. This was pressed forward to change down and back to change up. A second pedal on the right side of the floor panel but further to the rear next to the engine covers selected neutral if pressed down when the gearbox was in second gear.

The gearbox end cover which supported the shafts was an extension of the right side crankcase door and itself carried a small cover to enclose the positive stop mechanism.

The kickstarter arrangements were a little unusual. As a scooter, the machine required a forward working pedal as this was the convention on the great majority of scooters at that time. However, this moved its pivot position well away from the optimum at the gearbox to a point forward and below the crankshaft. A further difficulty lay in the need for the working shaft, which was concentric with the gearbox layshaft, to rotate in the opposite sense to the kickstarter pedal spindle. This was overcome by fitting small chain sprockets to both shafts and connecting the two by a short length of chain. By fitting the chain in the correct manner the direction of rotation of the shafts was reversed so that the pawl and ratchet rotated the layshaft bottom gear pinion as required.

The final drive was by an enclosed duplex chain running inside a single swinging arm which carried the rear wheel. The arm was built up from three light alloy castings and pivoted

Publicity picture of the times dated by hairstyle and the cigarette. The scooter has several of the available accessories fitted

The start of an ACU observed demonstration run for the BSA and Triumph scooter. The riders are both famous racing champions, John Surtees and Geoff Duke. Between them stands R J Fearon, BSA general manager, while to the right of Duke is Brian Martin who became BSA competition manager. On the extreme left is Bert Perrigo and on the right, Harry Clenshaw, a timekeeper and ACU observer for the occasion

on the gearbox mainshaft axis. The two main castings turned on a bush fitted to a flanged boss, bolted to the left side of the gearbox shell, while the third, an outrigger arm, was bolted to the case about half way along its length and pivoted on a bush fitted outboard of the primary drive cover. Thus the chain tension remained constant during wheel movement and was adjusted by means of a screw on the underside of the case which moved a slipper tensioner. An inspection cap in the outer case allowed the play in the top chain run to be checked.

The engine breathed through a single Zenith carburettor of the semi-automatic type with slide and needle. It also had a float which was concentric with the main jet and a starter slide rather than a strangler. The carburettor was fitted to an inlet pipe with a double crank in it which lowered its height to a point which ensured an adequate head of petrol even when climbing steep hills with a low fuel reserve.

The exhaust system was also a little unusual by motorcycle standards, the makers adopting the sensible principle that the appearance of the mechanical parts under the covers is of no importance on a scooter. Thus, an exhaust pipe ran back from each side of the cylinder head to a silencer box which was shaped to fit in the tail of the bodywork. From the box a single tailpipe protruded from the rear of the machine.

This engine unit was carried in a duplex frame which was bolted and clipped to the steering head at the front. From there the two main tubes swept under the floor to rise vertically behind the engine to support an oval

CENTRE OF ENGLAND
F. C. COLLETT.
SPAR
SPAR
MELLORS MINT
BAKED BEANS
TOMATO SOUP
15 COE
44 BUE

shaped structure which followed the seat outline. The main tubes were cross braced at several points and the seat frame was held square by a tube running back to the top suspension mounting point, there being of course, only one unit to match the swinging arm. The seat hinged up to disclose the one and a half gallon petrol tank and the rear structure was extended to support the silencer box and a small rear mudguard.

The front forks were designed to allow the use of stub axles—a normal scooter feature—but were telescopic in movement. This was achieved by placing two telescopic assemblies together on the same, left, side of the front wheel. Thus the stub axle, brake assembly and wheel were all carried by an alloy casting with two deep vertical holes in it. These slid on two tubes attached to a lower fork crown, the rear one of which contained a fork spring anchored both to the crown and the lower end of the slider casting while the front tube contained the fork's hydraulic damping unit. A pressed shroud fitted onto the two fork tubes and extended down over the slider casting.

The lower crown was fitted to a long steering column tube which turned on cup and cone head races and had the handlebars keyed to it.

Above **250 scooter at Earls Court in 1958. The actress is Jacki Pepper and the painter is using a shaver plugged into the BSA**

Left **Centenary Day at Small Heath in 1961. Centre is an Otto cycle, on the left the first all BSA motorcycle of 1910 and on the right the 250 cc scooter with R J Fearon seated on it. The cyclist is sixteen year old apprentice Brian Wright and the four standing are BSA directors**

The bars were welded to the pinch clamp above the top race and were held in place by the two nuts used for steering head adjustment. The steering lock was also welded to the bars to the left of the clamp in the same area.

Both brakes were conventional single leading shoe drum types of five inch diameter and one inch width. The wheels fitted on three studs protruding from each brake drum as in normal car practice so were interchangeable and, like cars, fitted with hub caps. The wheels were pressed steel and of 10 inch diameter fitted with 3·50 inch section tyres. The rear brake was operated by a pedal mounted above the floor on the left of the machine while a conventional lever and cable worked the front brake. Clutch and throttle were as motorcycle practice and the controls were completed by a combined dip switch and horn push mounted on the left handlebar, and two switches fitted either side of the speedometer on the machine's apron to control ignition, with both normal and emergency positions, and the lights. In addition to the starter knob in the centre of the apron, the cold start control was fitted on the left side.

The bodywork was built up from pressed steel parts bolted together to form the front shield, apron, mudguard, floor and rear body shell. All these parts were easily removed for major servicing but remained in place for routine maintenance.

The electrics were straightforward with the normal complement of head, pilot, rear, stop and speedometer lights, horn, ignition warning light and generation and ignition circuits. The 6 volt battery was carried under a cover on the rear of the apron on the left side. Where an electric starter was fitted, a 12 volt system was obtained by the addition of a second battery fitted on the right side of the apron.

A whole range of accessories were made available for the machines including a windscreen, spare wheel and its carrier. The usual scooter shopping bag hook was fitted to the rear of the apron as standard. When announced the machine weighed 240 lb and was listed as the model B2 with kickstarter at £187. 2*s*. 2*d*., and as the model B2S with electric starter at £200. 17*s*. 0*d*.

The model launch was held at Grosvenor House in London and was attended by numerous celebrities. Some prophecies of the future sales of the models were made but these proved somewhat optimistic for the venture into the scooter world was none too successful.

In the middle of 1959 *Motor Cycle* road tested a Triumph Tigress and gave it a good write-up. Starting was immediate whether the engine was hot or cold, acceleration brisk and cruising at 55 mph the normal gait. Handling, comfort and braking were also praised, although the rear brake had lost much of its efficiency after 1000 miles, which was not so good on a vehicle sold mainly to riders who would use the rear brake more than the front. The centre stand grounded on left hand corners on occasion, and other criticisms concerned the need to free the clutch first thing in the morning, an only partly effective neutral selector and a small fuel tank, although consumption was around the 80 mpg mark. The dual seat was judged to become rather hard after some three hours riding, and became warm as a result of engine heat, especially in traffic.

As a result of tax changes, the prices had fallen slightly to £194. 4*s*. 2*d*. and the test machine was fitted with the windscreen at £4. 19*s*. 6*d*., the rear carrier at £3. 15*s*. 6*d*., the spare wheel at £5. 9*s*. 0*d*. and the spare wheel cover at £2. 2*s*. 0*d*.

The various versions of the scooter continued on for some years with virtually no changes although for 1961 the BSA was made available in fuchsia red or sapphire blue as well as the usual polychromatic green, either as single colour finishes or combined with cream coloured weathershield panels. The Triumph was also offered in a further choice of colours and the prices remained at £180. 18*s*. 9*d*. for the model B2 and £194. 4*s*. 2*d*. when the electric starter was fitted. Accessories also included a front carrier, pannier frames and bags, and wheel discs.

The scooter had become involved with some sporting activities by this time as in 1960 a Tigress ridden by Don Leadbetter, David Hurst and Roy Banks broke Australian records for one, twelve and twenty-four hours in the 250 cc and 350 cc categories. The run was made at Caversham airstrip near Perth in poor conditions of rain, wind and sleet, and in the twenty four hours the machine covered 1135·4 miles at an average speed of 47·3 mph.

Meanwhile in England, R. B. 'Bunny' Ward used the twin cylinder engine to power a Greeves trials frame in scrambles. While no world beater, it proved a successful operation with the engine running without fan or cooling shroud. The power occurred where needed and it proved a reliable machine running in local events.

In the middle of 1961 prices rose by about £3 due to tax changes and remained there until a budget change in 1962 took them back to their original point.

A minor change was introduced to the exhaust system when the two pipes were Siamesed with the pipe from the right being carried across the front of the engine to join the left which swept down from the port. The single pipe continued down to fit into a silencer extension.

For 1963 the scooters received only detailed improvements and their prices again rose but only by a few pounds so the B2S reached £198.

This made little difference for the day of the scooter had passed by and sales were dropping. The public demand moved on to other fields and it was to be another decade and a half before scooter sales began to pick up again.

Thus once again the venture of BSA into the world of two tiny wheels went sour and in October 1964 the scooters were dropped from the range so the interesting 250 cc twin was no more.

By the river on two wheels. A publicity picture showing machine and riders to advantage

830
BOM

7 The final twin

The last major Press and trade launch of the BSA/Triumph group was held in November 1970 and among the many models shown was a completely new machine fitted with a 350 cc twin cylinder engine. The basic design work was carried out by Edward Turner who, although he

The 350 cc twin cylinder Fury in its street scrambler form with raised exhaust system

had retired from Meriden in 1964, still maintained his interest in motorcycles. He worked on the 350 twin as a freelancer. It was to be his last project and as the founder of the vertical twin success story with his 1938 Speed Twin, it was perhaps fitting that his final, albeit less successful design should also have two cylinders.

The design was to have been sold under two brand names as the BSA Fury and the Triumph Bandit, with only minor styling differences. Both machines were also to have been made available in street scrambler guise to suit the American market.

The engine was a completely new unit whose cylinders inclined forward slightly with twin overhead camshafts driven by chain. It was based on dimensions of 63 × 56 mm with a 180 degree crankshaft, so had the uneven firing intervals and rocking couple out of balance forces normal with that engine layout.

The crankshaft was forged with an integral central flywheel and was machined all over to ensure consistency of balancing. The machining included slots in the flywheel periphery which located on a removable peg for ignition timing. The crankshaft ran in two main bearings with the drive on the right a ball race and the timing a roller. The big ends were conventional shells of the same size as used in the triple and the connecting rods were aluminium alloy forgings with steel caps located by dowels, a typical group design. They carried conventional three ring pistons held by gudgeon pins working directly in the rods and retained by circlips. The compression ratio was 9·5 to 1.

The crankshaft was supported in a vertically split crankcase, the two halves being gravity die cast in aluminium. The inside gave considerable clearance to the crankshaft and flywheel and was free from ribs, so would have had minimal oil drag effect at high engine speeds.

The cylinder block was another gravity die casting in aluminium with the two alloy iron cylinder liners pressed in. The cylinder head was made by the same process and in the same material as the block, and was unusual in that the use of loose sand cores had been avoided except for the ports. The head casting contained the camshaft supports and was well finned with air passages provided beneath the camshaft housings through the vertical fins rising directly from the combustion chambers. Although the cooling arrangements appeared adequate, little attempt was made to join the fins to prevent them ringing, which would have reduced mechanical noise. This aspect was partially dealt with by means of rubber inserts.

The two camboxes were open at the top with the bearings for the camshafts in the end walls of the resulting trough.

The valves were set at an included angle of sixty degrees which gave a shallow, compact combustion chamber. They worked against cast-in seats and ran in valve guides which were pressed in and located by circlips. Dual valve

BSA
FURY

springs were fitted and retained by conventional collar and cotters while the valves were opened by inverted bucket tappets under each cam. Valve clearances were set by shims inserted between the tappets and the valve heads, the shims being available in two thou steps. Access for measurement of the valve clearance was by four screwed plugs in the sides of the cam boxes whose removal allowed the insertion of a feeler gauge.

The camshafts were formed in one with both cams and drive sprockets and ran directly in the cylinder head. As the shafts were assembled through one of the bearings, this limited the cam lift to some extent, although it would have been an easy problem to overcome.

The camshafts were driven by a chain on the left of the engine from a half speed gear meshed to the crankshaft. The chain was enclosed in a chamber that rose from the crankcase on the left side of the cylinder block but to its rear, so that it lay below the inlet camshaft. At cylinder head level the chamber ran forward to encompass the exhaust camshaft. The chain ran straight down from the inlet camshaft, having travelled across from the exhaust before returning round a long curved tensioner that passed it from half speed sprocket to exhaust camshaft, and in the process changed its direction of movement from vertical to horizontal. The tensioner was rubber-faced and thus acted as a jockey sprocket as well as being adjustable to set the chain tension. Fixed, rubber-faced guides helped to control the other two chain runs.

The styling of the camshaft tunnel was not very smooth as distinct joints occurred at both cylinder base and head joint level while the camshaft sprocket cover was retained by nine bolts and styled with two circular pads and five horizontal ribs. The two camshafts' wells in the cylinder head were enclosed by flat covers with fins which ran across the engine and can hardly have assisted the air flow.

Dry sump lubrication was employed with a double gear pump skew driven from the left end of the crankshaft. A full flow oil filter with replaceable paper element was located in the front of the crankcase on the left and covered by a cap which housed the oil pressure warning switch.

Oil passed from the pump through a large junction block to the hollow timing side mainshaft sealed by a lipseal in the timing cover and from there it was fed to the big ends via the removable sludge traps in the crankshaft. The timing cover also contained a small jet which sprayed oil onto the pump drive gears and the camshaft drive reduction gears. From the main feed a bypass was taken to a point behind the left end of the cylinder block and connected to the rear of the camshaft drive sprocket housing in the cylinder head by a very small bore pipe, external to the engine. This was intended to feed the camshaft bearings and, via them, the cams by means of cross holes on the cam base circle connected to the hollow camshafts.

The oil drained from the inlet cam box down through two holes which passed through the casting above the combustion chambers to reach the exhaust cam box. This was lower than the inlet by virtue of the inclined engine installation angle and from it the oil drained down the camshaft chain tunnel. It finally reached the sump from where it was scavenged by the pump. An upward extension of the oil pump shaft was used to provide the rev-counter drive take-off point.

Engine breathing followed the design of the triple and was through the drive side main bearing into the primary drive case and from there via a settling chamber to the air filter box. This satisfied the then current emission requirements, and the breathing was a minimal

Fury twin in road form on show. Fork and hubs are common to the range but the frame is unique to the 350. The exhaust pipes could not be any closer to the frame

problem anyway as the engine layout automatically gave nearly constant under piston volume.

The mixture was provided by two Amal Concentric carburettors which were joined by short rubber hoses to separate, parallel, inlet port adaptors screwed into the cylinder head. The exhaust ports were also parallel and connected to two separate exhaust pipes and silencers. On the road machines each pipe curved down and back to a point just behind and below the footrests. To them were clamped tubular megaphone style silencers of the same pattern as was adopted at that time for both BSA and Triumph 650 cc twins. The silencers were supported by a plate suspended from the pillion footrest.

On the street scrambler models the two exhaust pipes were both carried round to the right side of the machine at high level. They connected to two megaphone style silencers joined into one unit with the left cylinder pipe above that from the right cylinder. The whole system was finished in matt black and carried two chromium plated heat guards, one bolted to each system.

Although the contact breakers could easily have been driven from the half speed timing gear, BSA chose to mount them at the right hand end of the exhaust camshaft from where they controlled the coil ignition system.

An electric starter was announced as being available as an optional extra and when fitted was positioned behind the cylinders on top of the gearbox. The starter end cap contained an epicyclic gear reduction train and was con-

Nearside of Fury twin road model showing left foot kickstart lever. Another typical BSA Press photograph of the time

nected to the crankshaft by chain. The overall reduction ratio was fourteen to one and the crankshaft sprocket contained a one way roller clutch and was mounted on a needle bearing. This sprocket lay outboard of the primary drive and just inboard of a Lucas alternator positioned at the extreme right hand end of the crankshaft. This was a standard design mounted on three studs screwed into the crankcase wall, so overhung the right main bearing by some distance.

The primary drive was by a duplex chain which lay between the right main bearing and the starter sprocket. It was slipper tensioned and drove a conventional multiplate clutch incorporating a shock absorber of the rubber and vanes type, the assembly being adapted from the BSA Victor component. It carried a centre adjustor screw accessible through a screwed plug in the cast aluminium outer chaincase and was lifted by a triple ball and ramp mechanism which was then being used on most of the Group's machines.

The gearbox was a five speed device built in unit with the engine and of typical English design with the output sprocket mounted on a sleeve gear, concentric with the mainshaft and positioned behind the clutch. The layshaft lay behind the mainshaft and the selectors slid on a rod positioned above the shafts, and were controlled by a circular cam plate which pivoted on a pin fixed to the top of the gearbox casting. This was rotated by a quadrant moved by the positive stop mechanism which was controlled with a pedal on the left side. Pivoted at a point just below the gear pedal was the

Gearbox of the 350 twin. Also to be seen are the starter, inaccessible gearbox filler plug, angled slot pedals and general rather 'bitty' construction

kickstart lever, also on the left, with a folding pedal. The gearbox design was in essence a Triumph unit with an added fifth gear, but could have been more suited to the overall machine layout had it employed a crossover drive with the gearbox sprocket fitted to the layshaft. The final drive chain was positioned on the right side of the machine.

The power output of the engine was claimed to be 34 bhp at 9000 rpm with the maximum torque claimed to be 20 ft lb at 7000 rpm. The engine unit was fitted into a frame with well splayed, duplex down tubes which swept under the engine and up to the rear unit top mounting points. A second pair of tubes ran from the top of the headstock over the inlet cambox to angle down to join the first pair just above the swinging fork pivot. A further pair of tubes ran forward horizontally from the rear unit top mounting to the upper frame tubes and thus lay just below the line of the seat and tank. These tubes were extended rearwards by a smaller loop which ran back to support the rear mudguard and tail light assembly and had the seat grab rail fitted to it.

The swinging fork was controlled by a pair of suspension units with exposed springs and the front forks were the new slim line type with internal springs and two way damping. Front fork movement was $6\frac{3}{4}$ inches, a good figure for the time.

The two hubs were the new BSA/Triumph conical type, cast in aluminium alloy as used for much of the range that year. The front hub contained an eight inch, two leading shoe brake which was operated by two very short cam levers pulled together by the cable action. The cast aluminium alloy backplate carried a large air scoop and had small slots in it to let the air out while the brake was adjusted with snail cams, which were accessible through a hole in the brake cone. The rear hub was similar, but housed a seven inch, single leading shoe brake with floating cam action which allowed the shoes to move to their most effective position without hindrance. The brake, its operating

Right **Conical hub introduced in 1971 for the 350 twin. Also used on other BSA and Triumph models**

Below **Front brake for the 350 twin and others. The hub and forks were also new to the range in 1971**

pedal and the rod that connected them, were all mounted on the right side of the machine.

The wheels were of conventional spoked design with steel rims and both the road and street scrambler machines were pictured as having the same roadster tyres. Both mudguards were sporting in style and the front one was rubber mounted to the fork legs.

The lighting and electrics of the machines were up-to-date with indicators, side reflectors, headlight flasher and a four position ignition switch which allowed the machine to be parked with the ignition off and the parking lights on. Both speedometer and rev-counter were rubber mounted and warning lights were provided for oil pressure, headlight high beam and the indicators.

The seat and tank design of the two brands was different, the BSA being fitted with a smooth finish dualseat while the Triumph had the ribbed top typical of the marque. Both seats were nearly flat with a slight upturn at the rear.

The BSA tank was finished, along with the other painted parts, in a coarse flecked metallic purple colour called Plum Crazy. The tank carried a bold line across its top in front of the central petrol cap and this continued down the sides at an angle with a break for the BSA winged motif. The line continued to the rear of the tank along a form line in the tank side. The Triumph tank was given a more curved styling theme with a simulated impression of a kneegrip panel.

The side covers were also finished in different ways. The BSA versions had the upper major part painted to match the tank with a small lower part in a lighter colour. The panels carried the name Fury within a box line or Fury SS as appropriate. The Triumph covers were coloured in the reverse sense which matched the tank finish and were suitably identified.

The new machines weighed 345 lb dry and were initially promoted at £380 with optional electric starter available for a further £21.

Several of these machines had been seen about in the Birmingham area during the summer and autumn of 1970, prior to the launch, as the prototypes went through their testing. As the year ended, more people had an opportunity to ride them and found that they were quick but mechanically noisy. The cycle parts were very good as would be expected when forks and wheels were from much larger, faster and heavier machines.

At that time, late in 1970, the group was in serious financial trouble and partly as the result of this, the new 350 cc machine was tooled up for production before a number of development problems had been overcome. As a result of the ensuing delays and the subsequent company collapse, the Fury never reached the market.

By August 1971 the street scramblers had been dropped as part of a streamlining operation carried out to try to save the day, and at the same time the price was raised to £458 for the model with the electric starter.

Sadly this was to no avail and by the end of the year the final twin was no longer listed.

The pre-production prototypes lived on, and some of these machines eventually finished up in the hands of BSA dealers when the firm finally closed. One of these was briefly tested by *Motor Cycle News* in 1973, but this test was a limited appraisal only as the machine had not been used in the intervening period. It proved to be highly geared with the fifth speed acting as an overdrive ratio while the engine was smooth but transmitted some vibration through the footrests. The handling was described as taut although the bars were felt to be too wide and angled. The ride was not good, but this was more likely to have been due to the condition of the forks, tyres and dampers after some years without use.

A tantalising test, for many felt the machine had tremendous potential it had never had a real chance to show.

8 Competition

The BSA twin cylinder machines were not originally intended to be sports models but to provide reliable transport with all the rather boring attributes such vehicles have. So, as well as reliability, the accent was on economy, ease of maintenance, spares and service back-up and other utilitarian virtues. If you were sufficiently bold as to ask for more performance from the two cylinders, the Star Twin was offered, but the real sports machines in the

Chris Vincent on his kneeler sidecar. Vincent was the most successful of the riders who used the BSA twin engines and dominated British sidecar racing for a decade. He also won the 1962 Sidecar TT, BSA's only international Isle of Man win

1950s were considered to be the singles.

So the twin was left rather to its own devices for most of the time but for all its humble beginnings it was eventually to give BSA their sole international TT victory. It was also used in a good number of other competition spheres where it acquitted itself well.

Its first appearance in the Isle of Man was in the Clubmans TT held on Wednesday, 11 June 1947. This was the first such event run as a combined race for 1000, 350 and 250 cc classes, the larger two of which covered four laps. All machines had to be standard catalogue models of which at least twenty-five had been sold to the public. Racing tyres, brake air scoops and straight through exhaust pipes were allowed, but not megaphones.

Two BSA twins were entered and both riders were kept busy up to the last minute by changes in ruling from the scrutineers which necessitated modifications to the machines. In the race, N. Kirby was forced to retire at the end of the first lap with a split petrol tank and due to this his lap time was slow. However, J. E. Stevens made up for this with a first lap in 31 minutes 1 second which placed him fourth at 72·99 mph behind Eric Briggs. Sadly Stevens was forced to retire at Glen Helen on his second lap due to a cracked carburettor and so ended the BSA twin's first TT venture.

In 1948, two more twins entered the Clubmans but both retired. However, in the following year there were four entries and J. Wright came home in eleventh position. After this the twins ceased to be used in this event which ultimately became dominated by the BSA Gold Star.

For a little while the twin just carried on with its job of carrying riders and pulling sidecars along although occasionally there were less usual tasks for it to do. One such was that given to two A7s by Tornado Smith whose occupation was Wall of Death rider. The machines were basic twins in rigid frames stripped of all non-essential equipment such as mudguards and electrics. Long footboards replaced the normal footrests, the fuel tank was raised sufficiently for there to be a clear gap between its underside and the top of the engine while the seat was lifted some six inches or so by a rigid structure. Open pipes terminated near the rear of the machine to give a healthy crackle to the exhaust as the machines circulated in their wooden cage.

In a complete contrast, two other BSA twins ran down the straight line of the Bonneville Salt Flat timing strip in the autumn of 1951 in an attack on one mile records. This was organised by the BSA West Coast distributor Hap Alzina from California and the two machines were prepared by Gene Rhynne and ridden by Gene Thiessen.

The first machine was a 500 cc Star Twin which was prepared to comply with the Class C rules of the American Motorcycle Association. These covered machines that were basically standard and which appeared in the maker's current catalogue. The engine had to run on pump petrol and the maximum compression ratio allowed was limited to 8 to 1. Alterations from standard were restricted to the removal of lights and silencers while the engine alterations were limited to increases of valve sizes, changes to camshaft type and general polishing. The A7 engine was equipped with a special camshaft which gave both increased lift and extended timing, had its ports enlarged and was fitted with special valve springs to allow it to run to 7250 rpm. A single Amal TT carburettor of $1\frac{1}{16}$ inch choke was used and the carefully assembled engine produced over 40 bhp.

It was installed in the standard frame and forks with no front mudguard and the handlebars bent down so that the grips were nearly vertical.

For the attempt, the rider was required to wear normal riding clothing, crash helmet and gloves and thus clad, Thiessen took the totally unstreamlined machine over the flying mile at 123·69 mph, an impressive figure.

The second machine was a 650 cc Golden Flash prepared to the much less restrictive class A rules which allowed dope fuels and any compression ratio. The engine was modified

Above **The north turn at Daytona where the riders leave two miles of sand and start on two miles of tarmac. A unique circuit where BSA won in 1954**

Left **J E Stevens and his A7 before the 1947 Clubmens TT in which he retired after holding fourth place on the opening lap**

along the same lines as the 500 cc unit but had a compression ratio of 13·5 to 1 and was fitted with two 1 inch choke Amals. It ran on a fuel composed of ninety per cent methanol and ten per cent benzole, turned over at 6500 rpm and produced over 60 bhp. It was fitted to a standard rigid frame and again the handlebar grips were positioned near to the vertical. Neither front mudguard or front brake were fitted and the rear mudguard was cut short at the top of the wheel. Both hubs carried alloy rims and a shield was clipped to the duplex down tubes to protect the engine from salt thrown up by the front wheel.

The rev-counter was driven from the magneto gear as usual and the gear lever remained in its normal position pointing forward. Megaphone exhausts were used. The engine was tow started due to the use of alcohol fuel and for the attempt Thiessen wore minimal clothing, as the lack of restrictions in class A applied just as much to rider as machine. For the attempt he wore tights, tennis shoes, flying helmet and goggles and ran the machine just as unstreamlined as the smaller twin to take the one mile record at 143·54 mph.

Later in 1951 the BSA twins became involved in a very different branch of competition work when the teams for the ISDT were selected. The Trophy team captain was Fred Rist on a 650 cc twin and the Vase B team included Tom Ellis and Basil Hall on Star Twins while Johnny Draper was second reserve to the squad on a similar model. The machines were prepared in the traditional Six Days form of the time with quick release fittings to many parts, tool and card holder on the tank and air bottle tied to the frame, alongside the rear plunger unit. The trial was held at Varese in Italy and the British Trophy team scored its fourth consecutive victory.

The following year the BSA 500 cc twin was successful in yet another form of competition when Leopoldo Tartavini won the sidecar class of the Milan Taranto race. He was partnered over the 876 mile open course by Sergio Calza and they completed it in 17 hours, 3 minutes, 3 seconds to finish some five hours ahead of the next sidecar. The outfit was very firmly held together and the sidecar was little more than a racing platform with nose shell incorporating a Perspex window. It was attached on the left of the machine and carried a spotlamp on the passenger's grab handle.

1952 was also the year in which BSA won the Maudes Trophy, as described in the next chapter, by running three twins round Europe, taking in the ISDT on the way.

The next major triumph for the BSA twins came in March 1954 when they finished first and second in the 200 mile experts race at Daytona. This was held on the Beach circuit in Florida with its combined sand and tarmac surfaces. The course was 4·1 miles in length with a two-mile straight of foreshore being connected to the parallel road by turns at each end, bulldozed out of the sand into bankings. The race was run under the AMA rules of the time which limited compression ratios, allowed side valve engines of up to 750 cc while restricting ohv and ohc engines to 500 cc, and prohibited the then current Manx Norton. This was aimed to assist the home product, the Harley-Davidson which had a side valve engine and so had little interest in compression ratios much above the 8 to 1 that can be attained with that layout.

The BSA entries were originally barred as the frames were considered not to be factory produced, but under pressure from the BSA American distributors this ruling was reversed. Most of the entries were on BSAs or Triumphs with a few Harley-Davidson K and KR models among them. The start saw a field of 111 lined up in the usual rows with a cold twenty mph wind blowing down the beach to slow the riders. From the start on the sand the field headed into the north turn led by Joe Leonard on a Harley with Kretz on a Triumph in second place as they streamed down the two miles of tarmac. In six laps the vee twin was out and Bobby Hill and Dick Klamfoth on the BSA twins lay third and fourth. By lap twenty Hill was in the lead with Klamfoth in close attendance and he took over the front position for six laps before dropping back again. From then on Hill gradually extended his lead to over twenty seconds to come home the winner in 2 hours, 7 minutes, 22·7 seconds, a speed of 94·24 mph, just below the 1953 record average. Klamfoth was second giving the Star Twins a double and the next three places went to BSA Gold Star singles with another in eighth position. It was a complete success for the Company and the twin cylinder models.

Above right **Daytona Beach with a Triumph chasing a BSA single through a turn**

Below right **Daytona South turn and a BSA single caught in the act of changing gear**

Below **The special 650 cc engine used at the Bonneville Salt Flats by Gene Thiessen. Built to run on dope and fitted with twin carburettors**

120
85

46
46
46

A few weeks later the Star Twin was again successful in American racing when Ken Eggers, a twenty-four year old mechanic from San Jose, won the main event at Willow Springs. He held the lead up to the twenty-fifth circuit of the $2\frac{1}{2}$ mile course before stopping to refuel when Kretz on a Triumph moved ahead. By lap thirty Eggers had retaken the lead and stayed in front to the finish of the 125 mile race.

From then on during the 1950s less was heard of the twin cylinder BSA's in competition as the factory concentrated its efforts on the single cylinder Gold Star. However, in one field they began to move to the forefront and one name in particular began to become synonymous with the BSA twin and victory—Chris Vincent.

Vincent had first raced on the grass in 1954 using a speedway JAP engine but by 1956 had turned to the BSA that was to make him famous. That year he was third in the grass track national championship, moving up to second in 1957, the year he first raced on road

Above **A twin for the ISDT. Note the tools, spare cables and spare gear pedal. The dynamo regulator is rather exposed to the elements**

Right **The incomparable Mike Hailwood winning a production race at Silverstone in the wet in 1965. His A65 finished in front of the works Triumphs**

circuits. That winter he built a road racing outfit that reflected the lines along which he was thinking, which were to lower the centre of gravity and reduce frontal area in the manner pioneered by Eric Oliver. During this period he was also involved in sidecar speedway and achieved considerable success in this field.

The new outfit was used for road racing but during the year was converted to grass specification for the 1958 national championship which Vincent won. That was to be his last serious grass event and from 1959 onwards he concentrated on road racing.

That year he had the first of the Vincent kneelers with BSA twin engine and it was immediately successful. Two engines were used in the appropriate events, one of 500 cc and the other of 650 cc, both appearing to be almost standard although their performance was anything but. The inside of the engine remained a closely guarded secret but only one carburettor was fitted and both exhaust pipes with their reverse cone megaphones were routed onto the right side of the machine.

The engine and gearbox were separate units as normal with the A10 and A7 at that time but the engine was mounted very low in a completely special kneeler frame that allowed VIncent to exploit his technique of drifting the outfit under power through the corners and steering it more with the throttle than the handlebars.

The outfit was tremendously successful from the start and in 1962 a second machine was built following the same general pattern as the first. In this version the engine lay back in the frame so that the inlet tract was parallel to the ground and below the rider's seat. The outfit was much lighter than the first machine but could not be prepared fully in time for the start of the season.

Therefore Vincent used the older, heavier one and on this finished third in the French Grand Prix during May. At the end of that month he was in the Isle of Man for the TT but still with the older machine. It was his third visit, the earlier ones in the previous two years both having resulted in retirements.

No-one seriously expected anything other than the customary BMW victory as they had won every postwar sidecar race except the first in 1954, which Eric Oliver had taken on his Norton. The BSA twin was expected to be well in the running but the lead was thought to be between the BMWs of Max Deubel, the winner in 1961 and reigning world champion, and Florian Camathias the flamboyant Swiss driver. These two had dominated sidecar practice but

Above **Drifting by the master—Chris Vincent and Eric Bliss at Brands Hatch in 1961**

Right **Mudguard problems for an A65 during a long distance race. Dave Croxford is the rider and Tom Kirby is behind the machine**

the third potential leader board BMW pilot, Scheidegger, who had been second in 1961, failed to reach the Isle of Man due to severe mechanical problems.

Thus the first two men to start were Deubel and Vincent with Camathias and Kolle ten seconds behind. Deubel headed Vincent down Bray Hill and by Ballacraine, Camathias had made up the starting difference and led the BSA on the road. Deubel pulled away steadily into the lead and completed the first lap with a sixteen second advantage over Camathias who led Vincent by 1 minute, 38 seconds. Deubel had broken the lap record from a standing start and set the first over 90 mph lap by a sidecar. Vincent was trying equally hard and had nearly overdone things at the Thirty-Third where he went wide and hit the grass verge which bent the gear pedal inwards and made gear changing a little more difficult.

As the second lap continued, Camathias began to close up on Deubel but to no avail, for he hit the bank at Kerroomoor and was out of the race. Deubel's second lap was a little slower than his first but his lead over Vincent was nearly four minutes while the BSA was about fifty seconds ahead of Kolle so the race pattern seemed set.

Then sensation, for Vincent was signalled first at Kirkmichael, as Deubel had stopped at Ballig Bridge with a broken piston and the BSA was leading the race. Just about every British spectator had their fingers crossed for so many

TTs had been lost in the last twenty miles, but the twin carried on without missing a beat to win the Sidecar TT. It was the first time a BSA had won a TT, and the first British sidecar victory on the Mountain Circuit since 1925. Vincent completed the three laps in 1 hour, 21 minutes, 16·4 seconds at an average speed of 83·57 mph, and his fastest lap was his first in a time of 26 minutes, 52·2 seconds, a speed of 84·25 mph.

It was cruel luck for Deubel but Vincent was in front of five other BMWs at the end of the race, the closest being Kolle's in second place some 37 seconds adrift. The BSA finished the event in very good condition with little wear on the tyres and the rear chain in correct tension. There was some oil spread over the front of the frame and the forks, thought to have come from the engine due to overfilling and blown forward by eddy currents under the fairing. The left piston had a noticeably hotter appearance than the right, no doubt due to mixture bias from the single carburettor. Apart from the pedal bending episode on the first lap, Vincent had no trouble and at the evening's prizegiving thanked the opposition for doing their part by blowing up. It was a popular victory.

Although Vincent was not to win another Sidecar TT he continued to dominate British sidecar racing throughout the 1960s using BSA twins. The original A7 and A10 engines were

Chris Vincent winning the 1962 TT in the Isle of Man

finally superceded early in 1964 when a new version using the A65 engine appeared. This was built up from essentially standard parts which included a twin carburettor cylinder head then only specified for machines destined for the USA. The same source also obliged with the 10 to 1 compression ratio, special pistons and camshaft, and the close ratio gears. The ignition system was an energy transfer alternator with twin scrambles type coils. The two carburettors were Amal GP units of $1\frac{5}{32}$ inch choke bore supplied by no less than three float chambers to reduce surge effects. Both exhaust pipes were connected into a single megaphone on the right side of the machine.

Eventually three engines were used by Vincent, a 500 and a 654 cc both fitted with five speed gearboxes and a 750 with a four speed box. Over the years other riders built similar outfits but none were as successful for such a long period, partly because Vincent was first in the field and established a technical lead which kept him ahead for most of a decade. His task was made easier because he worked at BSA and although he had no official support he would naturally be able to draw on factory knowledge and data on both the good useful parts and on the ideas that did not work out, the latter a great time saver.

Other drivers of sidecars fitted with BSA twin engines included Terry Vinicombe, Norman Hanks, Mick Boddice and Peter Brown who campaigned the four stroke into the 1970s before finally having to give best to first the Konig and then the Yamaha TZ outfits. The Vincent machine was driven by another great sidecar expert in late 1964, Eric Oliver. It impressed him with its power, handling and stability. He impressed Chris Vincent and circulated Silverstone rapidly despite a wet track and a misfire from the engine.

Early in 1965 Derek Minter, one of the leading solo road racers at that time, also tried the BSA at Silverstone and lapped very quickly indeed. Later in the year he gave a demonstration run at Brands Hatch and at the time there was some talk of him racing the outfit when it became available although this never came to anything.

Back in 1962 the then new A50 was pressed into service for the ISDT, first being tried out in the Welsh Three Days Trial held in May. The rider was John Harris and the machine used a standard engine and gearbox unit fitted with an optional, USA market, 8·5 to 1 compression ratio. Gearing was lower than standard but a speedometer reading of 90 mph was still on. A high level, Siamesed exhaust system was fitted

The BSA twin at Daytona in 1966; not one of their successes

and the two pipes joined above the gearbox on the right side. The exhaust pipe then snaked back inside the main frame saddle tube to a short tubular silencer. Gold Star forks and wheels were fitted and the seat, silencer, headlamp and handlebar were all C15 competition parts. A steel sump shield went under the engine to protect the crankcase and two Lucas batteries were fitted in place of the usual one. A light alloy petrol tank completed the machine.

In the ISDT the only problems that occurred were a rear wheel puncture, the mending of which was conveniently combined with a mid-

Right **Engine unit of the 1966 Daytona machine**

Below **Jim Rice on his BSA flat tracker fitted with disc brakes all round**

Right **AMA number 3, Dave Aldana with flat track BSA**

Far right **Dick Mann completed the BSA team riding with AMA plate number 4. He has drum brakes**

Below **Sidecar in 1968, Terry Vinicombe at Thruxton with his BSA twin**

week change of tyre, and a broken front mudguard stay which was repaired with tape. John Harris won a gold medal and so gained the A50 its first competition success.

In 1965 another very famous rider was seen racing an A65, Mike Hailwood. The meeting was the Hutchinson 100 held at Silverstone in August and Mike once again demonstrated his incredible ability to ride any machine under any conditions. He was expected to win the 500 cc race using the MV4 on a drying track which he did with ease. He was not expected to win the 350 cc event riding a single cylinder AJS but after Bruce Beale had retired his 305 cc Honda twin with a suspected crankshaft breakage and Phil Read had his 254 cc Yamaha seize, it was Mike who led over the finish line by a whisker.

It was in the fifteen lap production race that Mike appeared on the BSA Lightning with opposition from the Triumph Bonnevilles ridden by Phil Read and Percy Tait. It poured with rain for the event, the BSA was less well suited for production racing than the Triumphs and it was a kickstart event. The three riders pulled away from the remainder of the field and at half distance Tait led from Read and Hailwood. Then Read took over and finally Mike inched past, never to be headed again, despite the efforts of the two Triumph riders. The BSA set the fastest lap at 85·81 mph and Hailwood's comment on the occasion was, 'Apart from winning three races, it wasn't much of a day'.

The following year, 1966, BSA was back at Daytona with four special 500 cc twins in racing frames with hydraulic steering dampers, oil

radiators in the fairings and 190 mm racing brakes on both wheels. For BSA it was not a succesful event for three of their riders went out with ignition trouble so the best they could manage was eleventh. Fortunately for the Group, the Triumphs that went out with them had more success and Buddy Elmore won, using exactly the same ignition set up. This was a special energy transfer system with modified Lucas contact breaker unit which ran on its own bearings and was driven by the camshaft through an Oldham coupling.

In 1967 they all returned in even greater strength with six machines from each factory. The BSAs were based on the American specifi-

cation Wasp model using the A50 engine. Once again the special ignition system was fitted and the engine breathed through two $1\frac{3}{16}$ inch GP Amals. Power output was given as 50·75 bhp at 8250 rpm, nearly two up on the Triumph. The whole machine was fairly special although based on standard parts, and a Fontana double, twin leading shoe, front brake was fitted. The rear hub was all alloy and carried a single disc, hydraulically operated. The central oil tank capacity was one gallon and a

Right **Vinicombe winning the 750 cc sidecar TT in 1968. Note the travelling marshalls' BSA in the background**

Below **Mick Boddice at speed on his BSA sidecar. Front tyre and wheel distortion shows up the cornering loads involved**

cooler was fitted inside the fairing while the megaphones had reverse cones and flat sides to improve ground clearance. Two very large plastic breather pipes ran from the back of the engine to the rear of the machine. The seat and fairing were made in glass-fibre and the well shaped fuel tank in alloy.

In the event held on 19 March the Triumphs were once again successful finishing first and second with all six machines finishing despite one of them crashing and so losing a probable third place. For BSA it was once again a disaster and must have produced visions of the 1921 TT for all six machines retired, the best only covering twenty-nine of the fifty-three laps.

Back in England Tony Smith, a BSA tester, continued to ride a 650 in production races with considerable success and he was also involved in the work on the 500 cc twin and a 350 cc single. The twins had many ideas tried out on them, one such was to tuck the exhaust pipes in under the crankcase to improve clearance. Smith also raced one of the Daytona machines on its return and continued its development with such features as an electron crankcase. Late in 1967 a modified frame of all-brazed construction was tried which had the five pint oil tank located behind the gearbox and which was reported to handle better.

Stock Rocket 3 at Daytona during a refuelling stop. The rider is Yvon du Hamel. **See page 140**

The sidecar riders continued to produce and try out new ideas. Chris Vincent produced a new low outfit to replace the old one and used 10-inch Mini wheels at side and back with disc brakes and a rubber rear suspension system used parts from a Triumph Tina scooter.

Not to be outdone, Peter Brown fitted his 654 cc BSA engine with $1\frac{3}{16}$ inch GP Amals with no float chambers. Each carburettor was flanked by two swill pots, one on each side, with weir control of the fuel level. All four were connected to a left hand twist grip which allowed the appropriate two to be shut off when cornering.

Right at the end of the year BSA had some success in America when Ron Gould won the main race at Riverside in California riding a two year old Daytona machine fitted with a Spitfire engine.

In 1968 the BSA-engined sidecars took the first three places in the 750 cc TT with Terry Vinicombe winning from Norman Hanks and Peter Brown after Vincent retired. The race was run concurrently with the 500 cc class and the apparent slight of starting the 750s five minutes after the smaller machines was shown to be a correct judgement when Schauza's winning speed on his 500 cc BMW was over five mph faster than that of the BSA.

The marque was not so successful in the Production TT although Tony Smith did take third place in the 750 cc class on his Spitfire at 93·82 mph.

From then on the twin was to take a back seat to the triple but continued to dominate English sidecar racing. In 1970 Chris Vincent won his sixth British championship by winning five of the first six of the eight rounds and most of his opposition was also propelled by the BSA twin engine.

In 1971 Barry Kefford built a sidecar outfit, powered by a BSA twin engine that set a new standard in lowness. He achieved this by cutting the gearbox off an A65 and laying the engine horizontal. A triplex primary chain drove the A65 clutch mounted on a Gold Star gearbox. Twin Gardner carburettors were fitted and long straight exhaust pipes terminated in megaphones with reverse cones. The unit was carried in a low frame with leading link front forks, Mini wheels and disc brakes on front and rear only.

The advent of the Rocket 3 in 1968 was quickly followed by its use in competition. One of the first to use it was Darrell Triber of Spokane, Washington, who made an attempt on what was known in America as the Three Flag Run. This was from Blaine on the US and Canadian border down to Tijuana in Mexico, a distance of 1394 miles and was first covered in August 1915 by the legendary 'Cannonball' Baker in 81 hours, 15 minutes. Triber's aim was to beat the time of 28 hours, 7 minutes set up in 1936 by Fred Ham on a Harley-Davidson. In this he was successful, completing the distance in 23 hours, 35 minutes to average just under 60 mph including all stops.

At home in England one or two of the triples began to appear in production races with success and in the USA it attacked some records at Daytona. The machines were 'str-

aight from the crate' the runs were observed by the AMA and new figures were set for 5, 15, 20, 25 and 50 miles at just over 130 mph; for 100 and 150 miles together with the one hour at over 127 mph and for the 200 miles at over 123 mph. The 5 mile average was the fastest at 131·723 mph, which was impressive for a 750 cc motorcycle without any streamlining, just with the handlebars turned down and some padding taped to the tank.

The first major race outing for the factory was at Daytona in 1970 and six machines were prepared, three with BSA and three with Triumph on the tank. The cylinders were inclined slightly forward as normal on the BSA but the timing cover was cut off to increase clearance and the Triumph type gearbox end cover fitted. Although this gave the engine the appearance of the Triumph, the timing cover had the characteristic BSA lines. The engines were very well worked on and power was up by twenty-five per cent on the standard unit. Much of this work was on the cams, valve gear and cylinder head while breathing was through three $1\frac{3}{16}$ inch GP Amals. All three exhaust pipes joined together under the gearbox to feed a long plain megaphone that terminated above and behind the rear wheel spindle. A capacitor ignition system triggered by points was fitted with the electronic box mounted behind the steering head and containing the zener diode

Left **The record team at Daytona in 1969. The machine is completely standard except for lowered bars and no front mudguard**

Below **Ray Pickrell on his Rocket 3. The front brake is definitely non-standard**

Above **Mallory Park hairpin in 1971 with John Cooper leading Dick Mann on Rocket 3s, followed by two further triples**

Right **Dave Aldana on the Rocket 3 at Daytona in 1971**

and capacitor. The condensers were attached to the top of the box while two coils were flexibly mounted on the timing side of the engine with the third on the drive side. A Quaife five speed gearbox was fitted and the whole unit was installed in a new fully duplexed frame of triangular loop design. The front brake was a double sided, twin leading shoe drum of 250 mm diameter and the rear a nine inch disc with hydraulically operated pads.

The fuel tank was of five gallons capacity and it and the seat were made in glass-fibre. The oil tank fitted beneath the seat and carried ten

BELL
Castrol

pints. Two variants of the fairing were produced and tried out during practice when the big triples showed they meant business with Gene Romero qualifying fastest around the two and a half mile speedbowl at 157·34 mph. He was timed through the speed trap on the main straight at 165·44 mph. Although qualification was on the speedbowl, the actual race included an infield section and at first things looked good for the group. Gary Nixon on one of the Triumphs and Mike Hailwood on a BSA went straight to the front and circulated in company, with the Triumph apparently the faster machine. It did not last for long, however, as after twenty-eight miles Mike was forced out with flames coming from the exhaust and gradually the BSA and Triumph efforts faded. It was a gruelling race with only sixteen of the original ninety-eight starters still running at the end and was won by Dick Mann riding a Honda CB750 with Gene Romero second on a Triumph. The best BSA was Dave Aldana in twelfth spot.

Two months later in May the position improved greatly in the 200 mile race at

Talladega, Alabama for Dave Aldana won the event at 104·5 mph, the fastest ever speed for an event of that length in the USA. The machine was the one Mike Hailwood had ridden at Daytona and the group had the added pleasure of seeing Jim Rice third and Dick Mann fifth on BSAs with Romero sixth on a Triumph triple.

In June the group gained a further success in America when Gary Nixon won a 100 mile event at Laconia riding a Triumph on the difficult 1·6 mile circuit.

1971 was to be the great year for the racing triple. The machines were further improved by modifications to the contact breakers to stop the ignition timing from wandering and with other changes the power output was up to 84 bhp at 8500 rpm. New frames were built by Rob North with a modified head angle, the oil cooler was moved into the nose of the fairing, hence the slot in it to feed air through on the

Above left **1971 Race of the Year at Mallory Park. John Cooper keeps his BSA 3 just in front of the MV ridden by Agostini. Cooper won by a short head after a race long duel**

Below left **A moment at the Mallory Park hairpin. From the left the riders are Castro, Emde and Aldana, all on triples, one Triumph and two BSA's**

Below **Jim Rice at Daytona on the Rocket 3. 1970 version fitted with special front brake**

1971 machines, and the drum front brakes were replaced by twin discs. The weight stayed at 370 lb dry but the handling was better and the machine was very durable.

The season kicked off at Daytona and BSA/Triumph was there in force with triples for Mike Hailwood, Jim Rice, Dick Mann, Don Emde, Paul Smart and Gene Romero among others. For this meeting the engines were on 12 to 1 compression ratio and the gearbox contained special ratios suitable for Daytona. The standard clutch was used but the Renold chain was of racing quality. The BSAs retained their engine inclination and all models had shortened forks with two way damping in special wide centre yokes made to accommodate the disc brakes. All three discs were ten inch diameter and both wheels had light alloy symmetrical hubs laced to 19 inch WM3 alloy rims. Dunlop racing tyres were fitted, the final drive sprocket was in light alloy and the spindle in titanium. Both tanks were alloy, the oil tank under the seat contained eleven pints and the petrol, five gallons.

The triples dominated the meeting with Smart taking pole position on the Triumph in practice. He took the lead on lap five but then Hailwood went past to head the field until lap fourteen when a valve dropped in. At that point the triples occupied positions one to five and Smart continued to draw ahead until lap forty-one when he stopped for a change of plugs but had to pull out with a holed piston. This left Mann comfortably in the lead he held to the end with Romero second on a Triumph and Emde third on a BSA after a race long duel.

Most of the triples returned to England and commenced to dominate Formula 750, production and endurance racing, setting lap records at many major British circuits during the year. Most stayed with the original name on the tank but that used by Ray Pickrell started as a BSA, being the one used by Hailwood at Daytona, but was later raced in the Triumph colours and won the 1972 Formula 750 TT in that guise. Smart and Tait had many successes with their Tridents while Jefferies won the Formula 750 TT in 1971 on his. Perhaps the most famous of the triples was the one that remained a BSA and was ridden by John Cooper who came into the picture later in the day. In fact, Doug Hele, the Group race chief was reluctant to take him on due to the work load the mechanics were under preparing some eight machines but the factory insisted that Cooper had a triple for the 1971 Race of the Year at Mallory Park.

A week earlier, Tait and Pickrell rode one of the triples in the 24 hour Bol d'Or held on the 2·8 mile Bugatti circuit at Le Mans. The original

entry was for a BSA but the machine used was a Daytona specification Triumph. Because this was not notified to the organizers until after the race, it went onto the records as a BSA and stayed that way. In the event the rain was pouring when the flag fell and the triple at first refused to start and than ran on two cylinders for a lap before it cleared. Despite this handicap, the riders had fought their way up into the lead by the sixth hour, still in heavy rain. They lost the lead three hours later and were also delayed with a broken rear chain but around the seventeen hour mark, the leading Guzzi broke a rocker and while it was being repaired, the triple made up the five laps it was behind and re-took the lead. The sun had by then dried out the circuit and the triple held its lead to the end, covering a total of 616 laps at an average speed of 70·48 mph.

And so to Mallory where the cream of the world's riders were entered for the big race over thirty laps. The big triples were opposed by a smaller triple, the 500 cc MV3 ridden by Giacomo Agostini and such riders as Hailwood, Read, Saarinen, Grant and Gould on Yamaha twins, and Sheene on a 500 cc Suzuki twin. It was one of Cooper's great races for he battled

No fairing and Peter Brown is trying hard on his BSA triple-engined sidecar

with Agostini for the whole race with the two machines seldom more than a foot apart before winning by a fraction of a second from the MV with Pickrell's BSA triple third, followed by Smart and Tait on Triumphs.

Two weeks later Cooper repeated the exercise at Brands Hatch and despite the additional 250 cc of the BSA, the MV had four valves per cylinder, twin overhead camshafts and a long racing lineage.

Then in October, the factory went to the Ontario circuit in California for the Champion Spark Plug 250 mile classic event run in two equal length legs. In the first leg Doug Hele sprung a surprise for he had been sharp enough to realise that his triples, ridden by Nixon and Cooper, would just run the distance without a refuelling stop. This they did, while their competition all stopped once, and they finished first and third, Cooper having been baulked at the start and finishing behind DuHamel on his Kawasaki. In the second leg Nixon and DuHamel both crashed on an oil slick and Cooper rode on keeping station behind Carruthers on a 350 cc Yamaha. What was not known was that in the confusion of the crash, Hele had lost track of the laps covered and Cooper was reading the signal tower scoreboard not realizing that this was two or three laps in arrears of the real situation. This only became clear when he was shown the last lap flag when lying some 100 yards behind Carruthers. This was a seemingly impossible distance to make up but Cooper pulled back most of it on the infield as he forced his way through the backmarkers to exit from the last corner only twenty yards behind the Yamaha. For once he was not so gentle to the engine and

it went up to five figures in the gears to snatch first place on the line.

This was not the end of the day's tension for the factory as an almost unknown West Coast rider, Bob Bailey invoked the claiming rule that allowed any finisher to bid for the winning machine. Bailey put down his £1000 and asked for the BSA, Steve Brown the BSA mechanic who had set the machine up for the race sat on it and looked determined not to be parted from it while Doug Hele argued that the machine's true value was ten times the offer made. In the end, a compromise was reached and Bailey gained a spare engine and chassis after it had been pointed out to him that spares for the Cooper engine might be a little hard to come by.

That tremendous win at Ontario was the end of the line for BSA as in 1972 the factory had its own problems so kept clear of racing. Daytona was a complete contrast to 1971 with Dick Mann the only official BSA rider, and he had a dismal ride into twenty second place when he stopped on lap forty-seven. Ontario was little better with John Cooper taking the BSA into ninth place in heat one and sixth place in heat two. This gave him fifth position overall, a far cry from the previous year's victory.

So BSA stopped racing (and winning) but BSA enthusiasts still kept some examples of the triples running and they were run in home events and the TT over the years.

Left **Dick Mann at Daytona in 1971, an event he won for BSA riding the Rocket 3**

Below **Rocket 3 powered sidecar ridden by Peter Brown**

9 The Maudes Trophy

The three Maudes' BSAs in Austria. Norman Vanhouse, Fred Rist and Brian Martin with three rather dirty motorcycles

This trophy has had a chequered history since its inception in 1923, sometimes being competed for by several companies and at other languishing for long periods, virtually unknown until interest in it revives and another generation of riders learns of the many arduous feats attempted in efforts to claim it. It originated due to the concentration on speed at events held after the Great War with a proliferation of meetings run on roads, hills, sand, grass and field, all becoming faster, with two pinnacles, the TT and Brooklands. The TT was first run to demonstrate reliability and economy, but this aspect had soon been surmounted by the speed factor, while Brooklands was designed for speed alone although often used for long distance record attempts.

With the general public hostility to motorcycles, this accent on speed worried a good number of people in the industry, and one of those who felt it was again time to emphasise the reliability and economy aspects of two wheelers was a George Pettyt of Maudes Motor Mart, Exeter, who presented the ACU with a large, handsome and valuable silver vase, originally called the Pettyt Cup and later the Maudes Trophy. This was to be awarded annually to the firm whose observed and certified test was considered by the ACU to be the best of the year, provided it was of an acceptable standard.

From the start there were some very difficult tests devised, usually running machines selected at random from stock or built up from spares on dealers' shelves to emphasise the high quality standards of the industry.

One of the strongest supporters of the precepts behind the award was James Norton, and it is fitting that his firm was the first to win the Trophy in 1923 and went on to take it for the following three years to make four in a row. They lost out to Ariel in 1927 who retained the Trophy for the following year and in 1929 it went to Dunelt who kept it for 1930 as well. Ariel won it back in 1931 but then the attempts became less frequent with Triumph successful in 1933 and Panther in 1934. There was then a short break before a spate of activity in the late thirties saw Triumph successful in 1937, BSA in 1938, and Triumph again in 1939 when they won the Trophy back against attempts by both Panther and BSA.

After the Second World War, interest in the Trophy waned for several years until BSA decided that it had been adorning the Triumph offices for far too long and set out to recapture it.

The BSA plan was simple, if audacious. It was to take three stock Star Twins and run them over nearly 5000 miles of European roads under strict supervision. The catch was that they would include the International Six Days Trial en route.

The riders selected for this adventure were Fred Rist who was a very experienced BSA factory rider in trials, scrambles and six days events. His machine carried registration number MOL 301 and in the ISDT his riding number was 193. With five gold medals from six events, the omission was in 1939 when the army team he was in was withdrawn, his experience was immense and he came out of competition retirement for the 1952 event. The second machine was ridden by Brian Martin, who later became BSA's competiton manager, and he rode MOL 302 with ISDT number 202. The third member was Norman Vanhouse who had just joined the BSA sales staff and was mounted on MOL 303 with ISDT number 209.

The ACU observer chosen to accompany the three riders was John McNulty, an income tax inspector, and from the start he showed that he was going to keep a strict eye on the proceedings. About a week before the riders were due to leave, he visited the factory and selected three machines from a batch of 37. These were then prepared for their arduous journey under his supervision and had a minimal number of changes carried out. The main change was to fit the 49 tooth sidecar rear sprocket in place of the solo 45 tooth one which also entailed fitting the appropriate rear chain and speedometer head, all of which were standard parts, of course. The saddle was removed and replaced with a standard BSA dualseat, and pillion footrests fitted. Various modifications were carried out to suit the ISDT needs and included the fitting of competition number plates, a clock and tank-top toolbag, and the drilling of holes in cylinder head, barrel and crankcase for ISDT seals. All the oils were changed to Essolube 40 and the petrol to the Esso brand.

The machines were then placed in a private lock-up garage and covered with a ground sheet secured with lead seals. They were also tied and sealed to one another until the party set out on Sunday, 7 September.

The official car carrying the ACU observer and the party's luggage was driven by the BSA sales manager, George Savage, and they were accompanied by a Golden Flash sidecar outfit ridden by a photographer whose efforts to make a cine film of the trip expired after two days when he was whipped into a local French hospital to have his appendix removed.

The party proceeded from Harwich to the Hook of Holland and from there ran through Belgium, France, Switzerland and on to Vienna. The ISDT started on 18 September and was centred on Bad Aussee in the Salzkammergut lake district. The three BSA riders were entered as a club team from the Birmingham MCC, not as a factory team, so did not have to run on the ten per cent higher speed schedule which applied to the factory runners. However, they did have to manage with the standard road silencers which frequently dragged on the shoulders of ruts in the glutinous mud, close fitting road mudguards and standard road tyres, the front a normal 19 inch diameter, not the 21 inch preferred for trials work.

Modifications carried out before the trial began were minimal and consisted of fitting security bolts to the tyres, crankcase shields, nail catchers, touring type handlebars, air bottles and tommy bars to the wheel spindles. In addition, normal adjustments and checks were carried out to points and fluid levels.

The trial was a disaster for Britain but a great success for BSA. While many British riders suffered trouble with their waterproofed magnetos the Star Twin standard contact breakers remained bone dry all week despite the very wet weather and the high altitudes involved in some parts of the course. It was a hard trial by ISDT standards and it speaks volumes both for the toughness of the machines and the abilities of the three riders that the trio of BSAs came through it all to win their gold medals, the only British team to do this.

This was not managed without one or two close moments for Vanhouse used virtually all his three minutes allowance at one time check but all three riders kept on time after the one really bad hill that nearly stopped the trial and was later deleted from the results. The final speed test in which the riders were required to cover 60 miles in the hour was not without its moments either for Martin's fuel tank began to leak and he ran low on petrol while Vanhouse had a plug lead come adrift at one stage and suffered a slight fuel tank leak.

The tanks were welded the next day and the three machines set off for the remainder of their tour taking in Germany, Denmark, Sweden and on into Norway. The test concluded at Oslo aerodrome where the machines were timed over a measured 400 metres. The standing start speeds for the three machines were 49·99, 47·98 and 50·15 mph while flying start speeds were 82·12, 84·43 and 80·27 mph. The best one way standing start speed was 51·44 mph and the best flying start was 85·23 mph.

During the run through Europe and Scandinavia, the machines were given normal maintenance in that tyres, chains and oil levels were checked but of course, during the ISDT the normal components were marked or sealed. In fact, contemporary photographs clearly show one of the seals on the wire connecting cylinder head to crankcase.

The only replacements fitted to the machines while they were under the jurisdiction of the ACU were listed in the official report and comprised two headlamp pilot bulbs, three rear bulbs, two frayed rear lamp leads which were replaced and one primary chaincase filler cap which was lost during the journey. The two welded petrol tanks were mentioned and on one machine a loose horn lead had to be fixed. During the final speed test, the main jets of two machines were found to be choked so were cleaned and then refitted.

The official distance for the trip was given as 4958 miles and the test was just finished before the deadline of 30 September by which date tests for any given year had to be completed.

It was a tremendous achievement in the best traditions of the Maudes Trophy and shortly after the team returned to England in October, the ACU announced that they had awarded the Trophy to BSA. It was the first attempt made for the Trophy since 1939 and the only one made in 1952 but this in no way detracted from the test and the cup was proudly exhibited at the Earls Court Show in November.

It remained with BSA for ten years before Honda ran a trio of 50 cc models round Goodwood for seven days and nights and the Maudes Trophy went foreign for the first time.

The three BSAs went their various ways and were long forgotten by the general public when the Vanhouse machine was found neglected and modified into a chopper. Subsequently it was restored to a faultless standard and complete with competition plates detailing the observed test was first seen by the public at a vintage race meeting at Mallory Park in 1978, and later exhibited at the Earls Court Motorcycle Show that year.

One curious anomaly remains. The competition plates and BSA advertisements in the press in October 1952 both refer to a trip of 4500 miles. The press report of the test in the same magazine, *The Motor Cycle* dated 16 October 1952, and later BSA advertisements, both give the distance as 4958 miles.

They were long hard miles!

Norman Vanhouse in the wet—a picture that captures the atmosphere of the ISDT in the 1950s

10 Oddments

When researching and writing this type of book, all sorts of odd items crop up which have little to do with the main theme but are part of the history. These items can be incorporated into the main theme but then become impossible to find easily. Rather than do that, they are collected together in one chapter.

Ready for 2000 miles to the Elephant Rally in 1965. Pat Slinn of BSA and Bob Bennett of Watsonian on the first hitching of a Lightning and a Monaco

Variations

BSA themselves did some rather outrageous things with the early twins. One A7 was cut in half and from that came some data used for the C15. Both A7 and A10 units did a stint in a projected BSA mini car for the group had serious four wheel connections. The internals from the A7 went to build the S10 prototype Sunbeam that followed the postwar range outline with the two cylinders in tandem but did away with the power sapping worm drive and substituted a hypoid bevel. The scooter twin engine was also used in the boot of a stylish open two seater bubble car that came to nothing as the bubble burst when the Mini was born.

Long distance

A comfortable, reliable machine is a favourite for any long distance rider as the secret is to keep going and not to be worn out by vagaries of the machine. The BSA twin was good for this and many were used over the years for such purposes.

In 1953 Scotsman W. Stirling set out from Ceylon with his wife on the pillion of his Golden Flash. They spent three months riding through India, Pakistan, North Africa and Europe before reaching England.

In 1966 a Lightning with Watsonian sidecar set off from the factory to the BSA Owners Club Rally in Vienna. Two years later two Thunderbolts were chosen for an overland trip from England to Australia. The riders were Stephen Hickson, son of the then BSA UK Sales Manager and Geoffrey Bourne.

Star miss

The title of Miss Federation 1965 was won by Jocelyn Aitken, twenty-two, who rode her Shooting Star to the fifth FNOMMCC rally at Woburn Abbey. This was of course the forerunner of the BMF annual event which attracts thousands of riders.

Shiny twin

In 1966 Walter Elcock decided that he wanted his 650 cc BSA to stand out in the car park at race meetings, so he had it chrome plated. The machine had a Road Rocket engine with high lift camshaft, needle roller bearings and polished internals. Starting with the frame just about every part that could be plated eventually went into the plater's vat. The result was an eye dazzling shine and a never-ending need for chrome cleaner.

Double twin

The Bacon family (no relation to the author) live in Nottinghamshire and collect motorcycles. Their collection began in a random fashion and for years they just retained every machine that came their way. Now they have a kaleidoscope of motorcycle history and among the 200 or so machines is a BSA four. This was concocted by someone else and bought unfinished. It comprises two 500 cc engines in tandem fitted to a stretched frame and once the engines were timed to fire together the coupling chain stopped breaking. It was a monster but docile and felt like an enormous twin to ride.

Triple twin

An even longer machine appeared in 1966 when Canadian tuner Dick Forest of Montreal built a sprint bike with three twin cylinder engines. These were joined by chains and drove through a BSA gearbox to an 18 inch Avon slick rear tyre. Each engine had an alloy head, high compression pistons, plain straight through exhaust pipes and a single racing Amal carburettor.

It was ridden by one André Benault and under the then existing NHRA rules, had one engine, the front one, immobilised. Despite this and the rider's own weight of 180 pounds, a time of 11·1 seconds was achieved over the standing quarter mile with a terminal speed of 127 mph.

BSA
4

BSA

The ride was described as hairy, as was starting the machine which was done with rollers, not such a common feature then.

The James Bond BSA

The Bond films starring Sean Connery in the title role were a tremendous success in the 1960s and created their own cult. In *Thunderball* a BSA Lightning was ridden by Chris Vincent dubbing for Luciana Paoluzzi in a short sequence, and much publicity made of its added rocket firing capability. This was done by adding a fairing to the machine and fitting four tubes into it, two on each side, pointing forward. The tubes carried projectiles which were fired electrically using NGK spark plugs and clips from the film show them streaming away from the machine trailing smoke.

The film sequence has Bond's car followed by a Spectre agent Count Lippe who in turn is followed by the BSA. The motorcycle closes up fires its rockets and the car crashes into the ditch in flames. No sooner had it done its job when the BSA was turned off the road and pointed at a gravel pit with the next shot showing the tail end of the machine disappearing under the muddy water. Fortunately, they did not drown the actual machine, which did a publicity tour when the film was released in 1965.

Above left **The double BSA A7 four. Brothers Harry and Alfred Bacon stand behind it while Harry Bacon Snr attends the rearwheel**

Below left **The modified BSA used in the James Bond film** *Thunderball* **with the hero's Aston Martin**

Below **Rocket firing tubes on the Bond BSA**

Simulating sidecar

At the Earls Court Show held in November 1966, the famous Chris Vincent BSA racing sidecar was linked to a simulator which depicted the Silverstone circuit. Visitors to the show sat on the machine and operated the controls in the normal fashion while in front of them the moving track was projected onto a screen. The system was built by General Precision Systems who normally specialised in flight simulators and a rider who just opened the throttle went completely off the track.

Although not totally convincing, especially to anyone who had actually ridden round Silverstone, it proved to be a highly popular feature and the stand was jammed with potential sidecar racers throughout the show.

A Japanese Flash

At the end of 1966 the last of the big four from Japan reached Europe when Kawasaki machines became available in Holland. The range included a machine which was based on the 1959 Meguro 500 cc twin model K1, an old established marque dating from 1937 that Kawasaki had absorbed in 1961. It was the

650 cc W1 with twin cylinder, ohv, engine that bore a remarkable resemblance to the Golden Flash. Engine dimensions were 74 × 73 mm so the actual capacity was 624 cc. From the timing side the engine was a dead ringer for the A10 with characteristic timing cover and single carburettor attached to an inlet manifold with slight downdraught. The drive side made a good job of following the BSA line as well.

This model, which was extensively used by the police in Japan, was shown at Earls Court in 1967 along with the W2SS, a five speed version. All were fitted with two leading shoe brakes and a hydraulic steering damper. The model remained in production until 1970 in various forms but was mainly sold into the Asian market.

Burmese BSAs

In 1968 the Burma Army placed an order worth £20,000 with the factory for 500 cc BSA twins.

BSA pieces

Sidecar front fork springs are common but for the A7 and A10 an extra heavy spring was available for use when a large double adult chair was attached. Its part number is 42-5145.

The breather valve of the A7 and A10 was improved near the end of its life. The newer item, part number 12967-0987 could be fitted to all the earlier engines but again required that the sealing cork washer fitted between it and the pinion face be under compression.

TriBSA

For scrambles use at one time the favoured front forks were either Norton which did not twist or BSA which did, but could easily be untwisted. BSA forks fitted best to a BSA frame and wheels but the engine was another matter. The Triumph twin was perhaps the easiest to tune and obtain 'quick' parts for, so was very popular with private owners.

Put together they became Tribsa, a very potent force to be reckoned with when four-

Kawasaki style A10, the 650 cc model W1 based on the earlier Meguro. Seen at Earls Court in 1967 and built up to 1970, mainly for the Asian market

stroke machines dominated scrambles. In the end, the light two-stroke won out but for a while a Triumph twin engine and BSA cycle parts were an easy way to a good scrambler.

Of course there were other engine/frame permutations too. Following the most popular Triton (Triumph engine in a Norton Featherbed frame) there was the Norbsa which could be either combination of engine/frame but most likely the BSA engine in Norton frame.

Bright lights

The early A50 and A65 twins were fitted with 6 volt batteries charged by an alternator. Like many of their contemporaries, it was possible to convert to 12 volts by changing the obvious parts such as battery, coils and bulbs along with the rectifier and by the addition of a zener diode. At a stroke better lights, fewer boiled batteries and, later, halogen bulbs resulted.

Selly Oak Flash

The Ariel company, which BSA had bought up in 1944, produced their own 500 cc twin late in 1947. Thus Val Page, the chief designer, was not far behind the parent firm and his engine had many differences from the A7. It was fitted with two chain driven camshafts and the cams were at the ends of the shafts so that the pushrods ran in holes in the corners of the cylinder block.

When it came to a 650 cc twin, Page was not given the same scope but used a cleverly disguised A10 engine with the timing cover changed to one styled on the lines of that used on the 500. A Burman gearbox was used along with Ariel's own frame and cycle parts so the machine looked like an Ariel although virtually all the engine was straightforward A10. The rocker box inspection caps were changed for ones retained by one bolt only and a cap was fitted to the top of the rocker box but internally it was all A10.

The 650 was announced as the Huntmaster in the Autumn of 1953 for the 1954 season and was built almost without change until 1959 when the factory stopped making fourstrokes. It was very nice and riders mourned its passing.

The Ariel Huntmaster built from 1953 to 1959 using an A10 engine with minor changes to alter the appearance

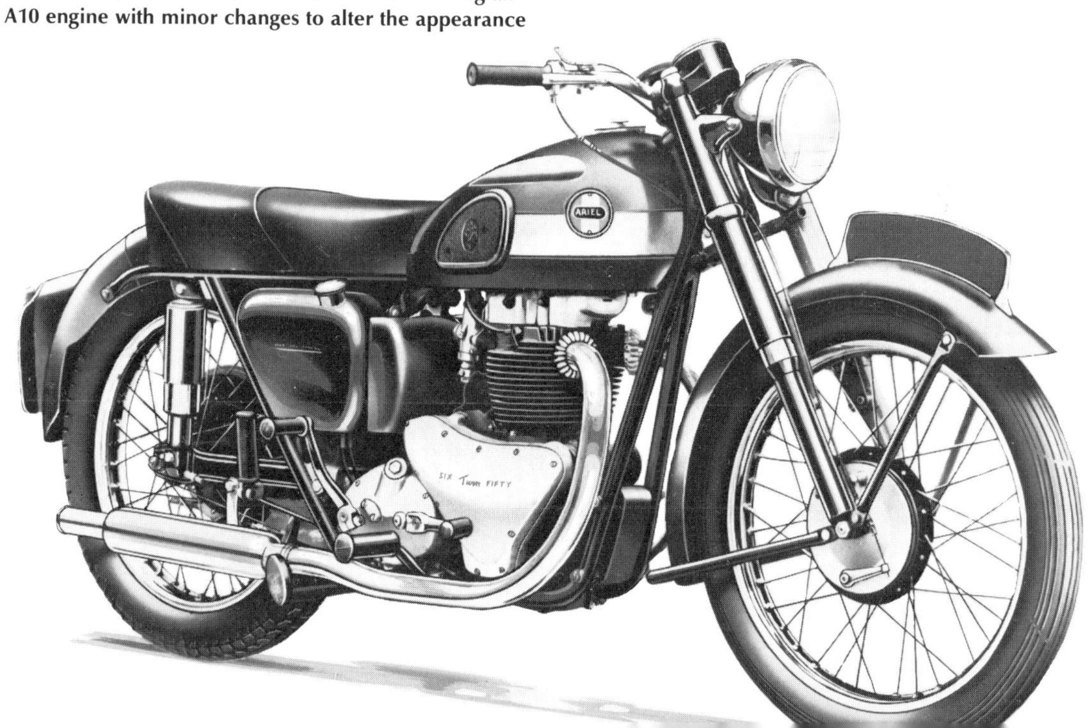

APPENDIX

Specifications

Model	A7/Star Twin	A7/Star Twin
Year from	1946/1949	1950
Year to	1950	1954
Bore (mm)	62	66
Stroke (mm)	82	72·6
Capacity (cc)	495	497
Inlet valve dia. (in)	1·25	
Exhaust valve dia. (in)	1·87	
Inlet valve inclination °	43	
Exhaust valve inclination °	38	
Valve stem dia. (in)	0·312	0·312
Pushrod dia. (in)	0·25	
Compression ratio (to 1)	6·6*/7·0	6·6/7·5*
Compression opt. high	7·5 & 8·6/7·5	
Spark plug (Champion)	L85/L5	L85/L5
Spark plug (NGK)	B7HS	B7HS
	*7·0 (1946–47)	*7·0 from engine AA7102

Late model A7, foundation of the line

Model	A7/Star Twin	A7/Star Twin
Year	1946–50/ 1949–50	1950–54
Valve timing:		
inlet opens BTDC	24	30/42
inlet closes ABDC	65	70/62
exhaust opens BBDC	60	65/67
exhaust closes ATDC	21·5	25/37
Valve clearance (time) (in)	0·015	
Valve clearance (cold) inlet (in)	0·015	0·010*/0·008
Valve clearance (cold) exhaust (in)	0·015	0·010*/0·012
Ignition timing piston (in)	0·313/0·375 full ad.	0·313/0·375 full ad.
Points gap (in)	0·015	0·010 to 0·012
		* See page 160
Piston rings:		
compression, width (in)	0·06	0·06
compression, gap (in)	0·010–0·015	0·008–0·013
oil control, gap (in)	0·009–0·013	0·008–0·013
ring vertical play (comp) (in)	0·002	0·002
ring vertical play (oil) (in)	0·002	0·002
Piston clearance top land (in)	0·0135	
Piston clearance top skirt (in)	0·006/–	
Piston clearance bottom skirt (in)	0·003	0·003
Valve seat angle °	45	45
Valve spring free length (in)	1·53	1·53
Valve spring free length (outer) (in)	1·87	1·87
Drive main ID (in)	1·12	30 (mm)
Drive main OD (in)	2·5	62 (mm)
Drive main width (in)	0·62	16 (mm)
Timing main ID (in)	1·37	1·37
Timing main OD (in)	Bush	
Timing main width (in)	1·09	1·06
Big end rod dia. (in)		1·461
Big end rod side play (in)	0·008/0·014	0·024 max.
Big end pin dia. (in)		1·4600

Model	A7/Star Twin		A7/Star Twin	
Year	1946–50/ 1949–50		1950–54	
Crank end float (in)	Nil		0·005 max.	
Cam bush dia. (in)	0·937–0·938/–			
Idler wheel bush (in)	0·7495/–			
Tappet guide dia. (in)	0·313/–			
Small end bush dia. (in)	0·6878–0·6881			
Oil pressure (psi)	50 (hot)/-			
Primary drive (in)	$\frac{3}{8}$ Duplex		$\frac{3}{8}$ Duplex	
No. of pitches	80		80	
Rear chain size (in)	$\frac{5}{8} \times \frac{3}{8}$		$\frac{5}{8} \times \frac{3}{8}$	
No. of pitches	102*		102	
Sprockets: engine (T)	27		27	
Sprockets: clutch (T)	54		54	
Sprockets: gearbox (T)	18		18	
Sprockets: rear wheel (T)	46**		46*	
Box ratios: top	1·0		1·0	
Box ratios: 3rd	1·211		1·211	
Box ratios: 2nd	1·759		1·759	
Box ratios: 1st	2·581		2·581	
O/A ratios: top	Solo	S/car	Solo	S/car
	5·111	5·444	5·111	5·444
O/A ratios: 3rd	6·190	6·593	6·190	6·593
O/A ratios: 2nd	8·990	9·577	8·990	9·577
O/A ratios: 1st	13·192	14·052	13·192	14·052
	*103T Sidecar gearing **49T—Sidecar		*49T—Sidecar	
Gearbox bearings:				
Layshaft bore (in)	0·698/–			
Layshaft gearbush bore (in)	0·7505/–			
Pinion sleeve bore (in)	0·813/–			
Kickstart quadrant bore (in)	0·563/–			
Gear operating spindle (in)	0·468/–			
Front tyre (in)	3·25 × 19		3·25 × 19	
Rear tyre (in)	3·50 × 19		3·50 × 19	
Pressure solo (psi)	16–17/17–18		18/20	
Pressure dual (psi)	18/26		18/28	

Model	A7/Star Twin	A7/Star Twin
Year	1946–50/ 1949–50	1950–54
Brake—front dia. (in)	7	7*
Brake—front width (in)	1·12	1·12**
Brake rear dia. (in)	7	7
Brake rear width (in)	1·12	1·12
		*8—1954
		**1·37—1954
Rear type	*/Plunger	Plunger*/ Plunger
Petrol tank (Imp. gals)	3·5**	3·5
Petrol tank (US gals)	4·2	4·2
Petrol tank (litres)	15·9	15·9
Oil tank (Imp. pints)	4	4
Oil tank (US pints)	4·8	4·8
Oil tank (litres)	2·3	2·3
Box capacity (Imp. pints)	1	1
Box capacity (US pints)	1·2	1·2
Box capacity (litres)	0·568	0·568
Chaincase (Imp. pints)	0·4	0·4
Chaincase (US pints)	0·48	0·48
Chaincase (cc)	227	227
Front forks/leg (Imp. pints)	0·25	0·25**
Front forks/leg (US pints)	0·3	0·3
Front forks/leg (cc)	142	142
	* Plunger option 1949–50	* Rigid avail 1950/51
	**3·0 in 1946	**1952/54—0·37

Model	A7/Star Twin	A7/Star Twin
Year	1946–50/ 1949–50	1950–54
Oil grade	SAE 40 or 50	SAE 40 or 50
Box oil grade	SAE 40 or 50	SAE 40 or 50
Case oil grade	SAE 40 or 50	SAE 40 or 50
Fork oil grade	SAE 20	SAE 20
Ignition system	Magneto	Magneto
Gen. type	E3H Dynamo	E3L Dynamo
Output (watts)	40	60
Battery (volts)	6	6
Earth	Neg.	Pos.
Wheelbase (in)	54·5/55	55
Ground clear (in)	6·5/5	4·5
Seat height (in)	29·5/31	30
Width (bars) (in)	29	
Dry weight (lb)	365/382	400*/382**
Wet weight (lb)	373/385	
Power (bhp)	26*/31	27/31
@ rpm	6000*/6000	5800/6000
Torque (ft lb)		
@ rpm		
	*27@5800 in 1949–50	*375—Rigid model **401 in 1953

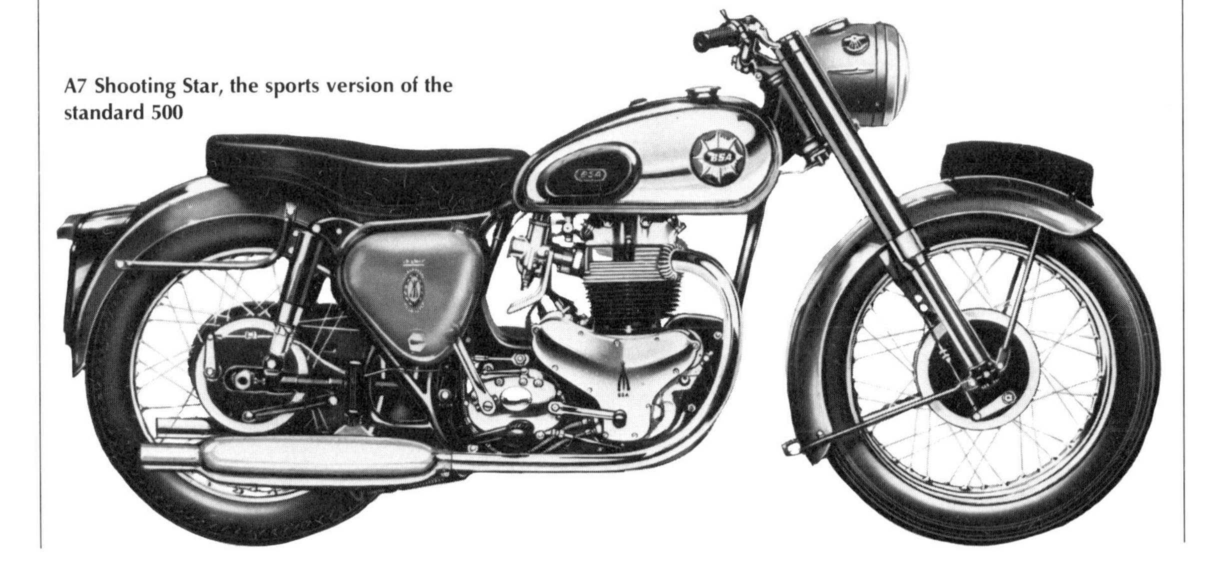

A7 Shooting Star, the sports version of the standard 500

Model	**A10/Super Flash/Road Rocket/A10**
Year from	1950/1953/1955/1955
Year to	1954/1954/1957/1961
Bore (mm)	70
Stroke (mm)	84
Capacity (cc)	646
Inlet valve dia. (in)	1·312/–/–/–
Exhaust valve dia. (in)	1·062/–/–/–
Valve stem dia. (in)	0·31
Compression ratio (to 1)	6·5/8·0/8·0/7·25*
Con rod ctrs. (in)	6·468
Spark plug (Champion)	L85/L5/N3/L85
Spark plug (NGK)	B6HS/B7HS/B7ES/B6HS
Gudgeon pin dia. (in)	0·750/0·7502/–/–/–
Valve timing:	
inlet opens BTDC	30/42/42/42**
inlet closes ABDC	70/62/62/62**
exhaust opens BBDC	65/67/67/67**
exhaust closes ATDC	25/37/37/37**
Valve clearance (cold) inlet (in)	0·010***/0·008/0·008/0·010****
Valve clearance (cold) exhaust (in)	0·010***/0·008/0·008/0·016****
Ignition timing °	34/35/35/34
Ignition timing piston (in)	0·34/0·37/0·37/0·34
Points gap (in)	0·010/0·012
	* 6·5 in 1957
	** 1955/1958 as 1950 A10
	*** 0·015—1950 only
	****0·008/0·010 1960/62
Piston rings:	
compression, width (in)	0·62
compression, gap (in)	0·008–0·013
oil control, gap (in)	0·008–0·013
ring vertical play (comp) (in)	0·002
ring vertical play (oil) (in)	0·002
Piston clearance bottom skirt (in)	0·004
Valve seat angle °	45
Valve lift—inlet (in)	0·310/–/–/–
Valve lift—exhaust (in)	0·300/–/–/–
Valve spring free length (in)	1·53
Valve spring free length (outer) (in)	1·87
Drive main ID (mm)	30
Drive main OD (mm)	62
Drive main width (mm)	16
Timing main ID (in)	1·3745/1·375
Timing main width (in)	1·070/1·075
Big end rod dia. (in)	1·461
Big end rod side play (in)	0·024 max

Model	**A10/Super Flash/Road Rocket/A10**
Year	1950–54/1953–54/1955–57/1955–61
Big end pin dia. (in)	1·4595/1·460
Crank end float (in)	0·005 max
Small end bush dia. (in)	0·7503/0·7506/–/–/–
Primary drive (in)	$\frac{3}{8}$ Duplex/$\frac{3}{8}$Duplex 0·5 × 0·305/ 0·5 × 0·305
No. of pitches	80/80/69/69
Rear chain size (in)	$\frac{5}{8} \times \frac{3}{8}$
No. of pitches	102/102/98/98
Sprockets: engine (T)	27/27/21/21
Sprockets: clutch (T)	54/54/43/43
Sprockets: gearbox (T)	19
Sprockets: rear wheel (T)	42*/42/42/42
Box ratios: top	1·0
Box ratios: 3rd	1·211
Box ratios: 2nd	1·759
Box ratios: 1st	2·581
	Solo S/car
O/A ratios: top	4·421 5·158/4·421/4·526/4·526
O/A ratios: 3rd	5·354 6·246/5·354/5·481/5·481
O/A ratios: 2nd	7·777 9·073/7·777/7·962/7·962
O/A ratios: 1st	11·41113/11·411/11·682/11·682 13·313
	*49T—Sidecar
Front tyre (in)	3·25 × 19
Rear tyre (in)	3·50 × 19
Pressure solo (psi)	18/20
Pressure dual (psi)	18/28
Rim—front (in)	–/–/WM2/WM2
Rim—rear (in)	–/–/WM2/WM2
Brake—front dia. (in)	8/8/7/8*
Brake—front width (in)	1·37/1·37/1·5/–
Brake rear dia. (in)	7
Brake rear width (in)	1·12/1·12/1·5/1·12**
	* 7 × 1·5–1955–57
	**1·5–1955–57
Rear—type	Plunger*/Plunger/ S/A/S/A**
Petrol tank (Imp. gal)	4·25***/4·25/4/4
Petrol tank (US gal)	5·1/5·1/4·8/4·8
Petrol tank (litre)	19·3/19·3/18·2/18·2
Oil tank (Imp. pint)	4/4/5·5/5·5
Oil tank (US pint)	4·8/4·8/6·6/6·6
Oil tank (litre)	2·3/2·3/3·1/3·1
Box capacity (Imp. pint)	1/1/0·7/0·7
Box capacity (US pint)	1·2/1·2/0·84/0·84
	*Rigid also available 1950–51
	** Plunger available to 1958
	***3·5 gal. available 1950–51

Model	A10/Super Flash/Road Rocket/A10
Year	1950–54/1953–54/1955–57/ 1955–61
Box capacity (litre)	0·568/0·568/0·398/0·398
Chaincase (Imp. pint)	0·4
Chaincase (US pint)	0·48
Chaincase (cc)	227
Front forks/leg (Imp. pint)	0·25/0·25/0·375/0·375
Front forks/leg (US pint)	0·3/0·3/0·45/0·45
Front forks/leg (cc)	142/142/213/213
Oil grade	SAE 40 or 50
Box oil grade	SAE 40 or 50
Case oil grade	SAE 40 or 50
Fork oil grade	SAE 20
Ignition system	Magneto
Gen. type	E3L Dynamo
Output (watts)	60
Battery (volts)	6
Earth	Pos.

Model	A10/Super Flash/Road Rocket/A10
Year	1950–54/1953–54/1955–57/ 1955–61
Wheelbase (in)	55/55/56/56
Ground clear (in)	4·5/4·5/6/6
Seat height (in)	30
Width (bars) (in)	28·12/28·12/31·37/28·12
Length (in)	84/84/85/85
Height (in)	40·5
Fork angle °	61
Dry weight (lb)	408*/–/418/430
Wet weight (lb)	**
Power (bhp)	35/42/40/34
@ rpm	5500/–/6000/5750
Torque (ft lb)	39/–/–/–
@ rpm	3900/–/–/–

* 380 with rigid frame
**395 with rigid frame

Super Rocket which succeeded the Road Rocket and ran to the end of the A10 line

Model	A7/Shooting Star	Rocket Gold Star Super Rocket
Year from	1955	1958/1962
Year to	1961	1963
Bore (mm)	66	70
Stroke (mm)	72·6	84
Capacity (cc)	497	646
Valve stem dia. (in)	0·31	0·31
Compression ratio (to 1)	6·6/7·25*	8·3*/9·0
Spark plug (Champion)	L85/N3	N3
Spark plug (NGK)	B7HS/B7ES	B7ES
Valve timing:		
inlet opens BTDC	42**/42	42
inlet closes ABDC	62**/62	62
exhaust opens BBDC	67**/67	67
exhaust closes ATDC	37**/37	37
Valve clearance (cold) inlet (in)	0·010***/ 0·008	0·008
Valve clearance (cold) exhaust (in)	0·016***/ 0·012****	0·008**/ 0·010
Ignition timing °		35/–
Ignition timing piston (in)	0·31/0·37	0·37/0·41
Points gap (in)	0·010/0·012	0·010/0·012
	*8—1958 on	*9·0 for 1962–63
	**1955–58 as 1950–A7	**0·010—1960–61
	***0·008/0·010 1960–61	
	****0·010—1960–61	
Piston rings:		
compression, width (in)	0·06	0·06
compression, gap (in)	0·008–0·013	0·008–0·013
oil control, gap (in)	0·008–0·013	0·008–0·013
ring vertical play (comp) (in)	0·002	0·002
ring vertical play (oil) (in)	0·002	0·002
Piston clearance bottom skirt (in)	0·003	0·005/–
Valve seat angle °	45	45
Valve spring free length (in)	1·53	2·0 in 1962/2·0
Valve spring free length (outer) (in)	1·87	2·12 in 1962/2·12
Drive main ID (mm)	30	30
Drive main OD (mm)	62	62

Model	A7/Shooting Star	Super Rocket/ RGS 1958–63/
Year	1955–61	1962–63
Drive main width (mm)	16	16
Timing main ID (in)	1·37	1·37
Timing main width (in)	1·06	1·06
Big end rod dia. (in)	1·461	1·461
Big end rod side play (in)	0·024 max	0·024 max
Big end pin dia. (in)	1·46	1·46
Crank end float (in)	0·005 max	0·005 max
Primary drive (in)	0·5 × 0·305	0·5 × 0·305
No. of pitches	68	69/70
Rear chain size (in)	$\frac{5}{8} \times \frac{3}{8}$	$\frac{5}{8} \times \frac{3}{8}$
No. of pitches	98	98/99
Sprockets: engine (T)	18	21/23
Sprockets: clutch (T)	43	43
Sprockets: gearbox (T)	19	19
Sprockets: rear wheel (T)	42	42/46
Box ratios: top	1	1/1*
Box ratios: 3rd	1·211	1·211/1·099
Box ratios: 2nd	1·759	1·759/1·326
Box ratios: 1st	2·581	2·581/1·754
O/A ratios: top	5·281	4·526
O/A ratios: 3rd	6·395	5·481/4·974
O/A ratios: 2nd	9.289	7·962/6.002
O/A ratios: 1st	13·629	11·682/7·939
		*Alt. ratios available
Front tyre (in)	3·25 × 19	3·25 × 19
Rear tyre (in)	3·50 × 19	3·50 × 19
Pressure solo (psi)	18/20	18/20
Pressure dual (psi)	18/28	18/28
Rim—front (in)	WM2	–/WM2*
Rim—rear (in)	WM2	–/WM2*
Brake—front dia. (in)	7/8*	8/8**
Brake—front width (in)	1·12	–/1·37
Brake rear dia. (in)	7	7
Brake rear width (in)	1·12**/1·12**	1·12
	*1955–57—7 in	*Alloy rims opt.
	**1956–57—	**190 mm option
Front suspension:	1·5 in	–/Gold Star
Rear type	S/A	S/A
Petrol tank (Imp. gal)	4	4/4*
Petrol tank (US gal)	4·8	4·8
Petrol tank (litre)	18·2	18·2
Oil tank (Imp. pints)	5·5	5·5
		*2 & 5 Imp. gal available

Model	A7/Shooting Star	Super Rocket/ RGS
Year	1955–61	1958–63/ 1962–63
Oil tank (US pints)	6·6	6·6
Oil tank (litre)	3·1	3·1
Box capacity (Imp. pint)	0·7	0·7
Box capacity (US pints)	0·84	0·84
Box capacity (litre)	0·398	0·398
Chaincase (Imp. pint)	0·4	0·4
Chaincase (US pint)	0·48	0·48
Chaincase (cc)	227	227
Front forks/leg (Imp. pint)	0·375	0·375
Front forks/leg (US pints)	0·45	0·45
Front forks/leg (cc)	213	213
Oil grade	SAE 40 or 50	SAE 40 or 50
Box oil grade	SAE 40 or 50	SAE 40 or 50
Case oil grade	SAE 40 or 50	SAE 40 or 50
Fork oil grade	SAE 20	SAE 20
Ignition system	Magneto	Magneto
Gen. type	E3L Dynamo	E3L Dynamo
Output (watts)	60	60
Battery (volts)	6	6
Earth	Pos.	Pos.
Wheelbase (in)	56	
Ground clear (in)	6	
Seat height (in)	30	
Width (bars) (in)	28·12	28·12/–
Length (in)	85	85/–
Height (in)	40·5	40·5/–
Fork angle °	61	63/–
Dry weight (lb)	425/416	418/–
Power (bhp)	28/32	43/46*
@ rpm	5800/6250	–/6250 *50 with special silencer

Model	A50	A50C Cyclone and A50CC Cyclone Clubman/ A50 Royal Star/ A50 Wasp
Year from	1962	1964/ 1965/ 1965
Year to	1965	1965/ 1970/ 1966
Bore (mm)	65·5	65·5
Stroke (mm)	74	74
Capacity (cc)	499	499
Inlet valve dia. (in)	1·41	1·45/ 1·45/ 1·47
Exhaust valve dia. (in)	1·31	1·31
Inlet valve inclination °	37	37
Exhaust valve inclination °	37	37
Valve stem dia. (in)	0·3095	0·3095
Compression ratio (to 1)	7·5*	9·0/ 9·0/ 10·5
Con rod ctrs. (in)	6	6
Spark plug (Champion)	N4	N4/N4/N3
Spark plug (NGK)	B7ES	B7ES/ B8ES/ B8ES
Gudgeon pin dia. (in)	0·750	0·750
Valve timing:		
inlet opens BTDC	40	51/40/51
inlet closes ABDC	60	68/60/68
exhaust opens BBDC	65	78/65/78
exhaust closes ATDC	35	37/35/37
Valve clearance (time) (in)	0·015	0·015
Valve clearance (cold) inlet (in)	0·008	0·008
Valve clearance (cold) exhaust (in)	0·010	0·010
Ignition timing °	34	34/34/23
Ignition timing piston (in)	0·305	0·305/ 0·305/ 0·143
Points gap (in)	0·015 *1964—8·5 Mid 1962–8·0	0·015
Piston rings:		
compression, width (in)	0·06	0·06
compression, gap (in)	0·007/0·012	0·007/0·012
oil control, width (in)	0·12	0·12
oil control, gap (in)	0·007/0·012	0·007/0·012
ring vertical play (comp) (in)	0·002	0·002
ring vertical play (oil) (in)	0/002	0·002
Piston clearance top skirt (in)	0·0048–0·0051	0·0048–0·0051

Styling of Royal Star and Thunderbolt for 1965 and 1966. Heavier than the A7/A10 series but still good reliable machines

Model	**A50**	**A50C and A50CC/ Royal Star/ Wasp**
Year	1962–65	1964–65/ 1965–70/ 1965–66
Piston clearance bottom skirt (in)	0·0012–0·0027	0·0012–0·0027
Valve seat angle °	45	45
Valve lift—inlet (in)	0·306	0·366/ 0·306/ 0·366
Valve lift—exhaust (in)	0·306	0·334/ 0·306/ 0·334
Valve spring load open		
Valve spring load closed		
Valve spring free length (in)	1·62	1·62/1·44/1·5
Valve spring free length (outer) (in)	2·03	2·03/1·75/1·62
Drive main ID (in)	1·125	1·125
Drive main OD (in)	2·812	2·812
Drive main width (in)	0·812	0·812
Timing main ID (in)	1·500	1·500
Timing main OD (in)	1·630	1·630
Timing main width (in)	0·950	0·950
Big end rod dia. (in)	1·688	1·688
Big end clearance (in)	0·001–0·0025	0·001–0·0025

Model	**A50**	**A50C and A50CC/ Royal Star/ Wasp**
Year	1962–65	1964–65/ 1965–70/ 1965–66
Big end rod side play (in)	0·024	0·024
Big end pin dia. (in)	1·687	1·687
Crank end float (in)	0·0015–0·003	0·0015–0·003
Cam bush dia. (left) (in)	0·810	0·810
Cam bush dia. (right) (in)	0·874	0·874
Small end bush dia. (in)	0·7505	0·7505
Small end bush width (in)	0·945	0·945
Oil pressure (psi)	50	50
Primary drive (in)	$\frac{3}{8}$ Triplex	$\frac{3}{8}$ Triplex
No. of pitches	80	80
Rear chain size (in)	$\frac{5}{8} \times \frac{3}{8}$	$\frac{5}{8} \times \frac{3}{8}$
No. of pitches	98	98/104/108
Sprockets: engine (T)	28	28
Sprockets: clutch (T)	58	58
Sprockets: gearbox (T)	17	17/18/20
Sprockets: rear wheel (T)	42	42/47/50
Box ratios: top	1	1
Box ratios: 3rd	1·18	1·14/1·14/ 1·107
Box ratios: 2nd	1·65	1·47/1·60/ 1·47

Model	A50	A50C and A50CC/ Royal Star/ Wasp
Year	1962–65	1964–65/ 1965–70/ 1965–66
Box ratios: 1st	2·56	2·03/2·51/ 2·03
O/A ratios: top	5·12*	5·12/5·41/ 5·18
O/A ratios: 3rd	6·04*	5·86/6·2/ 5·73
O/A ratios: 2nd	8·44*	7·52/8·67/ 7·61
O/A ratios: 1st	13·10*	10·39/13·6/ 10·52
	*1964—5·12, 5·85, 7·17, 12·82	
Gearbox bearings:		
Mainshaft sleeve ID (in)	1·25	1·25
Mainshaft sleeve OD (in)	2·5	2·5
Mainshaft sleeve width (in)	0·62	0·62
Mainshaft right ID (in)	0·75	0·75
Mainshaft right OD (in)	1·87	1·87

Model	A50	A50C and A50CC/ Royal Star / Wasp
Year	1962–65	1964–65/ 1965–70/ 1965–66
Mainshaft right width (in)	0·56	0·56
Layshaft left ID (in)	0·75	0·75
Layshaft left OD (in)	1	1
Layshaft left width (in)	0·75	0·75
Layshaft right ID (in)	0·75	0·75
Layshaft right OD (in)	1	1
Layshaft right width (in)	0·75	0·75
Front tyre (in)	3·25 × 18	3·25 × 19/ 3·25 × 19/ 3·50 × 19
Rear tyre (in)	3·50 × 18	3·50 × 19/ 4·00 × 18*/ 4·00 × 18
Pressure solo (psi)	18/20	18/20 / 23/21 / 23/21
Rim—front (in)	WM2	WM2/WM2/ WM3
Rim—rear (in)	WM2	WM2/WM3 WM3

1967 Thunderbolt with finned rocker cover and humped back seat

Model	A50	A50C and A50CC/ Royal Star/ Wasp
Year	1962–65	1964–65/ 1965–70/ 1965–66
Brake—front dia. (in)	7*	8
Brake—front width (in)	1·12	1·12/1·62/1·62
Brake rear dia. (in)	7	7
Brake rear width (in)	1·12	1·12
	*1964—8 in option	*1965 as A50
Front suspension	Tele.	Tele.
Front spring rate (lb/in)	32·5	32·5
Front movement (in)	5·75	5·75
Front trail (in)	3·12	3·12
Rear—rate (lb/in)	90	90
Rear—movement (in)	3	3
Petrol tank (Imp. gal)	4	4*/3·5**/1·67
Petrol tank (US gal)	4·8	4·8/4·2/2·0
Petrol tank (litre)	18·2	18·2/15·9/7·6
Oil tank (Imp. pint)	6*	5·5/5·0***/5·5
Oil tank (US pint)	7·2	6·6/6·0/6·6
Oil tank (litre)	3·41	3·12/2·84/3·12

Model	A50	A50C and A50CC/ Royal Star/ Wasp
Year	1962–65	1964–65/ 1965–70/ 1965–66
Box capacity (Imp. pint)	0·875	0·875
Box capacity (US pint)	1·05	1·05
Box capacity (litre)	0·5	0·5
Chaincase (Imp. pint)	0·25	0·25
Chaincase (US pint)	0·3	0·3
Chaincase (cc)	142	142
Front forks/leg (Imp. pint)	0·33	0·33
Front forks/leg (US pint)	0·4	0·4
Front forks/leg (cc)	190	190
Petrol grade	—	4/5 star
Oil grade	SAE 20–50	SAE 20–50
Box oil grade	EP 90	EP90
	*1963 on—5·5	*1964 option—2 **1969—4 Imp. gal 1968—2·75 Imp. gal ***5·5 to 1966

1969 Royal Star with USA styling adopted for all models

Model	A50	A50C and A50CC/ Royal Star/ Wasp
Year	1962–65	1964–65/ 1965–70/ 1965–66
Case oil grade	SAE 10–30	SAE 10–30
Fork oil grade	SAE 20	SAE 20
Ignition system	Coil	Coil/ Coil/ Energy transfer
Gen. type	Alternator	Alternator/ Alternator/–
Output (watts)	60	60/100/–
Battery (volts)	6*	6*/12/–
Earth	Pos.	Pos./ Pos./–
Wheel base (in)	54·12	54·12
Ground clear (in)	7	7
Seat height (in)	31·50	31·50
Width (bars)	28	28/28/–
Length (in)	81	81
Height (in)	39·75	39·75/–/–
Fork angle °	63	63
Dry weight (lb)	385	390/ 391/ 386
Wet weight (lb)	—	–/404/-
Power (bhp)	28·5	38·5/32**/–
@ rpm	6000	6750/6250/–
Torque (ft lb)	—	–/31/–
@ rpm		–/3500/–
	*12 volt option from 1963	*12 volt option **35 in 1969

Model	A65	A65R Rocket/ A65L Lightning/ A65LC Lightning Clubman
Year from	1962	1963/1964/ 1964
Year to	1965	1964/1965/ 1965
Bore (mm)	75	75
Stroke (mm)	74	74
Capacity (cc)	654	654
Inlet valve dia. (in)	1·47	1·47
Exhaust valve dia. (in)	1·41	1·41

Model	A65	A65R/ A65L/ A65LC
Year	1962–65	1963–64/ 1964–65/ 1964–65
Inlet valve inclination °	37	37
Exhaust valve inclination °	37	37
Valve stem dia (in)	0·3095	0·3095
Compression ratio (to 1)	7·5*	9·0/9·0*/9·0
Compression opt. low		
Compression opt. high	8·3*	
Con rod ctrs (in)	6	6
Spark plug (Champion)	N4	N4/N3/N4
Spark plug (NGK)	B7ES	B7ES/B8ES/ B7ES
Gudgeon pin dia. (in)	0·750	0·750
Valve timing:		
inlet opens BTDC	40	51
inlet closes ABDC	60	68
exhaust opens BBDC	65	78
exhaust closes ATDC	35	37
Valve clearance (time) (in)	0·015	0·015
Valve clearance (cold) inlet (in)	0·008	0·008
Valve clearance (cold) exhaust (in)	0·010	0·010
Ignition timing °	34	34
Ignition timing piston (in)	0·305	0·305
Points gap (in)	0·015	0·015
	*1962—7·25 1964—8·0 **US model	*1964 option 11·0
Piston rings:		
compression, width (in)	0·06	0·06
compression, gap (in)	0·008–0·013	0·008–0·013
oil control, width (in)	0·12	0·12
oil control, gap (in)	0·008–0·013	0·008–0·013
ring vertical play (comp) (in)	0·002	0·002
ring vertical play (oil) (in)	0·002	0·002
Piston clearance top skirt (in)	0·0048–0·0051	0·0048–0·0051
Piston clearance bottom skirt (in)	0·0012–0·0027	0·0012–0·0027
Valve seat angle °	45	45
Valve lift—inlet (in)	0·366	0·366
Valve lift—exhaust (in)	0·334	0·334
Valve spring free length (in)	1·62	1·62
Valve spring free length (outer) (in)	2·03	2·03

1967 Lightning with finned rocker cover

Model	A65	A65R/ A65L/ A65LC
Year	1962–65	1963–64/ 1964–65/ 1964–65
Drive main ID (in)	1·125	1·125
Drive main OD (in)	2·812	2·812
Drive main width (in)	0·812	0·812
Timing main ID (in)	1·500	1·500
Timing main OD (in)	1·630	1·630
Timing main width (in)	0·950	0·950
Big end rod dia. (in)	1·688	1·688
Big end clearance (in)	0·001–0·0025	0·001–0·0025
Big end rod side play (in)	0·024	0·024
Big end pin dia. (in)	1·687	1·687
Crank end float (in)	0·0015–0·003	0·0015–0·003
Cam bush dia. left (in)	0·810	0·810
Cam bush dia. right (in)	0·874	0·874
Small end bush dia. (in)	0·7505	0·7505
Small end bush width (in)	0·945	0·945
Oil pressure (psi)	50	50
Primary drive (in)	$\frac{3}{8}$ Triplex	$\frac{3}{8}$ Triplex
No. of pitches	80	80
Rear chain size (in)	$\frac{5}{8} \times \frac{3}{8}$	$\frac{5}{8} \times \frac{3}{8}$
No. of pitches	100	100
Sprockets: engine (T)	28	28
Sprockets: clutch (T)	58	58
Sprockets: gearbox (T)	20*	20/19/19
Sprockets: rear wheel (T)	42	42
Box ratios: top	1·0	1·0
Box ratios: 3rd	1·18	1·14
Box ratios: 2nd	1.65	1·60/1·46/ 1·46
Box ratios: 1st	2·55	2·57/2·02/ 2·02
O/A ratios: top	4·35	4·35/4·58/ 4·58
O/A ratios: 3rd	5·13*	4·98/5·22/ 5·22

Model	A65	A65R/ A65L/ A65LC
Year	1962–65	1963–64/ 1964–65/ 1964–65
O/A ratios: 2nd	7·18*	6·96/6·7/6·7
O/A ratios: 1st	11·10*	10·92/9·26/ 9·26
	*1964—19 4·56, 6·66, 7·29, 11·43	
Gearbox bearings:		
Mainshaft sleeve ID (in)	1·25	1·25
Mainshaft sleeve OD (in)	2·5	2·5
Mainshaft sleeve width (in)	0·62	0·62
Mainshaft right ID (in)	0·75	0·75
Mainshaft right OD (in)	1·87	1·87
Mainshaft right width (in)	0·56	0·56
Layshaft left ID (in)	0·75	0·75
Layshaft left OD (in)	1	1
Layshaft left width (in)	0·75	0·75
Layshaft right ID (in)	0·75	0·75
Layshaft right OD (in)	1	1
Layshaft right width (in)	0·75	0·75
Front tyre (in)	3·25 × 18	3·25 × 18/ 3·25 × 19/ 3·25 × 19
Rear tyre (in)	3·50 × 18	3·50 × 18
Pressure solo (psi)	18/20	18/20
Rim—front (in)	WM2	WM2
Rim—rear (in)	WM2	WM2
Brake—front dia. (in)	8	8
Brake—front width (in)	1·12	1·12
Brake rear dia. (in)	7	7
Brake rear width (in)	1·12	1·12
Front suspension	Tele.	Tele.
Front spring rate (lb/in)	32·5	32·5
Front movement (in)	5·75	5·75
Front trail (in)	3·12	3·12
Rear—rate (lb/in)	90	90
Rear-movement (in)	3	3
Petrol tank (Imp. gal)	4	4
Petrol tank (US gal)	4·8	4·8
Petrol tank (litre)	18·2	18·2
Oil tank (Imp. pint)	6*	5·5
Oil tank (US pint)	7·2	6·6
Oil tank (litre)	3·41	3·12
Box capacity (Imp. pint)	0·875	0·875
Box capacity (US pint)	1·05	1·05
Box capacity (litre)	0·5	0·5
Chaincase (Imp. pint)	0·25	0·25

1969 Lightning, the top twin of the range for that year

Model	A65	A65R/ A65L/ A65LC
Year	1962–65	1963–64/ 1964–65/ 1964–65
Chaincase (US pint)	0·3	0·3
Chaincase (cc)	142	142
Front forks/leg (Imp. pint)	0·33	0·33
Front forks/leg (US pint)	0·4	0·4
Front forks/leg (cc)	190	190
Oil grade	SAE 20–50	SAE 20–50
Box oil grade	EP90	EP90
Case oil grade	SAE 10–30	SAE 10–30
Fork oil grade	SAE 20	SAE 20
	*1963 on— 5·5	
Ignition system	Coil	Coil
Gen. type	Alternator	Alternator
Output (watts)	60	60
Battery (volts)	6*	6*
Earth	Pos.	Pos.
Wheelbase (in)	54·12	54·12
Ground clear (in)	7	7
Seat height (in)	31·5	31·5
Width (bars) (in)	28	28
Length (in)	81	81
Height (in)	39·75	39·75/–/–
Fork angle °	63	63

Model	A65	A65R/ A65L/ A65LC
Year	1962–65	1963–64/ 1964–65/ 1964–65
Dry weight (lb)	390	390 395 395
Wet weight (lb)	408	
Power (bhp)	38	45/48/51
@ rpm	5800	6250/6250/ 6750
	*12v option from 1963	*12v option

Model	A65T Thunderbolt/ A65L Lightning/A65S Spitfire II/ A65H Hornet
Year from	1965
Year to	1970/1970/1966/1967
Bore (mm)	75
Stroke (mm)	74
Capacity (cc)	654
Inlet valve dia. (in)	1·47
Exhaust valve dia. (in)	1·41
Inlet valve inclination °	37
Exhaust valve inclination °	37
Valve stem dia. (in)	0·3095
Compression ratio (to 1)	9·0/9·0/10·5/10·5
Con rod ctrs. (in)	6·00
Spark plug (Champion)	N4/N3/N3/N3
Spark plug (NGK)	B7ES/B8ES/B8ES/B8ES
Gudgeon pin dia. (in)	0·750
Valve timing:	
inlet opens BTDC	51
inlet closes ABDC	68
exhaust opens BBDC	78
exhaust closes ATDC	37
Valve clearance (time) (in)	0·015
Valve clearance (cold) inlet (in)	0·008
Valve clearance (cold) exhaust (in)	0·010
Ignition timing °	34/34/34/28
Ignition timing piston (in)	0·305/0·305/0·305/0·210
Points gap (in)	0·015
Piston rings:	
compression, width (in)	0·06
compression, gap (in)	0·008–0·013
oil control, width (in)	0·12
oil control, gap (in)	0·008–0·013
ring vertical play (comp) (in)	0·002
ring vertical play (oil) (in)	0·002
Piston clearance top skirt (in)	0·0048–0·0051
Piston clearance bottom skirt (in)	0·0012–0·0027
Valve seat angle °	45
Valve lift—inlet (in)	0·366
Valve lift—exhaust (in)	0·334
Valve spring free length (in)	1·44
Valve spring free length (outer) (in)	1·75
Drive main ID (in)	1·125
Drive main OD (in)	2·812
Drive main width (in)	0·812
Timing main ID (in)	1·500
Timing main OD (in)	1·630

Model	A65T/A65L/A65S Mk II/A65H
Year	1965–70/1965–70/1965–66/ 1965–67
Timing main width (in)	0·950
Big end rod dia. (in)	1·688
Big end clearance (in)	0·001–0·0025
Big end rod side play (in)	0·024
Big end pin dia. (in)	1·687
Crank end float (in)	0·0015–0·003
Cam bush dia. (in)	0·810
Idler wheel bush (in)	0·874
Small end bush dia. (in)	0·7505
Small end bush width (in)	0·945
Oil pressure (psi)	50
Primary drive (in)	$\frac{3}{8}$ Triplex
No. of pitches	80
Rear chain size (in)	$\frac{5}{8} \times \frac{3}{8}$
No. of pitches	106/106/106/109
Sprockets: engine (T)	28
Sprockets: clutch (T)	58
Sprockets: gearbox (T)	20/20/21/21
Sprockets: rear wheel (T)	47/47/47/50
Box ratios: top	1·0
Box ratios: 3rd	1·14
Box ratios: 2nd	1·60
Box ratios: 1st	2·52/2·52/2·51/2·52
O/A ratios: top	4·87/4·87/4·64/4·93
O/A ratios: 3rd	5·58/5·58/5·31/5·65
O/A ratios: 2nd	7·8/7·8/7·42/7·88
O/A ratios: 1st	12·27/12·27/11·65/12·40
Gearbox bearings:	
Mainshaft sleeve ID (in)	1·25
Mainshaft sleeve OD (in)	2·5
Mainshaft sleeve width (in)	0·62
Mainshaft right ID (in)	0·75
Mainshaft right OD (in)	1·87
Mainshaft right width (in)	0·56
Layshaft left ID (in)	0·75
Layshaft left OD (in)	1
Layshaft left width (in)	0·75
Layshaft right ID (in)	0·75
Layshaft right OD (in)	1
Layshaft right width (in)	0·75
Front tyre (in)	3·25 × 19
Rear tyre (in)	4·00 × 18
Rim—front (in)	WM2/WM2/Alloy WM2/WM2
Rim—rear (in)	WM3/WM3/Alloy WM3/WM3
Brake—front dia. (in)	8/8/190 mm/8
Brake—front width (in)	1·62/1·62/2/1·62
Brake rear dia. (in)	7

Model	A65T/A65L/A65S II/A65H
Year	1965–70/1965–70/1965–66/ 1965–67
Brake rear width (in)	1·12
Front suspension	Tele.
Front spring rate (lb/in)	32·5/32·5/32·5/34
Front movement (in)	5·75
Front trail (in)	3·12
Rear—rate (lb/in)	90
Rear—movement (in)	3
Petrol tank (Imp. gal)	3·5*/3·5*/2·0**/1·67
Petrol tank (US gal)	4·2/4·2/2·4/2
Petrol tank (litre)	15·9/15·9/9·1/7·6
Oil tank (Imp. pint)	5***/5***/5·5/5·5
Oil tank (US pint)	6/6/6·6/6·6
Oil tank (litre)	2·84/2·84/3·12/3·12
Box capacity (Imp. pint)	0·875
Box capacity (US pint)	1·05
Box capacity (litre)	0·5
Chaincase (Imp. pint)	0·25
Chaincase (US pint)	0·3
Chaincase (cc)	142
Front forks/leg (Imp. pint)	0·33
Front forks/leg (US pint)	0·4
Front forks/leg (cc)	190
Oil grade	SAE 20–50
Box oil grade	EP90
Case oil grade	SAE 10–30
Fork oil grade	SAE 20
	* 1968—2·75 gal 1969—4 gal **5 gal option ***5·5 to 1966
Ignition system	Coil/Coil/Coil/Energy transfer
Gen. type	Alternator/Alternator/ Alternator/–
Output (watts)	100/100/100/–
Battery (volts)	12/12/12/–
Earth	Pos./Pos./Pos./–
Wheelbase (in)	54·12
Ground clear (in)	7
Seat height (in)	31·5
Width (bars) (in)	28
Length (in)	81/81/81/85·25
Fork angle °	62
Dry weight (lb)	391/391/382/386
Wet weight (lb)	420*/420*/416/–
Power (bhp)	41*/53**/55/–
@ rpm	6250/7000/7000/–
Torque (ft lb)	–/37/–/–
@ rpm	–/6250/–/–
	*in 1969 **52 in 1969

Model	A65S Spitfire III/ A65S Spitfire IV/ A65FS Spitfire/ Firebird	A70
Year from	1966/1967/ 1967	1972
Year to	1967/1968/ 1970	—
Bore (mm)	75	75
Stroke (mm)	74	85
Capacity (cc)	654	751
Inlet valve dia. (in)	1·60	1·60
Exhaust valve dia. (in)	1·41	1·41
Inlet valve inclination °	37	37
Exhaust valve inclination °	37	37
Valve stem dia. (in)	0·3095	0·3095
Compression ratio (to 1)	10/–/–	9·5
Con rod ctrs. (in)	6	6
Spark plug (Champion)	N3	N3
Spark plug (NGK)	B8ES	B8ES
Gudgeon pin dia. (in)	0·750	0·750
Valve timing:		
inlet opens BTDC	51	51
inlet closes ABDC	68	68
exhaust opens BBDC	78	78
exhaust closes ATDC	37	37
Valve clearance (time) (in)	0·015	0·015
Valve clearance (cold) inlet (in)	0·008	0·008
Valve clearance (cold) exhaust (in)	0·010	0·010
Ignition timing °	34/34/28	38
Ignition timing piston (in)	0·305/0·305/ 0·210	0·444
Points gap (in)	0·015	0·015
Piston rings:		
compression, width (in)	0·06	0·06
compression, gap (in)	0·008–0·013	0·008–0·013
oil control, width (in)	0·12	0·12
oil control, gap (in)	0·008–0·013	0·008–0·013
ring vertical play (comp) (in)	0·002	0·002
ring vertical play (oil) (in)	0·002	0·002
Valve seat angle	45	45
Valve lift—inlet (in)	0·366	0·385
Valve lift—exhaust (in)	0·334	0·375

Model	A65S III/A65S IV/ A65FS	A70
Year	1966–67/ 1967–68/ 1967–70	1972
Valve spring load open (lb)		199
Valve spring load closed (lb)		71
Valve spring fitted length (in)	*	1·277
Valve spring fitted length (outer) (in)	**	1·37
Drive main ID (in)	1·125	1·125
Drive main OD (in)	2·812	2·812
Drive main width (in)	0·812	0·812
Timing main ID (uni)	1·500	1·499
Timing main OD (in)	1·630	1·630
Timing main width (in)	0·950	0·950
Big end rod dia. (in)	1·688	1·688
Big end clearance (in)	0·001– 0·0025	0·001– 0·0025
Big end rod side play (in)	0·024 *1·44 in free **1·75 in free	0·024
Big end pin dia. (in)	1·687	1·687
Crank end float (in)	0·0015– 0·003	0·0015– 0·003
Cam bush dia. left (in)	0·810	0·810
Cam bush dia. right (in)	0·874	0·874
Small end bush dia. (in)	0·7505	0·7505
Small end bush width (in)	0·945	0·945
Oil pressure (psi)	50	50
Primary drive (in)	$\frac{3}{8}$ triplex	$\frac{3}{8}$ triplex
No. of pitches	80	80
Rear chain size (in)	$\frac{5}{8} \times \frac{3}{8}$	$\frac{5}{8} \times \frac{3}{8}$
No. of pitches	106/106/–	110
Sprockets: engine (T)	28	28
Sprockets: clutch (T)	58	58
Sprockets: gearbox (T)	20/20/21	21
Sprockets: rear wheel (T)	47/47/50	47
Box ratios: top	1·0	1·0
Box ratios: 3rd	1·14	1·14
Box ratios: 2nd	1·60	1·60
Box ratios: 1st	2·52	2·52
O/A ratios: top	4·87/4·87/ 4·93	4·64
O/A ratios: 3rd	5·58/5·58/ 5·65	5·32
O/A ratios: 2nd	7·8/7·8/7·88	7·43
O/A ratios: 1st	12·27/12·27/ 12·40	11·69
Gearbox bearings:		
Mainshaft sleeve ID (in)	1·25	1·25
Mainshaft sleeve OD (in)	2·5	2·5
Year	1966–67/1967	1972
Mainshaft sleeve width (in)	0·62	0·62
Mainshaft right ID (in)	0·75	0·75
Mainshaft right OD (in)	1·87	1·87
Mainshaft right width (in)	0·56	0·56
Layshaft left ID (in)	0·75	0·75
Layshaft left OD (in)	1	1
Layshaft left width (in)	0·75	0·75
Layshaft right ID (in)	0·75	0·75
Layshaft right OD (in)	1	1
Layshaft right width (in)	0·75	0·75
Front tyre (in)	3·25 × 19/ 3·25 × 19/ 3·50 × 19	3·25 × 19
Rear tyre (in)	4·00 × 18	4·00 × 18
Pressure solo (psi)		21/22
Rim—front (in)	Alloy WM2/ Alloy WM2/ WM3	WM2
Rim—rear (in)	Alloy WM3/WM3/WM3	
Brake—front dia. (in)	190 mm/8/8	8
Brake—front width (in)	2·0/1·62/1·62	1·5
Brake rear dia. (in)	7	7
Brake rear width (in)	1·12	1·12
Front spring rate (lb/in)	32·5	25
Front movement (in)	5·75	6·75
Front trail (in)	3·12	4·47
Rear-rate (lb/in)	90	88
Rear—movement (in)	3	2·5
Petrol tank (Imp. gal)	4/4/1·67	2·5 or 4
Petrol tank (US gal)	4·8/4·8/2·0	3 or 4·8
Petrol tank (litre)	18·2/18·2/7·6	11·4 or 18·2
Oil tank (Imp. pint)	5	5
Oil tank (US pint)	6	6
Oil tank (litre)	2·84	2·84
Box capacity (Imp. pint)	0·875	0·875
Box capacity (US pint)	1·05	1·05
Box capacity (litre)	0·5	0·5
Chaincase (Imp. pint)	0·25	0·25
Chaincase (US pint)	0·3	0·3
Chaincase (cc)	142	142
Front forks/leg (Imp. pint)	0·33	0·33
Front forks/leg (US pint)	0·4	0·4
Front forks/leg (cc)	190	190
Oil grade	SAE 20–50	SAE 20–50
Box oil grade	EP90	EP90
Case oil grade	SAE 10–30	SAE10–30
Fork oil grade	SAE 20	SAE 20
Ignition system	Coil/Coil transfer/Energy/coil Transfer	

Model	**A65S III/A65S IV/ A65FS**	**A70**
Year	1966–67/ 1967–68/ 1967–70	1972
Gen. type	Alternator/ Alternator/–	Alternator
Output (watts)	100/100/–	108
Battery (volts)	12/12/–	12
Earth	Pos./Pos./–	Pos.
Wheel base (in)	54·12	57
Ground clear (in)	7	9
Seat height (in)	31·5	33
Width (bars) (in)		32·5
Length (in)	81	88
Height (in)		45
Fork angle	63°22′	61° 12′
Dry weight (lb)	382/408/411	390
Power (bhp)	55*/56·5/52	
@ rpm	7250/7250/ 7500 *56·5—mid 1967	

Model	**A50**	**A65T Thunderbolt/ A65L Lightning/ A65FS Firebird Scrambler**
Year from	1970	1970
Year to	1971	1973/1973/ 1971
Bore (mm)	65·5	75
Stroke (mm)	74	74
Capacity (cc)	499	654
Inlet valve dia. (in)	1·47	1·60
Exhaust valve dia. (in)	1·31	1·41
Inlet valve inclination °	37	37
Exhaust valve inclination °	37	37
Valve stem dia. (in)	0·3095	0·3095
Compression ratio (to 1)	9	9
Compression opt. low		7·5/7·5/–
Con rod ctrs. (in)	6	6
Spark plug (Champion)	N4	N4/N3/N3
Spark plug (NGK)	B7ES	B7ES/B8ES/ B8ES
Gudgeon pin dia. (in)	0·750	0·750
Valve timing:		
inlet opens BTDC	40	51
inlet closes ABDC	60	68
Model	**A50**	**A65T/ A65L/ A65FS**
Year	1970–71	1970–73/ 1970–73/ 1970–71
exhaust opens BBDC	65	78
exhaust closes ATDC	35	37
Valve clearance (time) (in)	0·015	0·015
Valve clearance (cold) inlet (in)	0·008	0·008
Valve clearance (cold) exhaust (in)	0·010	0·010
Ignition timing °	34	34/34/28
Ignition timing piston (in)	0·305	0·305/0·305/ 0·210
Points gap (in)	0·015	0·015
Piston rings:		
compression, width (in)	0·06	0·06
compression, gap (in)	0·008– 0·013	0·008– 0·013
oil control, width (in)	0·12	0·12
oil control, gap (in)	0·008– 0·013	0·008– 0·013
ring vertical play (comp) (in)	0·002	0·002
ring vertical play (oil) (in)	0·002	0·002
Valve seat angle °	45	45
Valve lift—inlet (in)		0·385
Valve lift—exhaust (in)		0·375
Valve spring load open (lb)		199
Valve spring load closed		71
Valve spring free length (in)	1·277	1·277
Valve spring free length (outer) (in)	1·37	1·37
Drive main ID (in)	1·125	1·125
Drive main OD (in)	2·812	2·812
Drive main width (in)	0·812	0·812
Timing main ID (in)	1·499	1·499
Timing main OD (in)	1·630	1·630
Timing main width (in)	0·950	0·950
Big end rod dia. (in)	1·687	1·687
Big end clearance (in)	0·0025– 0·001	0·0025– 0·001
Big end rod side play (in)	0·024	0·024
Big end pin dia. (in)	1·687	1·687
Crank end float (in)	0·0015– 0·003	0·0015– 0·003
Cam bush dia. (in)	0·810	0·810
Idler wheel bush (in)	0·874	0·874
Small end bush dia. (in)	0·7505	0·7505
Small end bush width (in)	0·945	0·945
Oil pressure (psi)	50	50
Primary drive (in)	0·37 Triplex	0·37 Triplex

Model	A50	A65T/ A65L/ A65FS
Year	1970–71	1970–73/ 1970–73/ 1970–71
No. of pitches	80	80
Rear chain size (in)	$\frac{5}{8} \times \frac{3}{8}$	$\frac{5}{8} \times \frac{3}{8}$
No. of pitches	110	110
Sprockets: engine (T)	28	28
Sprockets: clutch (T)	58	58
Sprockets: gearbox (T)	18	20/20/18
Sprockets: rear wheel (T)	47	47
Box ratios: top	1	1
Box ratios: 3rd	1·14	1·14
Box ratios: 2nd	1·60	1·60
Box ratios: 1st	2·51	2·51
O/A ratios: top	5·41	4·87/4·87/ 5·41
O/A ratios: 3rd	6·19	5·57/5·57/ 6·19
O/A ratios: 2nd	8·65	7·79/7·79/ 8·65
O/A ratios: 1st	13·58	12·23/12·23 13·58
Gearbox bearings:		
Mainshaft sleeve ID (in)	1·25	1·25
Mainshaft sleeve OD (in)	2·5	2·5
Mainshaft sleeve width (in)	0·62	0·62
Mainshaft right ID (in)	0·75	0·75
Mainshaft right OD (in)	1·87	1·87
Mainshaft right width (in)	0·56	0·56
Layshaft left ID (in)	0·75	0·75
Layshaft left OD (in)	1	1
Layshaft left width (in)	0·75	0·75
Layshaft right ID (in)	0·75	0·75
Layshaft right OD (in)	1	1
Layshaft right width (in)	0·75	0·75
Front tyre (in)	3·25 × 19	3·25 × 19/ 3·25 × 19/ 3·50 × 19
Rear tyre (in)	4·00 × 18	4·00 × 18
Pressure solo (psi)	21/22	21/22
Rim—front (in)	WM2	WM2/WM2/ WM3
Rim—rear (in)	WM3	WM3
Brake—front dia. (in)	8	8
Brake—front width (in)	1·5	1·5
Brake rear dia. (in)	7	7
Brake rear width (in)	1·12	1·12
Front suspension		
Front spring rate (lb/in)	25	25/25/–
Front movement (in)	6·75	6·75/6·75/–

Model	A50	A65T/A65L/ A65FS
Year	1970–71	1970–73/ 1970–73/ 1970–71
Front trail (in)	4·47	4·47/4·47/–
Rear—rate (lb/in)	88	88/88/–
Rear—movement (in)	2·5	2·5/2·5/–
Petrol tank (Imp. gal)	2·5	2·5*/2·5*/2·5
Petrol tank (US gal)	3	3
Petrol tank (litre)	11·4	11·4
Oil tank (Imp. pint)	5	5
Oil tank (US pint)	6	6
Oil tank (litre)	2·84	2·84
Box capacity (Imp. pint)	0·875	0·875
Box capacity (US pint)	1·05	1·05
Box capacity (litre)	0·5	0·5
Chaincase (Imp. pint)	0·25	0·25
Chaincase (US pint)	0·3	0·3
Chaincase (cc)	142	142
Front forks/leg (Imp. pint)	0·33	0·33
Front forks/leg (US pint)	0·4	0·4
Front forks/leg (cc)	190	190
Oil grade	SAE 20–50	SAE 20–50
Box oil grade	EP90	EP90
Case oil grade	SAE 10–30	SAE 10–30
Fork oil grade	SAE 20	SAE 20
		*4 gal in 1972
Ignition system	Coil	Coil/ Coil/ Energy transfer
Gen. type	Alternator	Alternator/ Alternator/–
Output (watts)	108	108/108/–
Battery (volts)	12	12/12/–
Earth	Pos.	Pos./Pos./–
Wheelbase (in)	57	57
Ground clear (in)	7	7
Seat height (in)	33	33
Width (bars) (in)	32·5	32·5
Length (in)	88	88
Height (in)	45	45/45/–
Fork angle °	61° 12′	61° 12′/ 61° 12′/–
Dry weight (lb)	390	390*/ 393**/ 395
Wet weight (lb)		–/420/–
Power (bhp)	31	46/52/54
@ rpm	6250	7000/ 7000/ 7250

*388 in 1972
**390 in 1972

Model	A50	A65T/A65L/A65FS
Year	1970–71	1970–73/1970–73/1970–71
Torque (ft lb)	31	36·5/39·4/39·4
@ rpm	3500	5750/6500/6500

Model	Scooter	Fury
Year from	1958	1971
Year to	1964	
Bore (mm)	56	63
Stroke (mm)	50·62	56
Capacity (cc)	249	349
Inlet valve dia. (in)	1	
Exhaust valve dia. (in)	1	1
Inlet valve inclination °	Nil	60
Exhaust valve inclination °	Approx 45	included
Valve stem dia. (in)	0·27	0·31
Compression ratio (to 1)	6·5	9·5
Con rod crts. (in)	3·875	4·740
Spark plug (Champion)	L85	
Spark plug (NGK)	B6HS	
Gudgeon pin dia. (in)		0·62
Valve timing:		
inlet opens BTDC	10	
inlet closes ABDC	50	
exhaust opens BBDC	50	
exhaust closes ATDC	10	
Valve clearance (cold) inlet (in)	0·005	
Valve clearance (cold) exhaust (in)	0·005	
Ignition timing °	5 full retard	
Ignition timing piston (in)	30	0·18
Points gap (in)	0·015	
Piston rings:		
compression, gap (in)	0·013	
oil control, gap (in)	0·013	
ring vertical play (comp) (in)	0·003	
Piston clearance bottom skirt (in)	0·001	
Valve seat angle °	45	
Valve lift—inlet (in)	0·28	0·332
Valve lift—exhaust (in)	0·28	0·332
Valve spring load open (lb)	67·5	
Valve spring load closed (lb)	45	
Valve spring free length (in)	1·5	
Valve spring free length (outer) (in)	1·56	
Drive main ID (mm)	25	30
Drive main OD (mm)	52	72

Model	Scooter	Fury
Year	1958–64	1971
Drive main width (mm)	15	19
Timing main ID (in)	1·12	30 mm
Timing main OD (in)	1·25	62 mm
Timing main width (in)	0·87	16 mm
Big end rod dia. (in)	1·12	1·62
Big end width (in)	0·78	0·81
Big end pin dia (in)	1·12	1·62
Drive mainshaft dia. (mm)	25	30
Time mainshaft dia. (in)	1·12	30 mm
Small end bush dia. (in)	0·56	
Small end bush width (in)	0·56	
Oil pressure (psi)		70–80
Primary drive (in)	Gear	Duplex $\frac{3}{8}$
No. of pitches	—	72
Rear chain size (in)	Duplex $\frac{3}{8}$	$\frac{5}{8} \times \frac{1}{4}$
No. of pitches		112
Sprockets: engine (T)	49	23
Sprockets: clutch (T)	98	52
Sprockets: gearbox (T)	2:1 ratio	17
Sprockets: rear wheel (T)		48
Box ratios: top	1·0	5th 1·0
Box ratios: 3rd	1·3	4th 1·156
Box ratios: 2nd	2.025	3rd 1·413
Box ratios: 1st	3·0	2nd 1·872
O/A ratios: top	4·0	1st 2·70
O/A ratios: 3rd	5·2	0/A 5th 6·38
O/A ratios: 2nd	8·1	4th 7·38
O/A ratios: 1st	12.0	3rd 9·02
		2nd 11·95
		1st 17·24
Front tyre (in)	3·50 × 10	
Rear tyre (in)	3·50 × 10	
Pressure solo (psi)	17/24	
Pressure dual (psi)	17/30	
Rim—front (in)	Pressed steel	
Rim—rear (in)	wheels	
Brake—front dia. (in)	5	8
Brake—front width (in)	1	
Brake rear dia. (in)	5	7
Brake rear width (in)	1	
Front suspension	Tele.	
Front movement (in)	4·375	6·75
Front trail (in)	3·75	
Rear—type	S/A	S/A
Rear—movement (in)	2·59	
Petrol tank (Imp. gal)	1·5	
Petrol tank (US gal)	1·8	
Petrol tank (litre)	6·8	
Oil tank (Imp. pint)	2·5	
Oil tank (US pint)	3·0	

Model	Scooter	Fury
Year	1958–64	1971
Oil tank (litre)	1·42	
Ignition system	Coils	Coil
Gen. type	Alternator	Alternator
Output (watts)		110
Battery (volts)	6 or 12	12
Earth	Pos.	
Wheelbase (in)	48	
Ground clear (in)	5	
Width (bars) (in)	24	
Dry weight (lb)	244	345
Power (bhp)		34
@ rpm		9000
Torque (ft lb)		20
@ rpm		7000

Model	A75R Rocket 3
Year from	1968/1970
Year to	1970/1973
Bore (mm)	67
Stroke (mm)	70
Capacity (cc)	740
Inlet valve dia. (in)	1·53
Exhaust valve dia. (in)	1·31
Valve stem dia. (in)	0·3095
Compression ratio (to 1)	9·5*/9·5*
Con rod ctrs. (in)	5·750
Spark plug (Champion)	N3
Spark plug (NGK)	B8ES
Gudgeon pin dia. (in)	0.6884
Valve timing:	
inlet opens BTDC °	50
inlet closes ABDC °	64
exhaust opens BBDC °	67
exhaust closes ATDC °	47
Valve clearance (time) (in)	0·020
Valve clearance (cold) inlet (in)	0·006
Valve clearance (cold) exhaust (in)	0·008
Ignition timing °	38
Ignition timing piston (in)	0·355
Points gap (in)	0·015
	*9·0–1968 only and 1971 on
Piston rings:	
compression, width (in)	0·06
compression, gap (in)	0·012–0·017
oil control, width (in)	0·12
oil control, gap (in)	0·012–0·017
ring vertical play (comp) (in)	0·0025

Model	A75
Year	1968–70/1970–73
ring vertical play (oil) (in)	0·0025
Piston clearance top skirt (in)	0·0045–0·0056
Piston clearance bottom skirt (in)	0·0018–0·0033
Valve seat angle °	45
Valve lift—inlet (in)	0·329
Valve lift—exhaust (in)	0·305
Valve spring load open (lb)	–/202
Valve spring load closed (lb)	–/88
Valve spring free length (in)	1·81/1·81 (free—1·468)
Valve spring free length (outer) (in)	1·229 (free—1·600)
Drive main ID (in)	1·125
Drive main OD (in)	2·812
Drive main width (in)	0·812
Timing main ID (mm)	25
Timing main OD (mm)	52
Timing main width (mm)	15
Centre main clearance (in)	0·0005–0·0022
Big end rod dia. (in)	1·624
Big end clearance (in)	0·0005–0·002
Big end width (in)	0·904
Big end rod side play (in)	0·008–0·014
Big end pin dia. (in)	1·624
Big end under sizes (in)	−0·01, −0·02, −0·03, −0·04
Crank end float (in)	0·0015–0·0145
Cam bush dia. (in)	1·061
Small end bush dia. (in)	0·689
Oil pressure (psi)	70–90
Primary drive (in)	$\frac{3}{8}$ Triplex
No. of pitches	82
Rear chain size (in)	$\frac{5}{8} \times \frac{3}{8}$
No. of pitches	107/108
Sprockets: engine (T)	28
Sprockets: clutch (T)	50
Sprockets: gearbox (T)	19/19*
Sprockets: rear wheel (T)	52**/53
Box ratios: top	1
Box ratios: 3rd	1·19
Box ratios: 2nd	1·69
Box ratios: 1st	2·44
O/A ratios: top	4·89***/4·98****
O/A ratios: 3rd	5·83/5·95
O/A ratios: 2nd	8·3/8·42
O/A ratios: 1st	11·95/12·15
	*18—1972
	**1970—53
	***1970—as 1970–71
	****1972—5·26, 6·52, 8·88, 12·83

Model	A75R
Year	1968–70/1970–73
Gearbox bearings:	
Mainshaft sleeve ID (in)	1·25
Mainshaft sleeve OD (in)	2·5
Mainshaft sleeve width (in)	0·62
Mainshaft right ID (in)	0·75
Mainshaft right OD (in)	1·87
Mainshaft right width (in)	0·56
Layshaft left ID (in)	0·69
Layshaft left OD (in)	0·87
Layshaft left width (in)	0·75
Layshaft right ID (in)	0·69
Layshaft right OD (in)	0·87
Layshaft right width (in)	0·75
Front tyre (in)	3·25 × 19/4·10 × 19
Rear tyre (in)	4·10 × 19
Pressure solo (psi)	26/28 / 22/28

Model	A75
Year	1968–70/1970–73
Rim—front (in)	WM2
Rim—rear (in)	WM3
Brake—front dia. (in)	8
Brake—front width (in)	1·62/1·5
Brake rear dia. (in)	7
Brake rear width (in)	1·12
Front spring rate (lb/in)	32·5/25
Front movement (in)	–/6·75
Rear-rate (lb/in)	110
Rear—movement (in)	2·5/3
Petrol tank (Imp. gal)	4·25/2·5
Petrol tank (US gal)	5·1/3
Petrol tank (litre)	19·3/11·4
Oil tank (Imp. pint)	6/5
Oil tank (US pint)	7·2/6
Oil tank (litre)	3·41/2·84

Carburettor settings

Year	Model	Type	Size*	Main	Pilot	Slide	Needle Pos.	Needle Jet	Float Chamber
1946/50	A7	276	$\frac{15}{16}$	140	—	6/3	3	·107	
1951/53	A7	276	$\frac{15}{16}$	140	—	6/4	3	·107	
1955/61	A7	376	$\frac{15}{16}$	210	25	$3\frac{1}{2}$	2	·106	Monobloc
1949/50	A7 Star Twin (two carbs)	275	$\frac{7}{8}$	110	—	5/4	3	·107	
1951/53	A7 Star Twin	276	1	160	—	6/4	3	·107	
1954	A7 Shooting Star	276	1	170	—	6/4	3	·107	15°
1952/54	A7 Star Twin	TT9	$1\frac{1}{16}$	350	—	6	4	·109	
1955/61	A7 Shooting Star	376	1	270	30	$3\frac{1}{2}$	3	·106	Monobloc
1950/53	A10 Golden Flash	276	$1\frac{1}{16}$	170	—	6/4	2	·108	
1954 1956/58	A10 Golden Flash	276	$1\frac{1}{16}$	170	—	6/4	2	·107	7°
1955/59	A10 Golden Flash, spring frame	376	$1\frac{1}{16}$	240	25	$3\frac{1}{2}$	3	·106	Monobloc
1960/61	A10 Golden Flash	389	$1\frac{1}{8}$	250	30	$3\frac{1}{2}$	3	·106	Monobloc

Model	A75
Year	1968–79/1970–73
Box capacity (Imp. pint)	2
Box capacity (US pint)	2·4
Box capacity (litre)	1·136
Chaincase (Imp. pint)	0·5
Chaincase (US pint)	0·6
Chaincase (cc)	284
Front forks/leg (Imp. pint)	0·33
Front forks/leg (US pint)	0·4
Front forks/leg (cc)	190
Petrol grade	4 star
Oil grade	SAE 20–50
Box oil grade	EP90
Case oil grade	SAE 20–50
Fork oil grade	TQF
Ignition system	Coil
Gen. type	Alternator

Model	A75
Year	1968–70/1970–73
Output (watts)	120
Battery (volts)	12
Earth	Pos.
Wheelbase (in)	58/58·5
Ground clear (in)	6·5/8·75
Seat height (in)	32/33
Width (bars) (in)	32·5/33
Length (in)	86·75/88
Height (in)	44/42
Fork angle °	–/61
Dry weight (lb)	468/444
Wet weight (lb)	495/–
Power (bhp)	58
@ rpm	7250
Torque (ft lb)	–/45
@ rpm	6900

Year	Model	Amal Type	Size	Main	Pilot	Slide	Needle Pos.	Needle Jet	Float Chamber
1954/57	Road Rocket	TT9	$1\frac{1}{16}$	340	—	6	4	·109	15°
1957/59	Super Rocket	376	$1\frac{1}{16}$	250	25	$3\frac{1}{2}$	4	·106	Monobloc
1957/58	USA Scrambles twin	376	$1\frac{1}{16}$	400	25	$3\frac{1}{2}$	4	·106	Monobloc
1958/59	Road Rocket, less air filter	389	$1\frac{1}{8}$	400	30	$3\frac{1}{2}$	3	·106	Monobloc
1958/60	Road Rocket	389	$1\frac{1}{8}$	290	30	$3\frac{1}{2}$	3	·106	Monobloc
1960/63	Super Rocket 1960/61, Super Rocket-home and Rocket Gold Star-home	389	$1\frac{5}{32}$	420	25	3	2	·106	Monobloc
1960/63	Super Rocket and Spitfire	389	$1\frac{5}{32}$	290	25	3	2	·106	Monobloc
1963	Rocket Gold Star	389	$1\frac{5}{32}$	310	25	3	2	·106	Monobloc
1960/61	Super Rocket and Spitfire	TT9	$1\frac{5}{32}$	410	—	7	4	·109	

Year	Model	Amal Type	Size	Main	Pilot	Slide	Needle Pos.	Needle Jet	Float Chamber
1962	Rocket Gold Star (USA)	389	$1\frac{3}{16}$	440	30	4	2	·107	Monobloc
1962/65	A50 home	376	1	250	25	$3\frac{1}{2}$	3	·106	Monobloc
1962/67	A50 USA 1962/65, Royal Star 1966/67	376	1	260	25	$3\frac{1}{2}$	3	·106	Monobloc
1964/65	A50 Cyclone	376	$1\frac{1}{16}$	170	25	$3\frac{1}{2}$	2	·106	Monobloc
1966	A50 Wasp	389/689	$1\frac{1}{8}$	200	25	$3\frac{1}{2}$	2	·106	Monobloc
1966	A50 Wasp (USA)	389/689	$1\frac{1}{8}$	190	25	$3\frac{1}{2}$	2	·106	Monobloc
1968	A50 Royal Star	626	26 mm	200	25	$3\frac{1}{2}$	2	·106	Concentric
1969/70	A50 Royal Star	626	26 mm	200	—	$3\frac{1}{2}$	2	·106	Concentric
1962/67	A65 home 1962/65,	389	$1\frac{1}{8}$	300	25	$3\frac{1}{2}$	3	·106	Monobloc
1962/63	Rocket home 1963/65,	389	$1\frac{1}{8}$	310	25	3	2	·107	Monobloc
	A65 USA Thunderbolt 1966/67								
1963/67	A65 Rocket (USA) 1963/65 Thunderbolt (USA) 1966/67	389	$1\frac{1}{8}$	310	25	$3\frac{1}{2}$	3	·106	Monobloc
1964/65	A65 Rocket, Lightning 1965	389	$1\frac{1}{8}$	220	25	$3\frac{1}{2}$	3	·106	Monobloc
1966	A65 Lightning and Hornet	389/689	$1\frac{5}{32}$	270	25	3	4	·106	Monobloc
1966/67	A65 Lightning and Hornet	389/689	$1\frac{5}{32}$	270	25	3	3	·106	Monobloc
1966	A65 Spitfire Mark II	GP2	$1\frac{5}{32}$	260	25	$5\frac{1}{2}$	2	·107	510/1
1967/68	A65 Spitfire Mark III	932	32 mm	190	20	3	2	·107	Concentric
1968	A65 Thunderbolt	928	28 mm	230	20	$3\frac{1}{2}$	1	·106	Concentric
1969/72	A65-T Thunderbolt	928	28 mm	230	—	$3\frac{1}{2}$	1	·106	Concentric
1968	A65L Lightning and Hornet	930	30 mm	190	20	$2\frac{1}{2}$	2	·106	Concentric
1969/70	A65L Lightning, Firebird	930	30 mm	180	—	3	1	·106	Concentric
1971	A65-FS, A65-SS S/bler	930	30 mm	220	—	3	1	·106	Concentric
1971/72	Lightning	930	30 mm	200	—	3	1	·106	Concentric
1972	A70L Lightning twin	930	30 mm	250	—	3	1	·106	Concentric
1958/64	Scooter 250 cc twin	Zenith 17 MXZ	82 mm	45	—	fixed	fixed	(200 starter slide)	
1971	Fury 350 cc twin	626	26 mm						
1969/70	A75R 740 Rocket 3	626	26 mm	150	—	3	2	·106	Concentric
1971/73	A75R 740 Rocket 3	626	26 mm	150	—	$3\frac{1}{2}$	2	·106	Concentric
1973	T150 Hurricane (carb finish-silver grey)	626	26 mm	150	—	$3\frac{1}{2}$	2	·106	Concentric

Colours

1946
19 September, original description of A7. General finish in red with chrome plating. Tank had chrome side panels with red panel ahead of knee grips. These were gold lined and carried winged BSA motif. Wheel rims were chrome with centre red with gold lines. Alternative finish—black with chromium.

December 1947–49
Black and chromium as standard, Devon red as option depending on colour supplies, i.e. the reverse of 1946 arrangement. Oil tank had level mark and tool box a BSA piled arms transfer.

1949
Star Twin Black and chromium except for tank which was chromium with silver panels, gold lined, carrying BSA star transfers, and wheels which were chrome with silver centres.

1950–52
A7 and **Star Twin** continued as above in black with red option for A7 applying to petrol tank only.
A10 polychromatic beige and chrome. Tank chromed with lined beige panels on top and side. Tank badge was circular with flying wing. Round part was red with BSA and zig-zag of lightning incorporated in it in beige. The A10 was also available in a black and chrome finish.

1953–54
A7 all maroon with chrome tank panels and badge as A10.
A10 all beige or black with chrome tank panels and badge as before.
A7ST two-tone green, dark for frame; pale polychromatic green for forks, mudguards, oil tank and petrol tank which had chrome panels and round **Star** badges.

1955
A7 All maroon with chrome tank panels and wheel rims. Round tank badge with piled arms insignia.
Shooting Star Forks, mudguards, oil tank and petrol tank in pale polychromatic green. Frame dark green. Tank side panels and wheel rims chromed. Round gold star badge.
A10 (S/A frame or plunger) All beige or all black with chrome tank panels and wheel rims. Tank badge as earlier A10 models.

1956
A7 Alternative black finish available, remainder as above plus **Road Rocket** Black cycle parts, tank silver or optional red with chrome side panels. Chrome mudguards and wheel rims. Tank badge as A7.

1957
No plunger A10 in list (special order only), others as 1956.

1958
Black frame and forks for all models; tank, mudguards, oil tank and toolbox in colours as before.

1959
A7 Princess grey for petrol and oil tanks, mudguards and tool box; frame and forks black, round tank badge with piled arms insignia on chrome side panels. Alternative all black finish.
Shooting Star in polychromatic green as from 1958.
A10 Golden beige for tanks, mudguards and tool box, round badge as A7 on chrome side panels. Alternative all black finish.
Super Rocket Red or silver sheen for tanks, mudguards and tool box, round badge on chrome side panels. Alternative all black finish. For export only chrome plate mudguards. All models have chrome wheel rims.

1960
A7 colour fuchsia red or black, **A7SS** continuing in polychromatic green. **A10** in beige with sapphire blue or black option. **A10SR** in red as before. Tanks fitted with chrome plated side panels and colours applied as from 1958. Pear shape tank badges and kneegrips without BSA insignia adopted.

1961
A7, A7SS, A10 as 1960.
A10SR in royal red or princess grey in 1960 style.

1962
Rocket Gold Star Black frame, forks, oil tank and toolbox. Chromed mudguards and wheel rims when steel. Round gold star badges with red background on silver tank with chrome side panels with red line to
Super Rocket Royal red or princess grey for tank and mudguards. Frame, forks, oil tank and tool box black.

Chrome wheel rims and tank side panels with pear shaped tank badges.

1962

A50 Star Frame, forks black. Tank, mudguards, side covers polychromatic green. Tank has chrome side panels with BSA pear shaped badge with black background. Kneegrips with name on them used. Side covers have circular BSA badge with flying wing. Black background, gold letters and wing (as used on A10 tank). Chrome wheel rims.

A65 Star As A50 but in polychromatic blue. Tank badge with blue background side cover badge as A50. Flamboyant red finish available as an extra on A65 only.

A50 and A65 Alternative black finish available.

1963

A50 and **A65** no change.

A65R Flame red petrol tank with chrome side panels and pear shaped badges. Flame red side panels with round winged badges. Chrome wheel rims, mudguards and top fork shrouds.

1964

A50, A65, A65R as above.

October 1964

A50C, A50CC, A65L, A65LC. Tank in metallic gold with chrome side panels lined in red. Pear shaped tank badges. Side panels gold finished glass fibre with flying BSA wing motif. Chrome wheel rims, mudguards, top fork shrouds and headlamp shell. Black frame and forks.

1965

As 1964.

September 1965

New range introduced. **A50 Royal Star**. Flamboyant red finish to side covers, mudguards and petrol tank which had chrome side panels and pear shaped star badge. Side covers had round, winged badge. Frame and forks black. Lining in white

A65T Thunderbolt As A50 but in flamboyant blue.

A65L Lightning As A50 in red with white lining and black frame and forks. Chrome mudguards and headlight shell

A65 Spitfire Mk II Ivory and gold lined flamboyant red glass-fibre tank with star transfer badge. Side covers in red with round winged badge. Black frame and forks. Chrome mudguards, headlamp shell and top fork shrouds.

A65 Hornet Mandarin red tank and side covers with badges as Spitfire. Black frame and forks, chrome mudguards and top fork shrouds.

A50 Wasp As Hornet but colour was sapphire blue.

November 1966

A50 as 1965 but in flamboyant blue,

A65T as 1965 but in black,

A65L as 1965 but in flamboyant red,

Spitfire Mk III as 1965 but in royal red.

November 1967

A50 Returned to flamboyant red for tank, side covers and mudguards. Tank has central filler cap and larger chrome side panels. Tank badge changed to light alloy die casting. Side covers have transfer of crossed flags design with model name. Frame and forks black. Chrome headlight. White lining on mudguards and tank.

A65T and **A65L** As A50 but with chrome mudguards.

A65 Spitfire Mk IV As Mk III in royal red for tank and side covers, Star transfer badge on tank and transfer of crossed flags on covers. Black frame and forks. Chromed mudguards, headlight shell and top fork shrouds.

February 1969

A50 Black frame and forks, chrome headlight shell. Tank has large chrome side panels with alloy star badge. Tank mudguards and side covers in Flamboyant Aircraft Blue. Mudguards and tank lined in white. Side covers carry name 'Royal Star'.

A65T As A50 but in black with 'Thunderbolt 650' on side covers.

A65L As A50 but in flamboyant red with chrome mudguards and '650 Lightning' on side covers.

November 1970

All models with dove grey frame and chrome plated mudguards and headlight shell. Air filter boxes and side covers in model colour. Two-tone tanks with winged BSA motif.

A65T in Sterling Moss green.

A65L and **A65FS** in bronze.

1972

Chrome mudguards, black frame. Tank, air filter boxes and side covers one colour. Chrome headlight shell.

A65T colour was Etruscan bronze.

A65L colour was firebird red.

Scooter

Introduced in 1958 in metallic green.

1961
Also available in fuchsia red or sapphire blue. All three finishes as single colours or with cream weathershield panels.

Triple
Late 1968 1969 1970
Black frame and forks. Chrome headlight shell. Tank, mudguards and side panels in red with white lines or lime green with red lines. Alloy tank badges combined with kneegrips. Rocket 3 motif on side panels in black on aluminium to match tank badge finish. Red side covers not lined but lime green ones were.

1971
New style. Dove grey frame. Chrome headlight shell and mudguards. Dove grey and chrome tank with pear shaped BSA Star badge. Plain side covers with Rocket 3 badges.

1972
Black frame, chrome headlight shell and mudguards. Tank style as in 1969 with Burgundy colour. Side covers plain with upper section in burgundy and lower in black. Motif changed to Rocket Three with 'Rocket' in white outline and 'Three' in white solid. Motif surrounded with white line. Front brake backplate coloured black.

Prices

The price for the original 1946 rigid A7 was £135.0*s*.0*d*. plus £36.9*s*.0*d*. purchase tax, giving a total of £171.9*s*.0*d*. To this had to be added the speedometer at £4.0*s*.0*d*. plus £1.1*s*.7*d*.

By 1947 the price had rise slightly to £177.16*s*.0*d*.

The prices of the A7 and A10 twins and their variants from 1946 to 1963 are set out in the following table. Prices often varied if an alternative finish was specified. Thus in 1955 the A10 with swinging fork frame was listed at £237.12*s*.0*d*. in black finish and £241.4*s*.0*d*. if in beige. The corresponding figures for the plunger frame version in the same colours were £228.0*s*.0*d*. and £231.12*s*.0*d*.

Accessories were often listed and in 1958 some prices were:

Prop stand for A7 or A10	£1. 0*s*. 7*d*.
Chaincase	£3. 4*s*. 0*d*.
Air-cleaner for Shooting Star	£1. 1*s*.10*d*.
Rev-counter for Super Rocket	£8. 2*s*. 2*d*.

The most popular model for accessories was the Rocket Gold Star and from the lists in 1962 could be chosen:

Air cleaner	£ 1. 5*s*.10*d*.
Ball end levers	£ 0.10*s*.10*d*.
Chrome mudguards	£ 4.15*s*. 2*d*.
Legshields	£ 4.14*s*.10*d*.
Prop stand	£ 1. 6*s*. 5*d*.
Rev-counter	£ 8.18*s* 6*d*.
Safety bars	£ 6. 5*s*. 9*d*.
Alloy rims	£12. 3*s*. 0*d*.
Clip ons	£ 2. 0*s*. 3*d*.
Racing tyres	£ 4. 0*s*. 2*d*.
2 gallon alloy tank	£ 8.10*s*. 5*d*.
5 gallon alloy tank	£26.15*s*.10*d*.
190 mm front brake	£ 5.19*s*. 9*d*.

Date	A7 rigid	A7 plunger and S/A	A7 Star Twin Shooting Star	A10 rigid	A10 plunger and S/A	A10 Rocket	Rocket Gold Star
19. 9.46	£171. 9*s*. 0*d*.						
5. 6.47	£177.16*s*. 0*d*.						
4.11.48	£177.16*s*. 0*d*.	£190.10*s*. 0*d*.	£203. 4*s*. 0*d*.				
24. 3.49	£182.17*s*. 8*d*.	£195.11*s*. 8*d*.	£208. 5*s*. 8*d*.				
9.11.50	£182.17*s*. 8*d*.	£195.11*s*. 8*d*.	£208. 5*s*. 8*d*.	£193. 0*s*.10*d*.	£205.14*s*.10*d*.		
1. 3.51	£194. 6*s*. 3*d*.	£203. 4*s*. 0*d*.	£210.16*s*. 5*d*.	£203. 4*s*. 0*d*.	£212. 1*s*.10*d*.		

Date	A7 rigid	A7 plunger and S/A	A7 Star Twin Shooting Star	A10 rigid	A10 plunger and S/A	A10 Rocket	Rocket Gold Star
4.12.52			£210.16*s.* 5*d.*				
Late '52		£220. 8*s.* 4*d.*	£230. 0*s.* 0*d.*		£227. 8*s.*11*d.*		
17. 9.53	£207. 0*s.* 0*d.*				£213.12*s.* 0*d.*		
7. 1.54	£207. 0*s.* 0*d.*		£216. 0*s.* 0*d.*		£213.12*s.* 0*d.*		
4.55		£228. 0*s.* 0*d.*	£240. 0*s.* 0*d.*		£241. 4*s.* 0*d.*		
7.56			£264. 2*s.* 5*d.*		£252. 6*s.*10*d.*	£269.14*s.* 0*d.*	
10.56		£238.14*s.* 0*d.*	£251. 2*s.* 0*d.*		£252. 6*s.*10*d.*	£269.14*s.* 0*d.*	
8. 1.57					£260. 8*s.* 0*d.*		
25. 4.57		£256. 1*s.* 3*d.*	£264. 2*s.* 5*d.*		£255. 8*s.*10*d.*	£281. 9*s.* 8*d.*	
6. 3.58		£257.12*s.* 2*d.*	£265.14*s.* 5*d.*		£261.19*s.* 6*d.*	£283. 3*s.* 8*d.*	
23. 4.59 } 21. 1.60 }		£249. 1*s.*10*d.*	£256.18*s.* 8*d.*		£253. 6*s.* 3*d.*	£273.16*s.* 5*d.*	
9.11.60		£255. 2*s.* 6*d.*	£262. 1*s.* 2*d.*		£259. 6*s.*11*d.*	£273.16*s.* 5*d.*	
30. 8.61 } 2.11.61 }		£259. 9*s.* 9*d.*	£266.10*s.* 9*d.*		£263.15*s.* 7*d.*	£280.19*s.* 2*d.*	
8. 3.62		£259. 9*s.* 9*d.*	£266.10*s.* 9*d.*		£263.15*s.* 7*d.*	£280.19*s.* 2*d.*	£299.19*s.* 5*d.*
28. 3.62							£314.19*s.* 5*d.*
18. 4.62		£267.17*s.* 7*d.*	£275. 3*s.* 3*d.*		£272. 6*s.* 3*d.*	£290. 0*s.*11*d.*	£309.13*s.* 6*d.*
7.11.62 } 6. 2.63 }						£303. 0*s.* 0*d.*	£323. 8*s.* 0*d.*

Standard Model—type B2
With electric start—type B2S

	B2	B2S
1958	£187. 2*s.* 6*d.*	£200.17*s.* 0*d.*
1959–60	£180.18*s.* 9*d.*	£194. 4*s.* 2*d.*
June 1961	£184. 0*s.* 7*d.*	£197.10*s.* 7*d.*
April 1962	£180.18*s.* 9*d.*	£194. 4*s.* 2*d.*
September 1962/63	£184.10*s.* 0*d.*	£198. 0*s.* 0*d.*

Scooter accessories in September 1962

Front carrier	£3. 2*s.* 6*d.*
Rear carrier	£3. 7*s.* 6*d.*
Wheel disc	£1.10*s.* 0*d.*
Spare wheel and tyre	£5.12*s.* 0*d.*
Spare wheel cover	£1.17*s.* 6*d.*
Spare wheel cover plate	11*s.* 0*d.*
Pannier bag	£2.12*s.* 3*d.*
Pannier bag carrier	£2. 0*s.* 0*d.*
Windscreen	£5. 0*s.* 0*d.*
250 cc model touring kit	£4.17*s.* 6*d.*

A50 and A65 series

When these models were introduced in 1962, the A50 was priced at £215 plus £49.7*s.*10*d.* purchase tax, making a total of £264.7*s.*10*d.* The A65 was £219 plus £49.13*s.*9*d.*, making £268.13*s.*9*d.* The prices over the years for the various models are given in the table.

	A50	A65	A65R Rocket	A65L Lightning	A65T Thunderbolt	A65S Spitfire
4. 1.62	£264. 7*s.*10*d.*	£268.13*s.* 9*d.*				
28. 3.62	£277.12*s.* 3*d.*	£282. 2*s.* 5*d.*				
18. 4.62 } 30. 5.62 }	£272.18*s.*11*d.*	£277. 7*s.* 7*d.*				

	A50	A65	A65R Rocket	A65L Lightning	A65T Thunderbolt	A65S Spitfire
6. 9.62 / 7.11.62 / 6. 2.63	£285. 3*s*. 0*d*.	£289.16*s*. 0*d*.				
23.10.63	£286.19*s*. 0*d*.	£293. 0*s*. 0*d*.	£308.11*s*. 0*d*.			
21. 3.64 / 14.11.64	£293.19*s*. 4*d*.	£304.14*s*. 4*d*.	£320.13*s*.10*d*.			
10.10.64	£293.19*s*. 4*d*.	£304.14*s*. 4*d*.	£320.13*s*.10*d*.	£341.16*s*. 0*d*.		
4. 9.65	£299. 0*s*. 0*d*.			£355. 0*s*. 0*d*.	£320.13*s*.10*d*.	£389.10*s*. 0*d*.
27. 7.66	£303.17*s*. 4*d*.			£360.15*s*. 7*d*.	£325.18*s*. 3*d*.	£395.16*s*.10*d*.
3.11.66	£303.17*s*. 4*d*.			£360.15*s*. 7*d*.	£325.18*s*. 3*d*.	£395.16*s*.10*d*.
10. 4.68	£315. 4*s*. 4*d*.			£374. 5*s*. 2*d*.	£338. 1*s*. 9*d*.	£398. 7*s*. 5*d*.
26. 2.69	£321.14*s*. 2*d*.			£381.19*s*. 3*d*.	£345. 0*s*.11*d*.	
Nov. 1970				£514. 0*s*. 0*d*.	£475. 0*s*. 0*d*.	
Aug 1971				£614. 0*s*. 0*d*.	£558. 0*s*. 0*d*.	

	A50C	A50CC	A50W	A65LC	A65H
10.10.64	£331.16*s*. 0*d*.	£335.16*s*. 0*d*.		£345.16*s*. 0*d*.	
1. 9.65			£325. 0*s*. 0*d*.		£339.10*s*. 0*d*.
27. 7.66			£330. 5*s*.10*d*.		£345. 0*s*. 6*d*.

Accessories for the A50 and A65 are listed below

4.1.62

Prop stand	£ 1. 4*s*. 7*d*.
Chaincase	£ 3. 4*s*. 9*d*.
Flamboyant red finish for A65	£ 2.15*s*. 0*d*.

28.3.62

Flamboyant red finish for A65	£ 2.17*s*.10*d*.

6.9.62

Flamboyant red finish for A65	£ 2.19*s*. 5*d*.

18.7.62

Handrail	£ 1.19*s*. 4*d*.
Legshields	£ 4.10*s*.11*d*.
Prop stand	£ 1. 5*s*. 4*d*.
Front safety bars	£ 6. 0*s*. 4*d*.
Whitewall tyres	£ 1.17*s*.10*d*.
Windscreen	£5.15*s*. 0*d*.
Rear chaincase	£3. 6*s*.10*d*.

23.10.63

Rev-counter for A65R	£8.18*s*. 6*d*.
12 volt lighting A65	£4. 0*s*. 0*d*.
Twin exhausts A65R	£2.12*s*. 3*d*.

10.10.64

Ball end levers A65R	11*s*. 5*d*.
Chaincase	£3.13*s*. 6*d*.
Flamboyant red finish A65	£3. 2*s*. 5*d*.
Handrail	£2. 3*s*. 4*d*.
Lifting handle	9*s*. 7*d*.
Rev-counter A65R	£9. 7*s*. 7*d*.
Front safety bar	£6.12*s*. 0*d*.
Rear safety bar	£6.13*s*. 6*d*.
Twin exhausts A65R	£2.15*s*. 0*d*.
12 volt system A65	£4. 4*s*. 0*d*.

A75 Road Rocket
This was introduced at £614.3*s*.5*d*. including purchase tax. In November 1970 this rose to £670 and in August 1971 to £714.

Gearbox ratios (A7 and A10)

As the gearbox fitted to the pre-unit construction twins (1955/63 A7 and A10 models with swinging fork frame) was the standard heavyweight unit, it was possible for it to be fitted with alternative ratios. It was normal for the Rocket Gold Star to have a close ratio box but it was as feasible for the RGS to have a trials box as for an A10 to have the extra close one. The numbers of teeth on each gear and the resulting ratios are shown below.

	Mainshaft				Layshaft			
Type	Sleeve	2nd	3rd	1st	Sleeve	2nd	3rd	1st
RRT2	25	22	24	19	18	21	19	24
RRT	25	22	24	18	18	21	19	25
Close	26	22	25	18	17	21	18	25
Scrambles	25	19	22	16	18	24	21	27
Standard	26	20	24	16	17	23	19	27
Wide	26	17	22	14	17	26	21	29

		Gear ratios			
	Marking	Top	3rd	2nd	1st
Ex/close	RRT2	1	1·099	1·326	1·754
Ex/close	RR or RRT	1	1·099	1·326	1·929
Close	DAY or DAYT	1	1·101	1·460	2·124
Scramble	SC or SCT	1	1·326	1·754	2·344
Standard	STD or STDT	1	1·211	1·759	2·581
Wide	TRI or TRIT	1	1·460	2·339	3·168

Speedometer gears (A50 and A65 in 1964)

Rear tyre size	Gearbox	Rear wheel	Driving gear	Letter marking	Driven gear
3·50 × 18	16	43	6	G	11
3·50 × 18	17	42	7	C	12
3·50 × 19	17	42	7	B	11
3·50 × 18	18	42	7	B	11
3·50 × 18	19	42	8	D	12
3·50 × 19	19	42	7	A	10
3·50 × 18	20	42	7	A	10
3·50 × 19	20	42	8	E	11
4·00 × 18	21	50	7	B	11

Torque wrench settings (A50 and A65)

dry in 1964	Torque in ft lb
Flywheel bolts	30
Connecting rod bolts	22
Cylinder head bolts ($\frac{3}{8}$ in)	25
Cylinder head bolts ($\frac{5}{16}$ in)	25
Cylinder head nuts ($\frac{3}{8}$ in)	26
Cylinder barrel nuts ($\frac{5}{16}$ in)	18
Oil pump stud nuts	7
Clutch centre nut	70–75
Kickstarter ratchet nut	60
Rotor fixing nut	60
Stator fixing nuts	10–15
Crankshaft pinion nut	60
Manifold stud nuts ($\frac{5}{16}$ in)	12·5
Manifold stud nuts ($\frac{1}{4}$ in)	6
Carburettor flange nuts	10

Engine and frame numbers

Year	Model	Engine	Frame
1946	A7	XA7-101	XA7-101
1947	A7	XA7-101	XA7-101
1948	A7	YA7-101	YA7-101
1949	A7	ZA7-101	ZA7-101
	A7 (S/F)	ZA7-101	ZA7S-101
	A7 Star Twin	ZA7S-101	ZA7S-101
1950	A7	ZA7-7001	ZA7-4001
	A7 (S/F)	ZA7-7001	ZA7S-6001
	A7 Star Twin	ZA7S-4001	ZA7S-6001
	A10	ZA10-101	ZA7-4001
	A10 (S/F)	ZA10-101	ZA7S-6001
1951	A7	AA7-101	ZA7-6001

Year	Model	Engine	Frame
	A7 (S/F)	AA7-101	ZA7S-14001
	A7 Star Twin	AA7S-101	ZA7S-14001
	A10	ZA10-4001	ZA7-6001
	A10 (S/F)	ZA10-4001	ZA7S-14001
1952	A7	AA7-5001	ZA7-8001
	A7 (S/F)	AA7-101	ZA7S-26001
	A7 Star Twin	AA7S-101	ZA7S-26001
	A10	ZA10-12001	ZA7-8001
	A10 (S/F)	ZA10-12001	ZA7S-26001
1953	A7	BA7-101	BA7-101
	A7 (S/F)	BA7-101	BA7S-101
	A7 Star Twin	BA7S-101	BA7S-101
	A10	BA10-101	BA7S-101
1954	A7	BA7-2001	BA7S-8950
	A7 Star Twin	BA7S-2001	BA7S-8950
	A10	BA10-7001	BA7S-8950
	A10 Super Flash (S/F)	BA10S-701	BA10S-701
	A7 (S/A)	CA7-101	CA7-101
	A7 Star Twin	CA7S-101	CA7-101
	A7 Shooting Star	CA7SS-101	CA7-101
	A10 (S/A)	CA10-101	CA7-101
	A10 Super Flash	CA10S-101	CA7-101
	A10 Road Rocket	CA10R-101	CA7-101
1955	A7 (S/A)	CA7-1501	CA7-7001
	A7 Shooting Star	CA7SS-501	CA7-7001
	A10 (S/A)	CA10-4501	CA7-7001
	A10 (plunger)	BA10-11001	BA7S-15001
	A10 Road Rocket	CA10R-601	CA7-7001
1956	A7 (S/A)	CA7-2701	EA7-101
	A7 Shooting Star	CA7SS-2301	EA7-101
	A10 (S/A)	CA10-8001	EA7-101
	A10 (plunger)	BA10-14001	BA7S-18001
	A10 Road Rocket	CA10R-2001	EA7-101
1957	A7 (S/A)	CA7-	EA7-
	A7 Shooting Star	CA7SS-	EA7-
	A10 (S/A)	CA10-	EA7-
	A10 Road Rocket	CA10R-	EA7-
	last A10 (plunger)	BA10-16036	BA7S-20289
1958	A7	CA7-5001	FA7-101
	A7 Shooting Star	CA7SS-4501	FA7-101
	A10	DA10-651	FA7-101
	A10 Super Rocket	CA10R-6001	FA7-101
1959	A7	CA7-5867	FA7-8522
	A7 Shooting Star	CA7SS-5425	FA7-8522
	A10	DA10-4616	FA7-8522
	A10 Super Rocket	CA10R-8193	FA7-8522
	A10 Spitfire Scrambles USA	CA10SR-776	FA7A-101
1960	A7	CA7-7101	GA7-101
	A7 Shooting Star	CA7SS-6701	GA7-101
	A10	DA10-7801	GA7-101
	A10 Super Rocket	DA10R-101	GA7-101
	A10 Spitfire Scrambles USA	DA10SR-101	GA7A-101
1961	A7	CA7-8501	GA7-11101
	A7 (generator)	CA7A-8501	GA7-11101
	A7 Shooting Star	CA7SS-8001	GA7-11101
	A10	DA10-	GA7-

Year	Model	Engine	Frame
		13201	11101
	A10 (generator)	DA10A-13201	GA7-11101
	A10 Super Rocket	DA10R-3001	GA7-11101
	A10 Spitfire Scrambles USA	DA10SR-401	GA7A-401
1962	A50 Star Twin	A50-101	A50-101
	A65 Star Twin	A65-101	A50-101
	A50 Star (rod brake)	A50-101	A50A-101
	A65 Star (rod brake)	A65-101	A50A-101
	A10	DA10-17181	GA7-21120
	A10 Super Rocket	DA10R-5958	GA7-21120
	A10 Rocket Gold Star	DA10R-5958	GA10-101
	A7	CA7-9714	GA7-21120
	A7 Shooting Star	CA7SS-9277	GA7-21120
	A10 Spitfire Scrambes USA	DA10R-5958	GA7A-536
	A7 (generator)	CA7A-9714	GA7-21120
	A10 (generator)	DA10A-341	GA7-21120
1963	A50 Royal Star (cable brake)	A50-823	A50-2288
	A50 Royal Star (rod brake)	A50-823	A50-2701
	A65 Star (cable brake)	A65-1947	A50-2288
	A65 Star (rod brake)	A65-1947	A50-2701
	A10 Golden Flash	DA10-17727	GA7-23643
	A10 (generator)	DA10A-17727	GA7-23643
	A10 Super Rocket	DA10R-8197	GA7-23643
	A10 Rocket Gold Star	DA10R-8197	GA10-390
	A10 Spitfire Scrambles USA	DA10R-8197	GA7A-748
1964	A50 Royal Star	A50A-101	A50-5501
A50 (Police)	A50AP-101		A50-5501
	A50 Cyclone (USA)	A50B-101	A50B-101
	A65 Star	A65A-1134	A50-5501
	A65 (Police)	A65AP-101	A50-5501
	A65 Royal Star (USA)	A65A-101	A50-5501
	A65 Rocket (less rev-counter)	A65B-101	A50-5501
	A65 Rocket (with rev-counter)	A65C-101	A50-5501
	A65 Thunderbolt Rocket	A65B-101	A50-5501
	A65 Lightning Rocket	A65D-101	A50B-101
	A65 Spitfire Hornet	A65E-101	A50B-101

Letter C after A50B- (Cyclone) indicates close ratio gearbox

Year	Model	Engine	Frame
1965	A50 Royal Star	A50A-101	A50-8437
	A50 (Police)	A50AP-121	A50-8437
	A50 Cyclone (road model)	A50D-101	A50B-4001
	A50 Cyclone Competition	A50B-507	A50B-4001
	A65 Star	A65A-1134	A50-8437
	A65 (Police)	A65AP-267	A50-8437
	A65 Rocket (less rev-counter)	A65B-334	A50-8437
	A65 Rocket (with rev-counter)	A65C-1082	A50-8437
	A65 Lightning Rocket	A65D-1742	A50B-4001
	A65 Spitfire Hornet	A65E 701	A50B 4001

Letter C after model indicates close ratio gearbox

Year	Model	Engine	Frame
1966	A50 Royal Star	A50R-101	A50C-101
	A50 Wasp	A50W-101	A50C-101
	A65 Thunderbolt	A65T-101	A50C-101
	A65 Lightning	A65L-101	A50C-101
	A65 Hornet	A65H-101	A50C-101
	A65 Spitfire Mk II	A65S-101	A50C-101

Letter C after model indicates close ratio gearbox

Year	Model	Engine	Frame
1967	A50 Royal Star	A50RA-	101

Year	Model	Engine	Frame
	A50 Wasp	A50WA-	101
	A65 Thunderbolt	A65TA-	101
	A65 Lightning	A65LA-	101
	A65 Hornet	A65HA-	101
	A65 Spitfire Mk III	A65SA-	101

Letter C after model indicates close ratio gearbox

1968	A50 Royal Star	A50RB-	101
	A50 Wasp	A50WB-	101
	A65 Thunderbolt	A65TB-	101
	A65 Lightning	A65LB-	101
	A65 Firebird Scrambler	A65FB-	101
	A65 Spitfire Mk IV	A65SB-	101

1969 on

1. First letter gives month of manufacture.
   Second letter gives year of manufacture.
2. Five numbers giving production number.
3. Last 3 to 5 digits or letters give model type.

Thus:

1. Date

Letter	Month	Year
A	January	1979
B	February	1980
C	March	1969
D	April	1970
E	May	1971
G	June	1972
H	July	1973
J	August	1974
K	September	1975
N	October	1976
P	November	1977
X	December	1978

2. Production number
   Each season starts at 00100. The numbers were taken consecutively within a range of models irrespective of model.
3. Model number code

Rocket 3	A75R
Lightning (home and USA)	A65L
Firebird Scrambler (USA)	A65F
Thunderbolt (home and USA)	A65T
Royal Star (home and USA)	A50R

Scooter numbers

Year	Model	Engine	Frame
1959	B2	W101	101B
	B2S	W101E	101B
1960	B2	W3201	4001
	B2S	W3201E	4001
1961	B2	W11790	18800B
	B2S	W11790E	18800B
1961	March		
	B2 (new exhaust)	W16582	27407B
	B2S (new exhaust)	W16582E	27407B
1962	B2	W17800	30140B
	B2S	W17800E	30140B
1963	B2	W18485	31825B
	B2S	W18485E	31825B